Contents

Introductory note

This volume consists of the proceeedings of a colloquium held in the Department of French, University of Durham, in April 1990, a few days before the 50th anniversary of the German invasion of France. Particularly welcome was the participation of Daniel Madelénat, *from the University of Clermont-Ferrand, whose contribution introduced a fascinating view of the defeat of France from the German side. M. Madelénat's presence explains, in part, why some of the papers are reproduced here in French, but if the result is certainly a* mixte *we trust it is not also a* macédoine. *Given the continuing importance, for the understanding of contemporary French history, of the event that provided the pretext for our colloquium, and the large number of researchers with an interest in the topic, we decided to invite colleagues from other institutions to what has hitherto been basically a departmental gathering. We were therefore delighted that William Kidd from Stirling, and David Gascoigne from St. Andrews were able to represent the Scottish Universities, and just as pleased to see an even nearer neighbour, Margaret Atack from Sunderland Polytechnic as well as a colleague from Cambridge, Michael Tilby. Though basically literary in focus, the colloquium was essentially concerned, of course, with writers' reactions to a momentous historical event. A spate of books, including Jean-Pierre Azéma's* 1940: l'année terrible *(published a week after our colloquium was held), provide much of the essential historical background of fact, but I was anxious to include amongst the papers a treatment of the ambiguous area where history and myth are hard to disentangle, and asked the historians Hilary Footit and John Simmonds to provide an account of this essential background, so important when fiction nourishes itself from personal reminiscence as well as historical fact. In conclusion, I should express my great pleasure in seeing four contributions from Durham, including an up-to-the-minute account of the rewriting of a very little known aspect of the history of the Occupation complete with eye-witness and carrier bags full of letters and documents. Our thanks to Dr Richard Maber, and his aunt, Dr Lesley Maber, for providing the final touch to a colloquium about not just literature and history, but living memory too.*

Anthony Cheal Pugh

WEEKEND A ZUYDCOOTE AND LA MORT DANS L'AME

HISTORY, POLITICS AND SEXUALITY

Margaret Atack

> La guerre n'était donc plus ce noble
> et commun élan d'âmes amantes de la
> gloire qu'il s'était figuré d'après
> les proclamations de Napoléon!
>
> *La Chartreuse de Parme*

On the battlefield of Waterloo, Fabrice experiences many emotions - among them, acute disappointment. He is seeking desperately to fight, his head is filled with aristocratic images of noble, manly friendships from the age of chivalry, and of imperial grandeur. But the reality does not match up to his expectations of what a war could or should be; a similar mismatch between received notions or cultural expectations of war and the experience of the defeat in May-June 1940 is a major factor in the two narratives under consideration here. In the writing of plot, episode, behaviour and attitudes, incongruity is being obsessively connoted throughout.

Literary discourse necessarily has its historical and political dimensions, and literary representations of the fall of France have had very specific historical and political impacts. Historical here has a dual sense, referring both to the way this event is being represented as a major one in the life of the French nation, as immediate History, history being made; and to the issue of writing the past, representing the past in the present. Literature is not a privileged discourse, but it is an extremely important one in a range of cultural discourses establishing the meaning or meanings of an event, helping to establish it as an event, and raising issues of where its boundaries lie. It is clear from *La Chartreuse*, for example, that the failed expectations of Fabrice are part of "the event" being narrated, and in that sense previous representations of war are present/absent in their non-realisation for the hero. In other words, narratives - or at least the interesting ones - tend, perhaps by their nature, to exclude the possibility that there might be such a thing as unmediated experience. Sartre himself offers a good example of the multi-layered nature of experience, representation and writing, and their interaction. During the *drôle de guerre* he is reading Jules Romains's *Prélude à Verdun* and *Verdun*, while writing and rewriting *L'Age de raison* and planning *Le Sursis*, both of which are set in 1938. Even more than *L'Age de raison*, *Le Sursis*, which covers the days of the Munich crisis, turns around the question of whether or not there will be a war. Sartre is also consigning his thoughts and reactions on a daily basis to letters and his carnets. He writes a "diary" of the *drôle de guerre*, not at the time but immediately after his return from captivity in March 1941 (to compensate for the notebooks he had lost), part of which was published in *Exercice du silence* in 1942 under the title '*La Mort dans l'âme*'.(1)

To have a concentrated burst of reading around the question of the fall of France is to rediscover once more the extent to which the late 1930s were dominated by the approach of war. Sartre puts it succinctly in 'La Fin de la guerre' which appeared after the war: 'Nous avons cru longtemps que la Guerre et la Paix étaient deux espèces bien tranchées, comme le Noir et le Blanc, comme le Chaud et le Froid. Ce n'était pas vrai et nous le savons aujourd'hui. Nous avons appris en 34 et 39 que la paix peut finir sans que la guerre éclate.'(2) The political history of this, nationally and internationally, is well known, and enough ink has been spilt on the out-dated views of the French état-major who thought they were going to be fighting the First World War again. But it may be worth repeating the extent to which the literary field was dominated by representations of warfare, be it contemporary wars or the First World War. One only has to start listing Malraux's L'Espoir (1937), Martin du Gard's Eté 14 (1936), Romains's Prélude à Verdun and Verdun (1938), Giraudoux's La Guerre de Troie n'aura pas lieu (1935), in conjunction with the extensive political analysis of the Munich crisis, to realise that no-one is going to be coming to the 1939 outbreak 'fresh'.

A useful illustration is Roland Dorgelès's writing from the front during the drôle de guerre, a phrase he claimed he was the one to coin (certainly Sartre and Beauvoir use "la guerre fantôme" in their letters at the time, which may show drôle de guerre is not an instant spontaneous collective phrase). These reports from the front(3) constantly refer to 'l'autre guerre',(4) in the context of the character, attitudes and behaviour of the soldiers and their officers. Another important factor which is also forcing comparisons with the First World War is the number of officers who were old enough to had fought, like Dorgelès himself, in 'l'autre'. This is not true of Weekend à Zuydcoote and La Mort dans l'âme; none of the main protagonists have fought in the First World War, which means there is an emphasis on the discovery of war and its reality rather than the continuity of national heroics and national character across the two wars which Dorgelès is able to construct. A further point to be made about the similarities Dorgelès stresses and which place the drôle de guerre within the frame of the 1914-18 conflict is that, while it is true that Dorgelès's writings were for public consumption, it is still striking how far this drôle de guerre is nonetheless a guerre compared to later representations. There is an enemy, with regular encounters, battles, victories, and losses; you have to pinch yourself to remember this is Jan-Feb 1940, since May-June 1940 are not like that in either Weekend à Zuydcoote or La Mort dans l'âme.

Sartre summed up philosophically the way war was more than just a possibility but was structuring the nature of the pre-war years, in describing their being as 'être-pour-la-guerre', a phrase formed from Heidegger's 'être-pour-la-mort'. But in the same way that the pre-war years only become such once war has broken out, this insight was revealed not by the approaching war, but by war itself.(5) Similarly we can cite the discrepancy between the contemporary experience and the well known discovery of historicity attendant upon the mobilisation of Mathieu in 1938 in Le Sursis(6) and equally famously attendant upon war itself in the pages of Qu'est-ce que la littérature?(7) In an interview which actually took place in 1938, looking forward to his next novel in the context of the very real possibility of imminent war and general mobilisation, Sartre says Antoine will discover, through mobilisation, his absolute freedom, and on returning from war will be able to carry out the perfect acte gratuit; not much room for historicity there.(8) In other words, these are constantly shifting perspectives, shifting grounds. My concern is both to try and avoid taking hindsight for the sight itself, and to avoid suggesting that there is some pure factual chronology. Part of the importance of literature is, as I've said, to raise questions around the boundaries and frontiers of events. And secondly to point towards the structuring role of narrative in relation to material which it does not totally control and is therefore also structured by.

The crucial determinant of the writing of the fall of France is that it is narrating a military defeat. Given that the conclusion is inscribed teleologically in the knowledge of the narration, writing this war is inevitably ~writing-for-defeat. This is not the case in Dorgelès's articles which can certainly be described as a case of writing-for-victory. Jean-François Sirinelli has argued(9) that the politicization of a generation was produced by the defeat of France, and the generation he is talking about is Sartre's, born in 1905. He is also referring particularly to the dominance of pacifism. But I think that in terms of perceptions of the coming war, and its nature, 'defeat' was not catered for, and the actual defeat therefore has a disturbing effect in many areas.

But to say that is really just pointing to where one starts from. It does not begin to deal with the history or the politics of this writing of war. Before considering the novels in detail, both of which are post-1945, it is worth mentioning that there were many novels and accounts of the defeat in the early days of the Occupation. *Les Lettres françaises* condemned many as 'des livres de guerre honteux'; the *Nouvelle Revue française* pointed out these novels were being read by the victor and the vanquished, which means that the accounts of defeat were part of the political programme of its aftermath: to sweep away the old order, (*Les Décombres*(10) offers a whole political programme in its title alone), depicting the rotteness of the defeated and the moral and physical superiority of the Germans, who will deign to re-make France and the French. Saint-Exupéry's *Pilote de guerre* (11) also stressed images of chaos, destruction and dismantling, but with a view to a reconstruction of the spirit of France, and was therefore considered wholly positive by the Resistance.

Weekend à Zuydcoote and *La Mort dans l'âme* were both published in 1949,(12) long after these battles. On the face of it they are very different. Merle's novel won the Prix Goncourt and great popularity,(13) while Sartre's depressed reaction to the relative lack of success and esteem for this third volume of *Les Chemins de la liberté* is well documented.(14) For several reasons, however, they can be considered typical of much postwar fiction of the fall of France. Firstly in the detailed use of dates - which is where one sees the *énonciation* structuring the *énoncé*, because at the level of the *énonciation* there is knowledge of the rapidity of the defeat. For example, *Déroute* by Jacques Debû-Bridel (15) dates nearly every chapter, and several subheadings, starting with Chapter 1: 'Les Douze ans de Claudine. Printemps 1939.' to Chapter X, 'Les Derniers Jours de Paris capitale, mai 1940', Chapter XI, 'Ils approchent, mai-juin 1940', Chapter XIV 'C'est fini, juillet-août 1940', to the final Chapter XV 'Dans les ruines du prieuré, octobre 1940'. The dates are carrying a sense of destiny, doom and tragedy, particularly in *Weekend à Zuydcoote* and *La Mort dans l'âme* where very little actually happens, to the extent that in *La Mort dans l'âme* one is irresistibly reminded of *Waiting for Godot* at times, as Mathieu and his fellow soldiers sit and talk, and others pass by, just stopping to talk for a time. Neither text covers the ground of *Déroute*. *Weekend à Zuydcoote* is set over one weekend, with 4 chapters: *samedi matin, samedi après-midi, dimanche matin, dimanche après-midi*. It is of course significant that it is using days rather than dates, this being part of the way it constructs

itself as adrift from real time and history, but the sense of a countdown
is maintained. The first part of *La Mort dans l'âme* (which presents the
process of defeat, whereas the second part depicts rather its result), is
dated from 15 June to 18 June. These narratives are therefore structured on
the basis of a closing of options, zooming towards The End, which may in
itself explain some of the difficulties Sartre had in opening his text out
to a fourth-volume and Resistance novel.

There are other common points which can be mentioned:

- The main protagonists: both are intellectuals, establishing rather
particular relationships with the other soldiers.

- The search for explanations as to what has gone wrong, and why they
are defeated. *La Mort dans l'âme* offers a full range of possibilities,
including betrayal by the bourgeoisie, the Popular Front, and 'no will to
fight'.

- The irony created by the discrepancy between the image of war and
the reality of this war, heightened by a tragic consciousness of the
absurdity of existence. War is not being carried out according to the
norms. Even the expression *drôle de guerre* implies that knowledge of how a
war should be conducted is being brought to bear. To mention a couple of
examples: soldiers are experiencing defeat without having seen an enemy;
the very title *Weekend à Zuydcoote*, suggests leisure. The incongruous
nature of the country landscape and fine weather, or the holiday scenery of
sea and sand, are repeatedly underlined in both novels.

- Social upheaval. This is perceptible mainly in neglect of the codes
and conventions of military behaviour; officers are ignored, or
aggressively demand respect of formalities, rather inappropriately.

- Both main characters die in a kind of self-destruction (of course,
we all know Mathieu does not die, since he figures in the fragments of the
fourth volume. However, I consider this to be a fiction not internally
supported by the evidence in *La Mort dans l'âme*). The narratives end (as
does Bost's *Le Dernier des métiers*) (16) with the eclipse of their
consciousness ('Maillat ne sut pas qu'il était en train de mourir' are the
last words of *Weekend à Zuydcoote*) which has been the primary, if not
unique, point of view. In each case, therefore, there is a kind of
deliberate shock to the reader. There is no obvious simple reason for this
pattern, but it suggests there may be a blurring of boundaries between
individual consciousness and consciousness itself.

Thematically many points of convergence can therefore be traced. What
are also thematised are the larger entities and values which are seen to be
brought down by this defeat. The controversies about the politics of
historical representations, in Resistance denunciations of what it saw as
collaborationist narratives of the defeat for example, bear particularly on
the kinds of values and perspectives being articulated through the
narrative. De Gaulle's *Mémoires de guerre* is another text which shows the
sequence of military events as part of a larger narrative: 'On peut dire
qu'en une semaine le destin était scellé. Sur la pente fatale où une erreur
démesurée nous avait, de longtemps, engagés, l'armée, l'Etat, la France,
roulaient, maintenant, à un rythme vertigineux.'(17) and the triad of
armée, *état* and *France* reappears three more times. Sartre takes a rather
different view in his 'prière d'insérer' for *La Mort dans l'âme*:

> Ils sont vivants mais la mort les a touchés; quelque chose
> est fini, la défaite a fait tomber l'étagère aux valeurs.
> Pendant que Daniel, à Paris, célèbre le triomphe de la
> mauvaise conscience, Mathieu, dans un village de Lorraine,

fait l'inventaire des dégâts: Paix, Progrès, Raison, Droit,
Démocratie, Patrie, tout est en morceaux, on ne pourra jamais
recoller les morceaux.*(18)*
These sentiments are echoed in the text as Mathieu shoots from the
belltower: 'Il tirait sur l'Homme, sur la Vertu, sur le Monde.'(19) Now, it
has become one of the truisms of the postmodern condition, that in the
Holocaust and the use of atomic bombs, what also came to grief were belief
in man, and the values of progress and humanism itself. But here, it is the
fall of France which is bringing down the Enlightenment - and *Weekend à
Zuydcoote* is not dissimilar in its sense of metaphysical absurdity. That
the defeat of the French nation can be linked to such considerations may in
part be pointing to the universalist values inherent in 'la patrie', a
notion which was forged in battle and in the universalist ideals of La
République,(20) or to the generally transcendent view of French culture.
Indeed, Dorgelès begins his account of the 10 mai offensive with the words:
'la guerre d'Europe *commençait* ce jour-là'.(21) But we are also dealing
with fictional narrative, realist conventions, and characterisation; with
representations of the defeat as lived by individuals, whose identity as
French (or not French), as soldiers and civilians, is also caught up in
this upheaval. Michel Contat reminds us that 'comme la plupart des romans
de guerre, *La Mort dans l'âme* est un roman d'hommes'(22) (though we might
be forgiven for forgetting this in *Weekend à Zuydcoote*). In other words, if
no analysis of representation of contemporary warfare, be it Vietnam or the
Falklands, is considered complete without looking at nationality, identity
and masculinity as a complex of themes,(23) *Weekend à Zuydcoote* and *La Mort
dans l'âme* teach us that this is not just a contemporary discovery.

Weekend à Zuydcoote is set near Bray-Dunes during the evacuation from
Dunkirk. Maillat has a kind of home base there camped out with three other
soldiers. They have done the war together. Alexandre is the cook who has
taken charge of their domestic life, Pierson is a priest, and Dhéry the
wheeler-dealer out for what he can make. Maillat makes serious attempts to
leave for England, in spite of the refusal by the British to embark French
soldiers. He also comes across two young women guarding their home. He
later returns to find one of them, Jeanne, being raped. He kills the rapist
and another man there, but soon afterwards he himself actually rapes
Jeanne. At the novel's end he returns for a third time and stays with her.

In terms of the writing of history, I would categorise this as a
metaphysical novel. It has a cosmic view of war and of history as
repetition, in part denying the narrative process: to tell the story of a
battle or a war produces an ending, with victors and losers. But there can
be no ending, we are told, as it is all to be repeated time and again.
There are very few precise historical references in this novel, but one is
an interview with a veteran of 1870 which Maillat remembers seeing before
the war, and which produces reactions of derision in him: 'Toute une
époque! pensa Maillat, toute l'actualité d'il y a soixante-dix ans! Et
comme on se passionnait alors! Que de haine, que d'espoirs, que de
mensonges! Que de sottises! Et maintenant, c'était fini! bien fini! ça
n'avait plus de sens. Peut-être, ça n'en avait jamais eu! ça n'existait
plus nulle part. ça n'existait pas plus que la guerre 14-18, que celle-ci
bientôt, que toutes celles qui avaient précédé, et toutes celles qui
suivront.'(24)

The scenes of disorder and chaos with the non-evacuation of the French
troops and the regular bombings by the Germans correspond to an overriding
lack of sense - in the primary opposition between order and disorder, sense

and nonsense, war and history are in the realm of nonsense, chance and
contingency. Narrative necessity and finality belong to peace-time, for
only in peace-time is the notion of a story meaningful: 'Les histoires se
nouent et se dénouent harmonieusement, comme des tragédies
classiques...'(25) Yet the need for and existence of order are in constant
tension with this chaos. It is repetition which constitutes domestic order
for Alexandre. Everything and everyone is in order, in its place, when they
are doing what's been done before. Jeanne's insistence on not leaving her
house is a similar quest for order. But both these behaviours are so
clearly grounded in their own logic alone that they are purely local
solutions within the prevailing disorder. The inability to adapt as a form
of order or conformity in itself is also taken to absurdist extremes, when
for example the English soldiers refuse to leave the burning ship they have
queued for so long to get on to. This is combined with a fierce narrative
finality which almost operates like a determinism. Alexandre is compared to
John the Baptist, Alexandre is decapitated; Maillat and Pierson sit next to
a half dug grave-like trench, Alexandre will be buried there. Another
aspect of the interrogation of absurdity can be traced in an anxiety around
'sequentiality', if I may be permitted the expression. Is there a logic
operating in a sequence of events? 'ça c'est passé comme ça'(26) is said to
reassure; characters are in the realm of pure contingency, Maillat is not
responsible for Alexandre's beheading, or his rape of Jeanne; on the other
hand, Alexandre had said to Maillat: 'ça te ressemble, tout ce qui t'arrive
et tout ce qui t'arrivera,'(27) which suggests not only a latent order, but
that it has the power of destiny. So the question of patterning and logic
in relation to history, which inevitably means narrative, is raised in a
variety of ways, without, I would argue, any kind of resolution.

This is in many ways a violent text, with much violence affecting
women. The novel opens with a soldier, Nittel, pushing a dead woman in a
cart. There's patterning here too - the dead woman's dress keeps riding up
and she is not wearing underpants. Nittel keeps pulling her dress down -
and Maillat is ashamed to catch himself doing the same to Jeanne's dress
after she has been raped. Sexuality and sexual violence concerning women
are major themes of the text. That this is also defining male sexuality and
identity is raised explicitly by Nittel. He is a taxi-driver in civilian
life and is describing to Maillat excursions to prostitutes with 'les
copains'. 'Moi, c'était assis, et la môme à genoux, à mes pieds. Tu m'as
compris! Comme un Pacha. Tu parles, je me donnais l'impression d'être un
grand patron pour une fois. Bien assis là, sur la banquette arrière, et la
môme à mes pieds! C'est là que tu te sens l'homme, dis donc!'(28) or, two
pages later with his wife: 'Il n'y avait plus que nous deux, bien au chaud
dans le plume, avec la petite lampe à côté. Et moi qui l'emboitais par
derrière, et lui caressais le ventre. Ah Bon Dieu! C'est là que tu sens
l'homme, dis donc, et ma femme, qui ne pipait pas mot (...). Elle
attendait, elle ne pipait pas mot (...). Et le vent dehors, un vrai temps
de salaud: le vent, la pluie, la grêle, le tonnerre, tout le bastringue,
quoi!'(29) So far, so conventional. But in relation to the links which can
be established at the level of episode and language, the scene of a man and
woman in bed together offering a refuge against an alien, hostile world,
recurs twice more, including the end, (though unfortunately on each
occasion a bomb drops on them). A closed space providing a feeling of
security for those who have retreated there, or an attitude of silent
expectancy, are elements which recur even more frequently.   In other
words, although one focuses 'sexuality' on the very obviously sexualised

scenes and descriptions of women, closer reading suggests that this applies just as much to men. If we take the opening scene of Nittel pushing the cart: 'Une femme y était étendue, jambes en avant. Sa robe, retroussée presque jusqu'au ventre laissait voir deux cuisses roses et grasses.'(30) This is preceded by the description of a car with two soldiers sleeping in it: 'étendus de tout leur long sur les coussins, [ils] dormaient côte à côte, les mains ouvertes, avec un air de satisfaction profonde.'(31) The pose is virtually identical, and announces a frequent image of the text, that of bodies lying in repose or dead, and sexualised. Open hands and palms are mentioned obsessionally in the descriptions of men. The fact that the 'main droite grande ouverte' of the rapist hides his exposed genitals, (32) suggests some kind of substitution. Maillat attacks the rapist, and in his fight has an explicit fantasy of being raped by this man, who has many similarities with 'son copain Alexandre' (who is identified with domesticity; Maillat also complains he is like a woman with all his questions).(33)

One final example of descriptions which reverberate and recur in various contexts can be given. At the beginning of 'samedi après-midi', Maillat goes past a dead horse and two others. One is wounded, making no sound. 'De nouveau, le cheval blessé leva la tête, puis il recula d'un pas, posa son museau sur l'encolure de son compagnon et ferma les yeux. Il resta ainsi quelques seconds, dans une attitude indéfinissable de lassitude et de tendresse.'(34) Maillat kills the rapist and his companion, and takes the corpse of the second, smaller man down the stairs: 'En se penchant, il approcha son visage de celui de la petite gouape et comme il tirait le bras à soi, la tête inerte glissa doucement vers lui, et vint se caler contre son épaule dans une attitude d'abandon et de tendresse.'(35)

The violence of war goes together with sexual violence, and the violence of war is itself sexualised. Identity is gendered and sexualised, and the aggression of dominator and dominated establishing that identity is operating between men as well as between men and women. Although *La Mort dans l'âme* is historically and politically very different, comparisons can certainly be made here. *L'Age de raison* opens with the man begging in the street who has been fighting in Spain, tapping straight into Mathieu's bad conscience. Mathieu is on his way to see Marcelle, who is pregnant, and the issue of the abortion will be a central one - and taps straight into Mathieu's bad conscience. The two run parallel, his lack of political and personal engagement and commitment, which is a fairly conventional public politics/private sexuality dichotomy. Like *Weekend à Zuydcoote*, *La Mort dans l'âme* will sweep aside that dichotomy.

Using documentary reportage techniques, dates and references, and newspaper headlines for the fall of Paris, for example, *La Mort dans l'âme* is immediately more rooted, historically, than *Weekend à Zuydcoote*.(36) Part of the 'metaphysical' perspective of *Weekend à Zuydcoote* can be found in the fact that, even though set at Dunkirk, and a realist text, it is clearly in a realm of pure fictionality. *La Mort dans l'âme* intersperses scenes of the non-war with others from France and USA, creating a more grandiose, epic dimension. Also, the characters are familiar from the previous two volumes, so it benefits from the specific effect of realism which that creates. Michel Contat has described at length the effect of the changed historical conjuncture on the writing of this third volume of *Les Chemins* and the perceived difficulties of moving towards a Resistance novel in relation to the political complexities and ambiguities of the postwar period.(37) *La Mort dans l'âme* was written in 1947-8. Also, as I suggested earlier, there could well be a discursive logic operating which is inhibiting an optimistic sequel.

This is an extremely rich text: I shall concentrate here on some aspects of its politics and sexuality.

It is a novel which in a sense advances pointing to its mask, since there is an early discussion about the role of political art, and the relationship' of art to politics outside literature. Ritchie believes in art as comfort, art as beauty. Gomez argues for art as disturbance, even if one should not mistake it for political action. But he also knows he can no longer create; perhaps because of the men he has killed. Art is a humanist enterprise, to kill is to pass to the other side; here as elsewhere, memories of *La Condition Humaine* in particular are inescapable. I have in mind the changes wrought in Tchen by the assassination in the opening pages, and the relationship of that transformation to the overall dichotomy between the human and the non-human; more particularly, the account of the individual soldiers - part animal, part thing - approaching the bell-tower carries many echoes of Hemmelrich watching the individual enemy, as much animal and insect as man, climbing towards him.(38)

This is quite consonant with the vision of the death of civilisation, of the disintegration of the human, which emerges from this account of the fall of France. Given the mention at one point that not only France, but Christendom is being effaced,(39) the title must I think be taken quite literally. The ancient laws are being swept aside, and a new, not necessarily human, order is being installed: the order of the absurd and the inhuman. War is described as a 'rêve de bourgeois'; defeat is taking down the bourgeois social order, nation and state, all that has forged the notion of man.(40) What is intriguing is the writing of this in 1947-8, in a text which explicitly raises the question of the politics of artistic endeavour. The novel ends on a truly apocalyptic vision: 'Au-dessus du mort et du wagon inerte, la nuit passe, seule vivante. Demain l'aube les couvrira de la même rosée, la chair morte et l'acier rouillé ruisselleront de la même sueur. Demain viendront les oiseaux noirs.'(41) Within the fictional chronology, Resistance optimism and solidarity is yet to come; but itself will be put into doubt by the holocaust, Hiroshima and Nagasaki. It is almost as if Sartre, in addressing 1949 from *1940*, is effacing that Resistance humanism; and re-instating the intuitions of 1939-1940 as a definitive historical break with civilisation.

But 'l'homme' is also a specific as well as a universalist term. 'Il fait son métier d'homme' says Mathieu of Pinette having sex with the *postière*.(42) These are soldiers who are learning to be defeated, to have failed in their 'métier d'homme' as soldiers. It is striking, the extent to which relations between the men and between the armies are mediated by the terms *aimer/haïr*. The group of men asks obsessively whether they are loved by the villagers and their compatriots, or whether they are pariahs. Similarly, they ask obsessively whether they detest or love each other. There are unusual scenes of male tenderness: Mathieu taking Pinette's hand; Brunet and Schneider hand-in-hand in the train at the end. The move beyond the human in killing is also accompanied by a desire for killing and the enemy. 'Un type rampait le long du mur, une grenade à la main. Mathieu visa cet être étrange et désirable.'(43) 'Un gros homme en bras de chemise apparut tout à coup à gauche du canon... Mathieu se redressa brusquement: ce petit homme à la gorge nue l'enflammait de désir.'(44) Like *Weekend à Zuydcoote*, sexuality is a crucial dimension of the depiction of warfare in *La Mort dans l'âme*.(45)

Characteristic of many postwar novels about the war and the Occupation is an at times cynical, at times angry interrogation of the sense of history, of the possibility of change and the efficacy of political action. The narrative of the defeat in *Weekend à Zuydcoote* and *La Mort dans l'âme* (whatever Sartre hoped to indicate in Part II of his novel) partake of this vision. Both novels show men who have become self-conscious actors in a sinister comedy, and who cannot act convincingly because they no longer believe in their role of soldier of the French nation, and the wider entities of nation, state and social purpose which that role sustains. In combining this with questions of the boundaries of sexual and gender identity, violence and desire, both novels chronicle the psychological, social and national disintegration at the level of the individual, particularly the individual soldier, under the catastrophic impact of a Blitzkrieg which is taking place off-stage.

Another reason why this presents a particular interest is the sexualisation of Resistance discourse on collaboration. The Resistance presented Drieu la Rochelle, Jacques Chardonne and other writers perceived as collaborating with the Germans, as effeminate, passive, and homosexual decadents. Sartre's clandestine article on Drieu in *Les Lettres françaises* is just one example among many.(46) In that sense, Daniel in *La Mort dans l'âme* is an emblematic figure, in his desire for the Germans as they enter Paris, and desire for them as carriers of a new order, installing a definitive realm of evil. *Weekend à Zuydcoote* and *La Mort dans l'âme* postdate the Resistance writings, but nonetheless suggest that homosexualisation might be fundamental to the discourse on collaboration and fraternisation with the enemy, because it is inherent in and dependent on contemporary representations of warfare, killing and combat. Paradoxically, it is the writing of defeat which illuminates the dynamic.

Notes

(The place of publication is Paris unless otherwise stated.)

1. Jean-Paul Sartre, *Les Carnets de la drôle de guerre*, Gallimard, 1983; *Lettres au Castor*, Gallimard, 1983; Appendice II, '*La Mort dans l'âme* (fragments de journal)', *Oeuvres romanesques* (henceforth OR), Bibliothèque de la Pléiade, 1981.
2. 'La Fin de la guerre', *Situations III*, Gallimard, 1949, p. 64.
3. Republished in Roland Dorgelès, *La Drôle de guerre 1939-1940*, Albin Michel, 1957, interspersed with chapters entitled: 'Ce que je ne pouvais pas dire'.
4. Which would be expected, no doubt, of the author of *Les Croix de bois*.
5, Lettre à Simone de Beauvoir', 26 octobre 1939, OR pp. 1895-6.
6. *Le Sursis*, OR pp. 805-9.
7. *Situations II*, Gallimard, 1948, pp. 242-3.
8. Interview with Claudine Chonez, OR p. 1697.
9. *Génération intellectuelle: Khâgneux et Normaliens dans l'entre-deux-guerres*, Fayard, 1989.
10. Lucien Rebatet, *Les Décombres*, Denoël, 1942.
11. Antoine de Saint-Exupéry, *Pilote de guerre*, Gallimard, 1942.

12. Robert Merle, *Weekend à Zuydcoote*, Gallimard, 1949; Jean-Paul Sartre, *La Mort dans l'âme*, Gallimard, 1949.
13. There was interesting discussion at the colloquium of genre conventions in *Weekend à Zuydcoote*, and the possibly chauvinist, populist basis of its appeal.
14. OR p. 1881.
15. Jacques Debû-Bridel, *Déroute*, Gallimard, 1945.
16. Jacques-Laurent Bost, *Le Dernier des métiers*, Gallimard, 1945.
17. De Gaulle, *Mémoires de guerre*, vol. I, Plon, 1954, p.29.
18. OR p. 2016.
19. OR p. 1344.
20. Philippe Contamine, 'Mourir pour la patrie' in Pierre Nora (ed.), *Les Lieux de mémoire*, volume II, *La Nation*, tome III, Gallimard, 1986, pp. 11-43.
21. Dorgelès p. 221 (my italics).
22. OR p. 1344.
23. See for example *The Falklands Factor: Representations of a conflict*, Manchester City Art Gallery/History of Art and Design Department of Manchester Polytechnic, 1989; and Klaus Thewelheit's very impressive work on the writings of the officers of the Freikorps, *Male Fantaises*, vol. I, 'Women, Floods, Bodies, History', translated by Stephen Conway in collaboration with Erica Carter and Chris Turner, Cambridge, Polity Press, 1987.
24. p. 203.
25. p. 29.
26. p. 201-2.
27. p. 251.
28. pp. 21-2.
29. p. 24.
30. p. 9.
31. ibid.
32. p. 200.
33. p. 34.
34. p. 74.
35. p. 209.
36. See also François Noudelmann, 'Histoire et idéologie dans *Les Chemins de la liberté*', *Etudes sartriennes, I, Cahiers de Sémiotique textuelle 2*, Paris X, 1984.
37. OR p. 1871.
38. André Malraux, *La Condition humaine*, Livre de poche, 1969, pp. 222-4 (Ist published 1933); OR p. 1335, p. 1337.
39. OR p. 1281.
40. This means that the "non-human" is more historicised, more rooted in ideological and cultural forms than in Malraux's Pascalian vision, as can be seen in the episode where Odette gazes at the immensity of sky, beyond humanity and language: 'C'était [Jacques] qui savait le nom des étoiles, la distance précise de la terre à la lune, le nombre des habitants de la région, leur histoire et leurs occupations (...) Elle courut à l'auto, elle voulait le réveiller tout de suite, réveiller la Science, l'Industrie et la Morale.' (OR p. 1312).
41. OR p. 1457.

42. OR p. 1282.
43. OR p. 1337.
44. OR p. 1341.
45. See also Andrew N. Leak, *The Perverted Consciousness: Sexuality and Sartre*, Macmillan, London, 1989, for a more psychological reading of the metaphors of sexuality in *La Mort dans l'âme*.
46. 'Drieu la Rochelle ou la haine de soi', *Les Lettres françaises* No. 6, avril 1943.

DESTROYING THE MYTHS OF DEBACLE

Hilary Footit and John Simmonds

The myths of the débâcle of 1940 were very much in the Sorelian mould of myth-making: 'une organisation d'images capables d'évoquer instinctivement tous les sentiments qui correspondent aux diverses manifestations de la guerre engagée contre la société moderne'.(1) They were - and to a large extent still are - living myths, not only guiding and influencing political behaviour, but at crucial times representing a major battlefield on which the struggle for France took place. Destroying the myths of the débâcle created by Vichy was not just an inevitable prelude to Resistance; it was, in the early days of the defeat, when isolated individuals, and small groups without armaments, constituted the sole opponents of the regime, *the only* form of Resistance. From the initial attack on the Vichy myths of débâcle, Resistance groups moved to the creation of their own counter myths which underlined much of Resistance preparations for the post-war period and shaped the proposals for post-war constitutions.

A catalogue of the myths begun in 1940 to account for the tragedy of defeat and assuage the trauma of national shame would take several volumes in its own right. This introduction will concentrate on some of the more potent and influential myths of 1940; ideas that the Resistance would have to counter if it were to break down resigned acceptance of defeat and encourage amongst the French a belief in the eventual victory of a sovereign France. Historians have, in recent years, picked their way fastidiously through this jungle of images, providing ironic or supportive footnotes, or calling on their contemporaries to radically re-appraise the myths they have inherited. Ironically, however, the sub-text to this paper is a recognition of the way in which many of the 1940 myths and their counter-myths are still being used by commentators on this period. In a sense the Resistance failed to destroy them.

Vichy and the Myths of the Defeat

Just as on the Free French side it was the single voice of de Gaulle on the B.B.C. which first articulated the Resistance message of a reverse not a defeat, so on the Vichy side it was the single voice of Pétain who articulated the capitulation myth of defeat. Pétain, unlike de Gaulle, was not a lone and unknown voice broadcasting over a rarely heard foreign French language service. He was a popular symbol of military heroism and fortitude, representing the victory of 1918 and all the virtues of traditional France. His words were awaited by the whole nation who sought to escape the horrors perpetrated by the Germans on defeated Poland. His ideas were thus almost universally disseminated and accepted, or at least assimilated, by a large majority of the French in the summer and autumn of 1940.(2) Pétain began to create his myth of the defeat before even the creation of Vichy and the National Revolution. He needed the Assembly to vote him full powers on July 11th as a means of legitimising his state and, as Azéma has pointed out,(3) he needed the armistice to sanction his regime as an international representative of France. But he also needed to create an interpretation of defeat which apportioned blame to all the elements of past regimes and societies that his new political, social and moral order would sweep away. This would justify the creation of a new authoritarian and conservative state overthrowing all the principles of liberty, justice and equality which had been won in a hundred and fifty years of republican struggle.

In the first broadcast on the 20th June, he launched the Vichy version of the military defeat.

'J'ai pris cette décision, dure au coeur d'un soldat, parce que la situation militaire s'imposait' ... 'Dès le 13 juin, la demande d'armistice était inévitable' ...'L'infériorité de notre matérial a été plus grande encore que celle de nos effectifs. L'aviation française a livré à un contre six ses combats. Moins forts qu'il y a vingt-deux ans, nous avons aussi moins d'amis. Trop peu d'enfants; trop peu d'armes, trop peu d'alliées, voilà les causes de notre défaite.'(4)

Pétain's myth was extended on the simple formula articulated during his 11th October broadcast.

'Le désastre n'est en réalité que le réflet sur le plan militaire, des faiblesses et des tares de l'ancien régime politique.'(5)

Thus the military was at fault but not to blame.

'Notre drapeau reste sans tâche. Notre armée s'est bravement et loyalement battue. Inférieure en armes et en nombre, elle a dû demander que cesse le combat'.(6)

Such was his reply to what he deemed a national insult from Churchill; the renewed offer of joint nationality. For Pétain the real culprits were:

'the coalitions of economic interests and ... teams of politicians and syndicalists falsely claiming to represent the working class. The political game played by these interests had led to a modern day "vassalage" of the people and since they were entirely devoted to domestic politics, these regimes were incapable of formulating and implementing a foreign policy worthy of France. Inspired in turn by paranoid nationalism or a doctrinaire pacifism, characterized by lack of understanding and weakness - at the very moment when our victory called upon us to be at once generous and strong, our foreign policy could only result in disaster'. ... One day in September 1939, without even daring to consult the chambers, the government declared war. This war was all but lost in advance'.(7)

The incompetence of Third Republican politicians and governments was mirrored for Pétain by the myth of the incompetence of the state and its civil servants.

'La démoralisation et la désorganisation qui, comme une gangrène, avaient envahi le corps de l'Etat en y introduisant la paresse et l'incompétence; parfois même le sabotage systématique aux fins de désordre social ou de révolution internationale'.

'Pendant les trois quarts du siècle qui ont précédé la guerre, le régime politique auquel étaient soumis les Français avait pour principal ressort la culture du mécontentment.'(8)

Pétain did say that the new order should not be a moral crusade, nor a revenge for the events of 1936, but his analysis belied his intention. One of the main themes of national decay was the failure of an increasingly godless and selfish people to produce children and promote family life.

Pétain's couplet, 'not enough children, not enough arms' was a powerful idea for people brought up on the propaganda of the missing generations and the pro-natalist legislation of the First World War and beyond. As an aside, the longevity of this myth can be seen in the recent writings of Henri Amouroux, who concluded:

'En vérité rien ne répare notre infériorité démographique, cause générale de tous nos malheurs, dès l'instant que nos alliées anglais n'apportent, ni sur terre, ni dans les airs, un concours digne du chiffre de leur population comme de leur puissance économique ... Trop peu de soldats, trop peu d'armes, trop peu de Français. Et trop peu d'alliées.'(9)

Of course for Pétain, despite disclaimers about moral retribution, there was always the vague moral condemnation of pre-war French society.

'Notre défaite est venue de nos relâchements. L'esprit de jouissances détruit ce que l'esprit de sacrifice a édifié'.(10)

Pétain even erected the first elements of the anti-capitalist and anti-worker myths:

'Le capitalisme international et le socialisme international qui l'ont exploité et dégradé (les Français) fut egalement partie de l'avant guerre ... Nous ne souffrons plus leur ténébreuse alliance'.(11)

The remarkable feature - and perhaps the most powerful persuasion - of the very early broadcasts by Pétain in the weeks after the defeat was their comprehensive nature. He appears to have touched upon virtually all the mythological interpretations that were later embellished and expanded by Vichy writers and collaborating propagandists. They were all broad but comforting analyses, easy to internalise, difficult to refute without hard fact, but useful as labels for a regime and a society which Vichy wished to demolish. Despite this onslaught, those writing in 1940 about the collapse of their country, even those writing in anger about the betrayal of France, saw Pétain as a dupe of more powerful and cunning forces. Elie Bois wrote in December 1940 (after the handshake at Montoire)

'I make a point of declaring here and now, however, that I rule out one name (from criticism); that of Marshal Pétain who has been imposed upon, deceived and gulled. He is a victim whom we must pity'.(12)

He was obviously not a 'victim' of anyone in 1940, not even Laval. He had a starkly articulated general hatred of the recent past in France whose politics, society and values he was determined to sweep away in a restoration of traditional values. If his early broadcasts are taken as examples of his political actions, then he was not a victim, but the single most powerful propagandist for the defeat and capitulation myths which blamed all France's failures on the regime from 1870 to 1940. It was these myths which justified the politics of the Vichy regime and acceptance of collaboration with the occupying forces in the north.

There were a set of other, more extreme, myths of which the surviving right-wing press and the newly established collaborationist papers were authors. They often took the early Petainist themes and radicalised them with violent popular imagery, but they established themes of their own which were generally in close ideological proximity to fascism.

The destructive and unpatriotic reputation of the French Communist Party (PCF) had been established well before the fall of France. Daladier, ably seconded by Tardieu, had banned the party's publications, its organisation and any form of communist activity. The government arrested

PCF militants for continuing communist activity and for sabotage; although there appear to have been only one or two real instances of anti-war sabotage in factories.(13) Parliamentary immunity was lifted and all the communist deputies, except the four in the army, were also held. These arrests, (Tardieu boasted of 10,000 in March 1940) and all the official anti-communist propaganda resultant from the Germano-Soviet Pact 'proved' the culpability of the French Communists. The far right did not need to pursue this theme, but instead launched a broader attack on the degenerative effects of left-wing pacifism and materialism. This was primarily the work of *Action Française* and its great literary orator, Charles Maurras. The target of *Action Française* was the Popular Front whose 'capacity for destruction was surpassed only by its impotence'.(14) Maurras' criticism was that whilst these pacificists had allowed the Saarland to go to Germany and Hitler to re-militarise the Rhineland, they simultaneously played at warmongering against Italy and Spain, who could have been two of France's most important allies. Democracy had not produced a strong and ardent France, indeed few wished to go to war on behalf of democracy in 1939 as they had gone to war on behalf of the nation in 1914. *Action Française* saw the return of the monarchy as the necessary figurehead for a new elite leadership system which France needed to clear out the demoralising influences of socialism and 'foreign ideas'.

The rapidly burgeoning collaborationist press spent much time denouncing those responsible for the defeat, because in the early days of the occupation it was easier to look for scapegoats and castigate the past than to explain the crushing measures of the armistice or the handshake between Pétain and Hitler at Montoire. Drieu la Rochelle, apart from celebrating the triumph of the anti-Dreyfusards, declared in *La Nouvelle Revue Française* that the French had become victims of rationalism and intellectualism - the worst of the Enlightenment and the French Revolution - and that 'la civilisation française a cessé d'être fondée sur le sens du corps'(15). He believed that it had no sense of physical, emotional and spiritual strength and no attachment to the nation. In his famous phrase France had been 'destroyed by the rationalism to which her genius had been reduced.'

'The France of the scouts, hikers and skiers was not strong
enough to overcome the France of the idlers, Pernod drinkers,
river bank fishermen and the salon, committee and *syndicat*
babblers.'(16)

Socialists, liberals, freemasons, jews, school teachers, civil servants, feeble upper classes, self-seeking bourgeois, deluded workers, and humiliated peasantry were all his targets for blame and scorn. No one escaped.

Marcel Bucard, the creator of *Francisme*, a fascist in the Mussolinian mould and representative of the 'tabloid' end of the collaborationist press condemned all and every republican,'[L]es bourreaux de la nation,' and called for the death penalty; 'où sont les guillotines?'(17). Louis Gillet in *Le Petit Journal* urged a new generation to rectify the natalist failings of the old.

'Mes fils qui venez de vous battre, résistez la tentation ...
L'amour est aussi le courage; on a plus de coeur à deux qu'à
soi seul. Le Maréchal l'a dit, si nous avions été soixante
millions au lieu de quarante, nos voisins y auraient regardé à
deux fois.'(18)

This may have been one of the earliest contemporary examples of the nineteen- sixties exhortation to make love not war. For Margueritte in *L'Effort*(19) and for *Le Cri du Peuple*(20) of Doriot's *Parti Populaire Français*, it was the Jews and the British together who had manufactured the defeat of France. Serpeille in *Paris Soir*(21) blamed the freemasons who had led the working classes to attack all that was good in traditional France and thus weaken the nation before the war. Jean Luchaire in *Le Matin*(22) attacked the parliamentarians and communists of the 'République des camarades', joining them to the British and the Jews in a European conspiracy against France.

An ironic feature of French history in 1940 was the support for the Vichy analysis of the débâcle which came from outside France. Many of the western nations - especially the United States and Britain - had French exiles, but instead of challenging the propaganda of the new Vichy regime, they often inadvertently gave succour to these notions. Of those who wrote in the heat - or cold - of the moment from the non-Vichy and non-collaborationist side of the argument, many directly attacked the Republicans of the inter-war period. They wrote from the uncomfortable position of being patriots who had abandonned their country and were not present to share the pain and anguish of their countrymen and women. So they tended to turn on great men of the past rather than the citizenry. Those in exile were among the first to write substantial pieces on the defeat and as they were eye-witnesses, they were translated, published and quite widely disseminated outside France. Elie Bois, writing in the winter of 1940, attacked Daladier and Reynaud. For the latter he reserved particular venom as a representative of the corrupt and indolent Third Republic. The President, Lebrun, who faded from the scene at the crucial moment, was attacked in a cry of pain and anguish; almost risible in translation:

'Has any other Head of State performed such a vanishing trick?
Albert Lebrun! Come here, give account of your stewardship!
Speak! Explain yourself! What have you done with France?'(23)

Jacques Maritain in *A Travers le Désastre* (1941)(24) blamed the army for its treachery and for bringing down the government of Reynaud, which he thought might have provided a last-ditch defence against the Germans. Pertinax in *Les Fossoyeurs*(25) continued his satirical attack against the men of the 1920's and 1930's, lampooning their age and their infirmities. Henri de Kérellis in *Français Voilà la Vérité* blamed 'la Main diabolique de la cinquième colonne' whom he seemed to identify as almost everyone in inter-war politics.(26)

In a sense such analyses spread support for the Vichy myths of defeat precisely in those places where they should have been weakest, the United States and Great Britain.(27)

Resistance Myths and Counter-Myths

Destroying these myths of débâcle was not just a prelude to resistance, it was, in the early days of defeat, *the only* form of resistance which was possible. The two central myths that the resistance began by attacking were that of the military defeat and that of Vichy's 'higher moral ground'. The most immediate and potentially pernicious interpretation for the defeat as far as future Resistance was concerned was that of the superhuman foe who had dealt a mortal blow to the country - the invincibility of the Germans - which had been taken as axiomatic in the Vichy myths.

De Gaulle's classic 'Appel du 18 juin' of course confronted this myth squarely: the defeat was neither caused by the inherent invincibility of the Germans, 'ce sont les chars, les avions, la tactique des Allemands qui nous fait reculer' nor was it final,

'La défaite est-elle définitive? Non! ... Les mêmes moyens qui nous ont vaincus peuvent faire venir un jour la victoire'(28).

The same attempt to question the assumption of automatic and total German invincibility is evident in early Resistance tracts from inside France: Jean Texcier's pamphlet, written in July 1940, used humour to dent the image of the perfect German soldier:

'C'est entendu. Ils savent chanter en choeur et d'une voix juste. Mais c'est au commandement, comme pour un exercice respiratoire.'(29)

Kedward makes the point that the supporters of Pétain and Vichy had every interest in presenting the defeat as a cataclysmic event which marked an enormous and total break with the past. Such a view was fed by the general confusion of the period, so that: 'France in the second half of 1940 was fragmented into a mass of individual experiences and regional differences'.(30) In effect, the discontinuity was more apparent than real - the attitudes of those who wanted outright collaboration with Germany for example, or those like Maurras who would provide some of the ideological underpinning for the Vichy regime, were consistent with their pre-war attitudes. The same is true of those who began, often as lone individuals, to question the myth of the total military defeat. Ideological considerations were stubbonly consistent. Kedward gives the example of Christian Democrats who attacked the myth of total military defeat as part of their continuous ideological opposition to nazism. Monseigneur Saliège, the Archbishop of Toulouse, for example, had been president before the war of the *Association Catholique d'Aide aux Etrangers* set up to support refugees from the Spanish Republic, whose cause he had supported, unlike most of his fellow prelates in France. Saliège's public reaction to the propaganda of Vichy and the Germans was swift - his weekly *Semaine Catholique de Toulouse* warned on the 7th July 1940 against: 'suspect propaganda and erroneous judgements'. On the 8th September he reflected that:

'Nothing is final on earth ... while hope continues. Coffee, alcohol and other things may be lacking, but such restrictions do not prevent a nation's recovery, nor a Goliath from finding his David.'(31)

Equally, some men who had been career soldiers found the concept of 'total military defeat' to be improbable and questioned the myth from, as it were, a professional perspective. Cochet with his first tracts, Frenay with his embryonic intelligence organisation, Loustaunau-Lacau, declaring it was his duty as a soldier to fight to the very end.(32) In these cases, destroying the myth of débâcle meant re-affirming, usually as isolated individuals, the continuity of their commitment - ideological or professional - with the past. To call such behaviour 'whistling in the wind' sounds insulting, but is not intended to be. Destroying the myth of the military defeat was bound, in 1940, to be rather akin to an act of faith; an initial and largely individual refusal to accept the apparent 'facts', what Cassou called 'un refus absurde'. Absurd or not, the myth of total defeat had to be challenged, as did the Vichy claim that the regime under Pétain had assumed a higher moral ground than that of his predecessor.

The major myth of the débâcle which provided moral underpinning for the Vichy regime and its National Revolution was that of the sinful, corrupt France which had deserved to be beaten. An individualist, pleasure-seeking, irreligious, inter-war period, strongly influenced by left-wing ideologies and by the actions of the Popular Front Government, had been, in this scenario, both responsible for, and swept away by the débâcle of defeat. The Vichy regime purported to be based on the opposite of this: individualism was replaced by the community, and at its root the family, working and sacrificing together:

'Le droit des familles est en effet antérieur et supérieur à celui des individus. La famille est la cellule essentielle; elle est l'assise meme de l'édifice sociale; c'est sur elle qu'il faut bâtir, si elle fléchit, tout est perdu; tant qu'elle tient, tout peut être sauvé'.(33)

As the moral bankruptcy of the Third Republic was shown by its failure to protect its citizens in 1940, so the moral credibility of the Vichy regime depended on its ability to safeguard and enhance its families and communities. Many studies have now shown that there is little validity in talking about the Vichy regime as one monolithic whole. But the nature of images and myths is to present a common front and in the case of the 'higher moral ground' to portray a unified regime - above politics - intent only on 'saving France', particularly its soul.

From individuals refusing to accept the definitive nature of defeat, the Resistance was thus forced to move to an attack on the moral stance taken by the Vichy regime. This was particularly significant for the case of women who featured prominently in Vichy's catholic moralist, pro-natalist and 'femme au foyer' propaganda. Resistance clandestine papers were quick to point out to women the falsity of Vichy propaganda, which extolled motherhood, when there was not enough food for mothers to feed their children and mouthed platitudes to the wives of prisoners of war, whilst leaving their families to starve.(34) In this context women were called upon by the Resistance to band together to demand higher wages and increases in benefits to wives of POW's.(35) There is evidence that in many places women did indeed form defence committees and take public action on food and that the authorities, embarrassed by their claimed respect for mothers, were forced to accede to their demonstrations. Thus one hundred women demonstrated outside the town hall in Nogent for meat, which they were duly given and at Montreuil several hundred mothers went day after day to the authorities demanding milk, which again, they were finally given.(36) It should be said of course that sections of the Resistance realised that such demonstrations were not only embarrassing to the regime, but also extremely difficult to deal with in a public order sense:

'Un policier français oserait-il arrêter une mère de famille réclamant à manger pour ses petits?'(37)

With the introduction of *Service du Travail Obligatoire (STO)* in early 1943, it was clear that the moral ground on which the Vichy regime stood was increasingly insecure. As *Franc-Tireur* trumpeted

'Ils veulent rafler un peuple ... toute notre jeunesse est recensée, marquée, comme de bétail, parquée, expédiée. Comment ont-ils [the authorities] encore le front de regarder les visages crispés des mères et des pères de France, comment ont-ils l'audace d'écrire et de parler encore, comment le vieillard Pétain peut-il encore se montrer?'(38)

Here, Vichy's myth of the débâcle - a Third Republic so morally corrupt

that it could not even protect its children - was nicely stood on its head.
'Ils ont peur. Peur de la défaite .... peur de la France
aussi. Alors ils veulent la vider des ses hommes.'(39)
 Interestingly, historians in more recent times have taken on the Vichy
notion of community - attacked by the Resistance - in order to re-examine
what we mean by Resistance. Historical interest has focussed on the way
particular communities or groups experienced the aftermath of defeat, with
the realisation that traditional notions of 'collaboration' and
'resistance' need to be re-assessed and redefinded. One thinks of Sweet's
study of Clermont-Ferrand, of Kate Glazier's work on Alsace-Lorraine and of
Roderick Kedward's developing study of maquis communities.(40) Kedward
points out that a positive culture of the outlaw community was created in
some areas of France to counteract the Vichy culture of a community from
which certain people had been excluded. The public sympathy created by STO
in 1943 for those on the run, acted - claims Kedward - as a dissolvent of
normative attitudes towards law and order. Perhaps one of the most
interesting developments in this exploration of antithetical moral
communities has been the work of women historians, both examining the
National Revolution's view of women and considering the attitude of the
Resistance towards women as well as their role in it.(41) In a sense, by
taking and adapting the so-called 'apolitical' Vichy line of communities,
historians have been able to free the resistance from the notion of
'resistance by action' and by political group only, which underlay much of
the early Comité d'Histoire de la Deuxième Guerre Mondiale historiography.
Resistance, as Paula Schwartz notes, involved whole communities and this
was validated by the German insistance on punishing communities or groups
which helped the Resistance, aided escapers, or held demonstrations and
strikes. In this respect women were, as Schwartz says 'on the ground floor
of the Resistance', providing a network of support which was not only vital
to the Resistance, but which *was* resistance.(42) In setting up
counter-communities they were directly challenging the Vichy propaganda of
community.
 Alongside the initial attacks on Vichy myths of débâcle by the early
Resisters, went a longer, more insistent analysis of reasons for the
defeat. After the first realisation that the 'invincibility' thesis could
be challenged, and a growing understanding that the moral claims of Vichy
were spurious, resisters looked again at the débâcle and began to feed
their own interpretations into discussions on post-war planning.
Interestingly, Resisters outside France were less likely initially to see
the defeat of 1940 as an institutional watershed, than those within France.
Thus the Free French Judicial Committee, set up to consider legal
institutions for the post-Liberation period, produced early plans which
still sought to respect the institutional apparatus of 1940. These plans
were soon to be taken over by the Resistance counter-myths of the defeat.
 The first, and in a sense the most potent, accepted that (according to
the particular point of view) certain politicians of the Third Republic,
its supporting institutions, classes and groups were in some measure
responsible for the events of 1940. Léon Blum, writing to de Gaulle in
1943, accepted that the Third Republic had grave faults; 'l'épreuve a fait
apparaître les défauts et les lacunes'.(43) *Défense de la France* denounced
 'ces sympathies intéressées des partis de droite ou de gauche
 pour les idéologies ou les trésoreries étrangerès, qui
 condamnaient la France à l'impuissance politique'.(44)

Libération Nord condemned the

'scandaleuses assemblées qui, chargées de veiller sur les destinées de la Patrie et de la République, ont un soir ... abandonné l'une et l'autre pour faire le jeu des aventuriers de la défaite'.(45)

Here, it should be noted, the analysis of the responsibility of the Third Republic extended beyond the armistice (at which point the Vichy myths generally stopped) to the fateful days of the 9th and 10th of July.

More importantly, the acceptance of institutional responsibility for the defeat was seen within the context of an almost visceral Republicanism - 'Vive la République quand même!' - which would be used to attack the 'illegal' regime of Vichy. In this way the recognised faults of the Third Republic merged with its treacherous betrayal by Vichy. Vichy was anti-republican; what was needed in the future was a Republic, but a new Fourth Republic. In 1943 the Comité d'Etudes de la France Combattante did a survey among Resisters to find out what was the nature of their republicanism. The answers were strongly traditional and underlined how important 'La République' was as a unifying notion in the Resistance.

'L'idée de la République allait se dégager d'elle-même, purifiée et renouvelée, des sacrifices, des souffrances, des camaraderies de la Résistance' ... 'L'amour de la République est la forme que revêtent spontanément le culte de la patrie, la passion de la liberté' ... 'La République apparaît aux Français comme le régime de tous'...'Je suis républicain parce que français'... 'Je suis républicain parce que socialiste'.(46)

All sections of the Resistance press echoed this republican tradition, linked to the French Revolution - 'La grande Révolution, la vraie, la nôtre'(47) - as opposed to the ersatz National Revolution of Pétain and Vichy.

If however the counter-myth of the purified Republic was a powerful unifying agent in the Resistance, the actual form that it would take in post-war France was hotly debated. There was general agreement that a complete change of personnel would be needed and publications of the metropolitan Resistance gave earnest and increasing attention to the need for an exclusion of all collaborators from public (and private) posts of responsibility, and their punishment as traitors in order to wipe the slate clean.

The C.N.R. indeed emphasised the urgency of this 'épuration' by placing it as a preamble to its March 1944 programme of measures to be applied at the Liberation. Beyond this, there was much less agreement. Some groups envisaged a total return to the constitution of 1875, once the personnel had been changed, or else only very minor changes to the Third Republic document. Others advocated an American style presidential regime. Still others, influenced by the Communist Party, suggested a variant on the Convention model, prefiguring the 'people's democracies' of eastern Europe. Some approaches were less constitutional and more overtly political, aiming to produce a society in which economic and social relationships had been profoundly altered. The C.N.R. programme for example called for the nationalization of the principal means of production, of insurance companies and of banks. There should be worker-participation in industry, wage improvements, the re-establishment of a strong trades union organization, social security and pension coverage, and the extension of political and economic rights to the colonies.

Often, a convenient shorthand for the purified Republic to come was 'Révolution', a revolution which stood in sharp contrast to the bogus National Revolution of Vichy. What this actually meant in practice, understandably differed from group to group. Compare for example the 'Révolution nécessaire' of *Combat* and de Gaulle's 'la France qui combat entend que la victoire soit le bénéfice de tous ses enfants',(48) with the sharper demands of a paper like *Franc-Tireur*.(49) This powerful counter-myth of 'Revolution' became an important factor in later historical analyses of the Liberation. To many French men and women who had lived through the Resistance with the image of 'Révolution', the aftermath of the Liberation seemed to be a betrayal of the bright hopes of the Resistance. 'The mountain has given birth to a mouse'.(50) Much of the work of historians in examining the conduct and the results of the 'épuration', and in judging the scale and nature of the political, social and economic reforms instituted has, to an extent, been overshadowed by the sense of an opportunity lost. For the right, an opportunity to heal the wounds and provide the country with a workable constitution, and here the Aron critique of the 'épuration', bizarrely stands with the large Gaullist literature on the failures of the Fourth Republic.(51) For the left, an opportunity to change the face of France had been lost, and here much of the polemic has centred on the role of the French Communist Party at the Liberation. For some, most notably de Gaulle in his memoirs, the Communist Party had been prevented from seizing power by the presence of the Gaullists:

'Si décidément, "le parti" n'avait pu en saisir l'occasion,
c'est parce que je m'étais trouvé là pour incarner la France
tout entière.'(52)
- with or without the aid of the Allies.

Communist historians like Elleinstein have generally reflected the Party's own interpretation, that conditions in France were unpropitious for the seizure of power, that de Gaulle was extremely popular, that the Communists, while experiencing a dramatic upturn in their fortunes, were still nowhere in the majority. The P.C.F. insists that it was always a patriotic and democratic party, which had no revolutionary intent, but only a policy of radical re-structuring.(53) Non-communist historians, it should be said, have often taken a more sceptical view of the validity of this interpretation.(54) As the polemic on the French Communist Party had ebbed and flowed, and papers from the Archives Nationales have begun to be released, historians have started to look in more detail at the actual moments of Liberation (June 1944 - April 1945) to see the way in which power passed in the early days, to better understand what happened later, and here they have met another strong Resistance counter-myth, the myth of France victorious.(55)

Given the appalling trauma of the French defeat and the scarring nature of its aftermath, it is hardly surprising that one of the counter-myths the Resistance sought to establish was that of 'France victorious'; a France which had freed itself and conquered its former enemy. De Gaulle, recreating his thoughts at the time of the June 18th appeal for his memoirs, put it well:

'Poursuivre la guerre? oui, certes! mais pour quel but et dans
quelles limites? Beaucoup ... ne voulait pas qu'elle fût autre
chose qu'un concours donné, par une poignée de Français, à
l'empire britannique demeuré debout et en ligne. Pas un
instant, je n'envisageai la tentative sur ce plan-là ... Je

pensais, en effet, que c'en serait fini de l'honneur, de l'unité, de l'indépendance, s'il devait être entendu que, dans cette guerre mondiale, seule la France aurait capitulé et qu'elle en serait restée là.'.(56)

Whilst some of the metropolitan Resistance press took up the same theme - *Combat* for example claiming that, 'Nous gagnerons par notre participation au Combat notre droit à la victoire'(57) - it was generally not until just before the Liberation that the Gaullist insistence on the primacy of 'France victorious' was reflected in internal Resistance groups. The myth then began to be sedulously cultivated by de Gaulle from August 1944 onwards, with the victory parade in Paris and the exhortations for the French to complete the Liberation of their own country and continue the war into Germany. Its potency as a counter-myth can be seen even today at places like Marckolsheim, where one of the remaining parts of the Maginot Line, overrun by the Germans in 1940, is preserved, with alongside it tanks and armaments of the Leclerc Division which liberated the village in 1945.

This particular counter-myth is at the heart of the historical argument today, about what actually happened at the Liberation, and about how power passed from one group to another, and which France, if France at all, *was* victorious. Anglo-Saxon historians, for example, tend to concentrate almost exclusively on the role of the Allies, their armies, their Civil Affairs officers, their political leaders. The French are seldom given more than a walk-on part: a 'problem' in David Eisenhower's study of his grandfather,(58) and weirdly absent from George Patton's bizarre chapter 'Touring in France with an Army'.(59) For Anglo-Saxon military historians, it is evident that it was Allied armies which liberated France - Hastings for example in his book on *Overlord* manages only one reference to 'difficult' issues such as the role of de Gaulle.(60) Those historians who have chronicled the work of the military civil affairs efforts in 1944-45, do make some attempt to analyse the role of the French and the question of political sovereignty, but even then, it is largely in the disruptive effects that this had on Allied military operations.(61)

French historians on the other hand have tended to present a picture of the French liberating themselves, virtually devoid of Allied help, although who 'the French' are in this context varies according to the view of the commentator. Those on the Left suggest that France was victorious largely because of the efforts of the internal Resistance and stress the role played by the local and departmental liberation committees: France liberated by local Resistance groups and militia, as representative of mass action and popular will. Willard, for example, in the PCF's *Cahiers d'Histoire*, claims that, 'une vaste région couvrant près des 3/5 du pays - au sud de la Loire et à l'ouest du Rhône - fut libérée entièrement par la Résistance seule.'(62) Gaullist historians and especially de Gaulle in his memoirs, give great prominence to the preparations and debates of the CFLN and the GPRF, and to the differences of opinion between the Allies and the Gaullists at key moments of the Liberation. In this optic, France was liberated virtually without Allied help and with a relatively minor role accorded to the domestic Resistance.(63) Our own work, attempting to bring together Allied and French documentation on the Liberation, and examine the process 'on the ground', suggests that there was not one Liberation, but many. Given the vacuum in Allied military planning, it was often in the chaotic passing of power to the French by quite junior officers, that an independent French state was established at the Liberation. To this extent, political decision making lagged well behind the decisions made 'on the ground', where everything depended on the balance of forces locally, the speed with which the Allied and French personnel arrived, and the judgements made by those who witnessed the events. In a very real sense, post-war France was built from the communes upwards.

'France victorious' and the triumph of the Resistance, which were counter-myths established during the war and retailed at the end of the conflict for political validation of the regime, became another orthodoxy for later historians. The Communist Party carried the myth of mass Resistance creating a popular Liberation through into their historiography of the period until very recent times.(64) De Gaulle founded the orthodoxy of his movement when he told Resistance leaders in 1944 'Grâce à vous, la France aura sa place plus glorieuse dans le monde'.(65) This nationalistic theme was to be continued and even revived during the Fifth Republic, by pro-Gaullist historians.(66) It also dominated generations of work after the war sponsored by Henri Michel and the *Comité D'Histoire de la Deuxième Guerre Mondiale*. One of the most recent (perhaps the last) expression of this romantic view, can be found in the remarks of Mr. Soufflet, a Free French airman, Fifth Republic deputy and Prime Minister Jacques Chirac's delegate to the C.N.R.S. Colloque on the Liberation in 1974. Declaring that the spirit of the Liberation was born in 1940 (superfluous to state that Soufflet was a Gaullist deputy) he went on to point out the lessons for subsequent generations. 'L'Obstination nationale', 'la ténacité victorieuse' and 'la volonté efficace' had restored France to its post-war eminence and all that was needed was more of the same.(67)

This Liberation orthodoxy has been challenged more recently by work which looked outside the heroic struggle of the armed groups, of the liberation committees, the political daring of the Gaullists and the new political map of electoral France in 1945. Typical of recent historiography, and seminal in the field, is the work of Roderick Kedward,(68) who has pointed out that not only was there no rupture in 1944-45, but that the forces of cultural change which might have brought it about were deliberately forgotten or obscured, precisely because they did challenge the *status quo ante*. Work on women in the Resistance shows greater and greater involvement at all levels and the development of new roles for women in French society.(69) But, despite the vote in 1945, women seem to disappear from French history until the 1960's. There was no great renewal and no great revival of French morale in 1945; the Ophuls flm *Le Chagrin et la Pitié* exposed that falsehood in 1969. Azéma notes that continuity was more evident than rupture(70) and Becker in *Histoire Politique de la France depuis 1945* says that 'le maintien des clivages anciens semblait donc conduire a ce que la réstauration du passé l'emporte sur le renouvellement'.(71) In a companion volume, *Histoire de la Société Française depuis 1945*, Borne concludes that in 1945 'la France traditionnelle co-existe avec les forces de renouveau; le corps social, s'il adhère au nouvel imaginaire social retrouve vite les habitudes anciennes'.(72)

After the trauma of 1940 and the complete disintegration of the Third Republic, the France which emerged from the Liberation was recognizably the same country as that which had plunged headlong to defeat. It is perhaps this continuity, 'la France éternelle', which is the final irony in the destruction of the myths of the débâcle. The restoration of the past however can in no way detract from the unique war of liberation fought by the Resistance and the Free French from 1940 to 1945, and from their heroic contribution to 'des lendemains qui chanteraient'.

Notes

1. Quoted by Robert Brasillach in 'Les Sept Couleurs' *Oeuvres Complètes*, Vol. II (Paris: Au Club de l'Honnête Homme, 1963-64).
2. See for example P. Laborie, *Résistants, Vichyssois et autre; l'Evolution de l'Opinion Publique et des Comportements dans le Lot de 1939 à 1944* (Toulouse: CNRS, 1980).
3. Jean-Pierre Azéma, *From Munich to the Liberation, 1938-1944* (Cambridge, C.U.P., 1984).
4. Maréchal Philippe Pétain, *Actes et Ecrits* (ed. J. Isorni) (Paris: Flammarion, 1974) pp. 449-450 and M. & J. Paillaud (Eds.), *Messages d'Outre Tombe du Maréchal Pétain* (Paris: Nouvelles Editions Latines, 1983), pp. 16-17.
5. *Messages*, Ibid.
6. 23rd June 1940, *Actes et Ecrits*, Ibid., pp. 450-451. *Messages, Ibid.*, pp. 17-18.
7. Speech on the 11th October, 1940, in Samuel Osgood, *The Fall of France, 1940* (Boston: Heath, 1965).
8. 13th August 1940, *Messages,* op. cit., p. 24.
9. Henri Amouroux, *La Grande Histoire des Français sous l'Occupation*, Vol. 1, 'Le Peuple du Désastre', p. 117 (Paris: Laffont, 1976).
10. 25th June 1940 in *Messages*, op. cit., p. 20.
11. 11th July 1940 in *Messages,* op. cit., p. 22.
12. Elie J. Bois, *Truth on the Tragedy of France* (trans. H.S. Wilson) (London: Hodder, 1940).
13. See Chapter 2 of J-P Rioux et al. (Eds.), *Les Communistes Français de Munich à Chateaubriant* (Paris: FNSP, 1987).
14. Quoted in Osgood, *The Fall of France, 1940* op. cit., p. 14.
15. Article in February 1941 from *La Nouvelle Revue Française* in *Le Français de L'Europe* (Paris: Balzac, 1944).
16. Quoted in Osgood, *The Fall of France 1940* op. cit., p. 50.
17. *Francisme* 30th June 1941.
18. *Le Petit Journal* 28th June 1940.
19. *L'Effort* 27th August 1940.
20. *Le Cri du Peuple* 2nd July 1940 and 5th Sept. 1940 for example.
21. *Paris Soir* 23rd November 1940.
22. *Le Matin* with Jacques Roujon several articles in July 1940.
23. Elie J. Bois, *Truth on the Tragedy of France* op. cit.
24. Jacques Maritain, *A Travers le Désastre* (New York: Voix de France, 1941).
25. (A. Geraud) Pertinax, *Les Fossoyeurs* (New York: Voix de France, 1943).
26. Henri de Kerillis, *Français Voilà la Vérité* (New York: Doubleday, 1942).
27. See also, Pierre Maillaud, *Over to France* (trans. F. Cowper) (London: Collins, 1946); André Maurois, *The Battle for France 1940*, also *Why France Fell* (London: Bodley Head, 1940); Marc Bloch, *L'Etrange Défaite* (Paris: Colin, 1947).

28. *L'Appel du 18 Juin* (Anglia Higher Education College Archive) (hereafter AHEC).
29. Jean Texcier, *Les Conseils à L'Occupé*, 14th July 1940 (AHEC).
30. Roderick Kedward, *Resistance in Vichy France: A Study of Ideas and Motivation in the Southern Zone, 1940-1942* (Oxford, O.U.P., 1978), p. 21.
31. Ibid., pp. 24-25.
32. Ibid., p. 38.
33. Maréchal Philippe Pétain, 'La Politique Sociale de l'Avenir' *Revue des Deux Mondes*, nos. 59-60, September 1940, pp. 114-115.
34. See for example *Jeunes Filles de France*, May 1941, *Femmes de Prisonniers*, *Comité des Femmes de Prisonniers* (AHEC).
35. *La Voix des Femmes*, November 1941, *La Femme Comtoise* (nd) (AHEC).
36. For the Reference to Nogent see *Aube* (nd) (AHEC).
37. *La Marseillaise*, February 1944 (AHEC).
38. *Franc-Tireur*, 20th March 1943 (AHEC).
39. Ibid.
40. John Sweets, *Choices in Vichy France* (Oxford: O.U.P., 1986); Kate Glazier, paper to the 1989 conference of the ASCMF and Roderick Kedward, 'Maquis and the Culture of the Outlaw' in Roderick Kedward and Roger Austin (Eds.), *Vichy France and the Resistance. Culture and Ideology* (London: Croom Helm, 1985).
41. See for example Miranda Pollard, 'Women and the National Revolution' in Kedward and Austin (op. cit.), M.F. Brive, 'L'Image des Femmes à la Libération' in *La Libération dans le Midi de la France*. Colloque tenu à Toulouse, Juin 1985, Eche Services des Publications, UTM, 1986, and P. Schwartz, 'Redefining Resistance: Women's Activism in Wartime France' in M.R. Higonnet and J. Jenson (Eds.), *Behind the Lines: Gender and the Two World Wars* (Yale University Press, 1987).
42. Paula Schwartz, ibid.
43. Letter, Léon Blum to de Gaulle, 15th March 1943, quoted in H. Michel and B. Mirkine-Guétzevitch, *Les Idées Politiques et Sociales de la Résistance*, (Paris: P.U.F., 1954).
44. *Défense de La France*, No. 33, 20th May, 1943 (AHEC).
45. *Libération* (Nord), No. 91, 28th August 1942 (AHEC).
46. *Les Cahiers Français*, No. 50, November 1953, (London), Special Number, 'La Pensée de la Résistance, Pourquoi je suis Républicain', p. 7.
47. *Le Père Duchesne*, April 1942, (AHEC).
48. *Combat* (Supplément local pour Lyon) undated, early December 1942 and de Gaulle's speech in London, 18th June 1942, quoted in H. Michel and B. Mirkine-Guétzevitch, op. cit.
49. *Le Franc-Tireur*, 20th January 1943, No. 14.
50. Pierre Hervé, *La Libération Trahie* (Paris: Editions 1945), p. 12.
51. Raymond Aron, *Histoire de l'Epuration* (Paris: Plon, 1968) and *Histoire de la Libération de la France juin 1944 - mai 1945* (Paris: Plon, 1968).

52. Charles de Gaulle, *Mémoires de Guerre*, Vol. 3, 'Le Salut, 1944-1946', (Paris: Plon, 1959), p. 314.
53. See for example, G. Willard, V. Joannes, F. Hincker and J. Elleinstein, *De la Guerre à la Libération, La France de 1939 à 1945* (Paris: Editions Sociales, 1972).
54. Auguste Lecoeur, *L'Autocritique Attendue* (St. Cloud: Girault, 1955); André Marty, *L'Affaire Marty* (Paris: Deux Rives, 1953), Charles Tillon, *On Chantait Rouge* (Paris: Laffont, 1977), Annie Kriegel, *Communismes au Miroir Francais*, (Paris: Gallimard, 1974); Stephane Courtois, *Le P.C.F. dans la Guerre* (Paris: Ramsay, 1980).
55. See for example, G. Guingouin, *Quatre Ans de Lutte sur le Sol Limousin* (Paris: 1974) and P. Guiral, *Libération de Marseilles* (Paris, 1974), Charles-Louis Foulon, *Le Pouvoir en Province à la Libération: les Commissaires de la République, 1943-1946 (Paris: Colin, 1975) and* Grégoire Madjarian, *Conflicts, Pouvoirs et Société à la Libération*, (Paris: Union Général d'Edition, 1986).
56. Charles de Gaulle, *Mémoires de Guerre*, Vol. 1, (Paris: Plon, 1954), p. 88.
57. *Combat* (Supplément local pour Lyon) undated, early December, 1942 (AHEC).
58. David Eisenhower, *Eisenhower at War, 1935-1945* (London: 1986).
59. General George Patton, *War As I Knew It* (London: Allen, 1948).
60. Max Hastings, *Overlord: D-Day and the Battle for Normandy* (London, Michael Joseph, 1984).
61. F. Donnison, *Civil Affairs and Military Government, North-West Europe, 1944-1946* (London: HMSO, 1961) and H.L. Coles and A.K. Weinberg, *Civil Affairs: Soldiers Become Governors* (Washington: U.S. Government Publications, 1964).
62. Germaine Willard, 'Le Rôle des Masses Populaires dans la Libération' *Cahiers d'Histoire de l'Institut Maurice Thorez*, Nos. 8-9, 1974.
63. Charles de Gaulle, *Mémoires de Guerre*, Vol. 3, op. cit.
64. R. Bourderon et al. (Eds.), *Le P.C.F. Etapes et Problèmes: 1920-1972* (Paris: Editions Sociales, 1981).
65. Charles de Gaulle, *Discours et Messages: Juin 1940 - Janvier 1946* (Paris: Plon, 1970), pp. 443-451.
66. One of the typical examples is François Mauriac, *De Gaulle* (Paris: Grasset, 1964).
67. M. Soufflet, discours d'inauguration, Henri Michel (Ed.), *La Libération* (Paris: CNRS, 1975).
68. op. cit., note 40.
69. op. cit., notes 41 and 42.
70. Jean-Pierre Azéma, op. cit.
71. Jean-Jacques Becker, *Histoire Politique de la France depuis 1945* (Paris: Colin, 1989).
72. Dominique Borne, *Histoire de la Société Française depuis 1945* (Paris: Colin, 1989).

LES NOYERS DE L'ALTENBURG: MALRAUX AND 1940

David Gascoigne

Les Noyers de l'Altenburg, written between 1940 and 1942, is Malraux's last novel,(1) and it has generally been discussed by critics in terms of its position and importance in the whole sequence of his writings rather than as a work shaped by the wartime circumstances in which it was written. Joseph Hoffmann's comment is typical of this diachronic approach: 'Ce roman apparaît à la fois comme l'épilogue de l'oeuvre romanesque de Malraux et comme le prologue de son oeuvre esthétique, éclairant simultanément les deux versants de l'oeuvre.'(2) Roger Caillois, in a review written in 1944, perceives in fact a disjunction between the work and the conditions from which it emerged: he expressed his surprise at the 'sérénité de l'oeuvre', a serenity which contrasts with 'les circonstances de la publication du livre si propres à conseiller à un combattant la violence et la haine.'(3) Denis Boak goes further: 'The most evident feature of *Les Noyers de l'Altenburg* is that it is not, as it stands, a novel of the Second World War at all, much less one of the Resistance. It is as if Malraux had deliberately turned his back on current events (...) There is, for instance, no explicit anti-Fascism in the novel, which can only be intentional.'(4) If Boak's judgment is accepted unconditionally, then it is indeed a surprising one, since all Malraux's novels, and especially his most recent and longest work up to then, *L'Espoir*, can be seen as drawing much of their substance from the tensions of contemporary events, and not least the struggle against Fascism. While the relationship of *Les Noyers* to the turbulent world of 1940-42 is a deliberately detached and distanced one (for reasons that will be touched on in this paper), it is nevertheless fascinating and illuminating to place the novel firmly within its historical context and to read it as a response to this dramatic moment in European history. The purpose of this paper is to show how, if this is done, central elements of the work emerge as powerfully expressive of Malraux's reactions to the war and to the threat of the Third Reich.

The first step towards such a reading is to sketch in the biographical background for the period from 1939, which itself contains a central problem for Malraux's biographers.(5) Like many another leading intellectual who had spoken and fought alongside the Communists in the struggle against the rise of Fascism, Malraux was disgusted by the Nazi-Soviet pact, which he saw as sacrificing the proletariat of the West to Soviet national interest. 'La révolution à ce prix-là, ... non' was his reported reaction. But he refused to add his voice to the anti-communist furore or to break with Russian friends, such as Ilya Ehrenburg: 'Je ne dirai, je ne ferai rien contre les communistes tant qu'ils seront en prison.'(6) At the outbreak of war he was turned down for active duty in the Air Force, despite his experience in Spain, but was accepted into an armoured unit based at Provins (Seine et Marne). When Jean Lacouture asked him many years later about his combat experiences in 1940, Malraux's reply was blunt: 'Ma guerre de quarante? Dérisoire... Nos chars de Provins étaient hors d'état de nous porter hors du polygone d'entraînement. En mai, nous avons fait mouvement à pied avec des anti-chars. Nous avons un peu tiraillé. J'ai été très légèrement blessé le 15 juin. Et le 16, nous étions faits prisonniers comme des fantassins, à mi-distance à peu près de Provins et de Sens, où on nous dirigea.' Conditions in the improvised POW camp at Sens were, he said, tolerable: 'Ce n'est pas à recommander comme vacances,

mais il ne faut rien exagérer.'(7) In October 1940 he escaped, and joined
his beloved Josette Clotis with their new-born son at her parents' house at
Hyères, between Cannes and Toulon, in the unoccupied zone. In January 1941,
they moved on to a villa at Roquebrune Cap Martin belonging to Simon and
Dorothy Bussy, friends of Roger Martin du Gard, and then rented a luxury
villa at Cap d'Ail, partly on the strength of advances from the US
publishers, Random House. From this point onwards, however, conditions in
the 'zone libre' became more difficult and dangerous, with arrests of Jews
and Allied sympathisers. Malraux, as a prominent anti-Fascist, was
obviously at risk. At the end of 1942, they left for the Dordogne. By early
1944 Malraux was quite heavily involved in coordinating local Resistance
groups in the Corrèze, and he went into hiding in mid-March 1944. As he
declared to Roger Stéphane in February 1945, 'Quand on a écrit ce que j'ai
écrit et qu'il y a le fascisme quelque part, on se bat contre le fascisme.
Quand on a écrit ce que j'ai écrit et qu'il y a la guerre en France, on la
fait.'(8) The biographical problem referred to above is clearly that of
explaining why, if he was so committed to struggle against the occupying
forces, he stood on the sidelines for something like three years. Since his
participation in the Spanish Civil War, his personal courage and commitment
to the anti-Fascist cause could scarcely be in doubt: the reason must lie
elsewhere.

Certainly, there had been no lack of opportunities for active
participation. A number of Resistance groups had sought to recruit him:
Boris Wildé, on behalf of the Réseau du Musée de l'Homme, Sartre and
Beauvoir for the Socialisme et Liberté group, Roger Stéphane for Combat,
Emmanuel d'Astier, Jean Cassou, and Francis Crémieux who offered him in
January 1942 the command of l'Armée Secrète de R4 (Toulouse), which
included many Spanish expatriates. Malraux's answer, according to Crémieux,
was that, since his Spanish experiences, he had lost any confidence in the
efficacy of a popular force in an occupied country. 'Pour moi, il n'y a que
deux choses, l'aviation ou les tanks. Si vous pouvez me garantir des armes,
je suis avec vous.'(9) There is a consistency here: we recall that those
were his first two choices for service as a volunteer in 1940, and in
L'Espoir he had constantly stressed the tragedy of heroism in the face of
absolute technical superiority. To Stéphane in 1941 he said that he did not
believe much in nationalism which is 'un sentiment, une idée, pas un
régime',(10) an unfashionable view which, as will be shown, finds
significant expression in Les Noyers. When he could be guaranteed
deliveries of arms by the RAF, he did join the Maquis. And when nationalism
could become a régime and not just 'un sentiment, une idée', he did join de
Gaulle.

During the period in which he was declining to join the Resistance,
Malraux was writing, and it is interesting to ask how far this was a
substitute for or an equivalent to practical involvement. He refused to
allow any of his works to be published in France. He was working on three
books at this period: a biography of T.E. Lawrence of which only a fragment
ever appeared, the three volumes of the Psychologie de l'art which would be
published after the war, and a three-volume novel, La Lutte avec l'Ange, of
which only the first, Les Noyers de l'Altenburg, saw the light of day. Of
these, it is clearly Les Noyers that has most to tell us about Malraux's
reaction to contemporary events.

Of all Malraux's novels, it is the most loosely-knit in structure and
chronology. The book starts and ends with self-contained episodes from the
narrator's life in 1940, printed in italics. These episodes serve therefore

as a kind of substantial prologue and epilogue, framing a central section, which is distinguished by being printed in roman type and which is divided into three numbered chapters. This whole central section is concerned with the life of Vincent Berger, the narrator's father, in the decade up to 1915, as recounted by his son. The narrative voice of Berger *fils* thus links central and outer sections, as he implicitly matches his own experiences in 1940 against episodes of his father's life; this narrative counterpoint across the divide of a generation establishes an analogy between father and son, between the events of their lives as they interpret them, between the insights afforded to each of the two men by the brutalities and revelations of war.

All five sections offer pointers to Malraux's reactions to the post-1940 situation. The first 'prologue' section, headed simply 'Chartres, 21 juin 1940', describes the hundreds of French prisoners of war, first held under guard in the cathedral itself, and then transferred to an improvised camp in open country. The description of this camp is clearly based on the camp at Sens where Malraux himself was a prisoner on that very date. A first obvious question suggests itself: why, in drawing on his own experiences, does Malraux substitute Chartres for Sens, and begin his narrative in the cathedral? One answer is that this novel will be substantially concerned with an investigation of the meaning of culture, and Malraux wishes to launch this theme with an evocation of one of European culture's most prestigious sites, 'ce haut lieu entre les hauts lieux de la terre' (p. 17), viewed in the stark light of war (the stained glass has been removed). It is an image of civilisation at risk: the whole edifice, shot through with the shafts of light from the plain temporary windows, trembles with the vibration from the passing German tanks. But it is also an image of the presence of the past, an assurance of a profound continuity even in a disrupted and turbulent present: the shouts from prisoners and guards echo back from the vaulted roof: 'cent voix fêlées répercutées par les voûtes' (p. 16), 'leurs voix répercutées par les voûtes historiques' (p. 18). The clamour of the present strikes a resonance from the structures of the past. The whole book is structured to remind us that the turmoil of 1940, of the *débâcle* which seemed for the moment to overshadow everything, only acquires proper perspective when set against the legacy of our forbears. The 1940 episodes, placed as prologue and epilogue, function literally as a frame through which to view the past - the past of a generation ago and, in the central section, the past of the whole human adventure. Interestingly, Malraux does not, as a more specifically Resistance writer might have done, make of Chartres a symbol of France (civilised) threatened by Germany (barbaric): on the contrary, the narrator very early on hears a German soldier speak of Bamberg, and calls to mind that cathedral, "la Chartres allemande" as he calls it (p. 15). This is the first of many indications that Malraux wishes, even in 1941, to transcend a narrowly patriotic view. The section ends movingly with the prisoner-narrator's words 'Ici, écrire est le seul moyen de continuer à vivre' (p. 30), words which may well reflect Malraux's own feelings as a non-combatant in the France of 1941.

The first of the central sections opens the journey into the past with a portrait of the narrator's grandfather, Dietrich Berger. At odds with the Church on the relaxation of Lenten observance, Dietrich continues to attend mass, but only at a distance, standing outside in the mud and nettles of the churchyard. Like his grandson-narrator, he thus embodies the notion of fidelity to the heritage of the past in the face of the slippages of current orthodoxy. In another gesture of rugged independence, he offers accommodation to Jews and circus-folk who are shunned by everyone else. An ultra-conservative Catholic from a doubtless anti-Dreyfusard milieu, he is shown nevertheless as taking an exemplary stand against anti-semitism and social prejudice. Malraux has accepted that Dietrich Berger is a portrait of his own grandfather, but again there is a transposition: the Malrauxs came from Dunkerque, while the fictional Bergers are an established Alsatian family. Malraux's choice of Alsace is significant: it is that of a setting where French and German cultures meet and mingle, a space of interchange, resistant to any exclusive loyalty to a nation-state. This resistance is exemplified by the fact that the Bergers, like many Alsatian families, have fought on both sides at one time or another. The rest of this section tells of Vincent Berger's experiences as a representative of the German government attached to Enver Pasha's staff in Turkey in about 1908-10. His story resembles that of T.E. Lawrence, and like Lawrence his ties to his European masters weaken as his enthusiasm for the nationalist cause he has adopted (Turkish in this case) waxes stronger. He undertakes a long journey to Afghanistan, negotiating to establish the basis for a new pan-Turkish empire, but he finally recognises that this aspiration is hopelessly unrealistic. This episode suggests a scepticism about political imperialism and its claims, and it may well, as Lucien Goldmann suggested, be coloured by Malraux's disillusion with communism.(13) One piquant detail is that the event which triggers Vincent Berger's recognition of failure is a frenzied attack on him by a madman in a bazaar - he is not allowed to fight back because of the traditional Islamic veneration of the insane. Embittered and furious at being defenceless in the face of a savage attack by a madman - such is the state of mind of Vincent Berger, but it could also be a fair description of Malraux's own feelings after his 'dérisoire guerre de 40' and his helplessness in the face of the Blitzkrieg.

In the central episode of the whole novel, Vincent Berger is invited in June 1914 by his uncle Walter Berger to attend a colloquium of international scholars at the old Priory of Altenburg in Alsace, which is now Walter's residence.(14) The place is filled with portraits and mementoes of Pascal, Montaigne, Beethoven, Tolstoy, Nietzsche - 'ces messieurs de la famille' as Walter calls them. The 'family' of cultural ancestors evoked here, therefore, is not French but European, and with Defoe, Shakespeare, Cervantes and the Greek classics also figuring in the discussion, it would seem at first as if any notion of nationalism within European culture was being wholeheartedly set aside. As befits the Alsatian setting, French and German scholars engage in open and lively debate on no less a topic than the permanence of man, on the question of what, if any, characteristics can be seen as common to human beings of every culture, past and present. The most eagerly awaited contribution is from the German ethnologist Möllberg, recently returned from Africa, and who is known to be completing a book entitled *La Civilisation comme conquête et comme destin*.

Malraux revealed to an American professor, Armand Hoog, that the character of Möllberg was based, intellectually, on the German ethnologist Leo Frobenius, and indeed Hoog traced the source of a number of the examples of strange cultures quoted by Möllberg in the Altenburg discussion to Frobenius's early work *The Childhood of Man* which appeared well before the First World War. His *Histoire de la civilisation africaine* was translated into French in 1926, and, more significantly still, his book Le *Destin des civilisations* was published by Gallimard in 1940 (note the similarity of title to Möllberg's projected work). Another feature common to both Möllberg and Frobenius is a fervent intellectual nationalism. The narrator of *Les Noyers* anticipates with some trepidation the impact on the German public of Möllberg's theories, if he succeeds in his ambitious synthesis: 'Il était facile de prévoir quelle audience trouverait son système lorsqu'il atteindrait la culture générale et les passions qu'elle traîne avec elle, car il faisait de la pensée allemande l'interprète désignée de l'histoire; et l'Allemagne a depuis Hegel, pour tout ce qui la veut révélatrice du destin, une reconnaissance inquiète et passionnée.' (pp. 109-110) Another German scholar at the colloquium, Stieglitz, speaks of this Hegelian project of a universal cultural history in these terms: 'Il s'agit d'intégrer au *Weltgeist* les faits apportés par les nouvelles connaissances, et je ne vois pas du tout pourquoi ce que vous appelez l'aventure humaine ne deviendrait pas une histoire, comme l'histoire d'Allemagne est une histoire, bien que formée d'éléments qui paraissent d'abord hétérogènes! J'affirme même que nous, Allemands, (...) sommes particulièrement qualifiés pour mener à bien une telle histoire!' This talk of 'intégration au *Weltgeist*' of 'éléments qui paraissent hétérogènes' would surely have had sinister political echoes in 1941: it is the language of an arrogant cultural imperialism, readily translatable into the brutality of military annexation. The same rhetoric of national vocation is frequently to be found in Frobenius. In the opening pages of *Histoire de la civilisation africaine* he argues that modern man is 'sollicité par une conception nouvelle, - l'unité de la civilisation humaine'. It is in particular Spengler, he says, who has initiated this new era of enlightenment for 'l'homo europaeus, et particulièrement l'homme allemand' who can now attain 'une virtuosité dans la compréhension des faits'. 'Nul peuple aussi qualifié que le peuple allemand pour accepter ce changement de conception.' (pp. 7,25,29) In his *Destin des civilisations*, Frobenius continued to proclaim his faith in this synthesis: 'Pour moi, tout se passe comme si les plus grands événements de l'histoire mondiale ne se distinguaient des plus petits que par leur dimension et comme si l'homme, depuis les peuplades de la steppe africaine, du désert arabe ou de la jungle indienne, jusqu'aux nations dominatrices du monde, vivait les mêmes expériences. Il ne s'agit pas ici de la civilisation matérielle, mais du Destin.' (p. 15)

It is at this point that Malraux's character parts company from his model. When Möllberg finally rises to speak, he delivers himself of a powerful and bitter speech about the lack of any common ground between the primitive cultures he has studied, the lack of any possible dialogue or continuity between primitive man and our own day. Like Vincent Berger he has journeyed in search of a unifying principle, and has found none. In a final gesture of surrender, he has left the pages of his book scattered across the desert. 'Selon l'usage,' he concludes sardonically, 'le vainqueur porte les dépouilles du vaincu'. (p. 110) Malraux makes this change, I would suggest, because it is important in 1940 to assert the failure of German imperialism, in whatever guise: Möllberg's defeat is necessary to prepare the way for more humane, less arrogant conceptions, just as Germany's defeat is necessary for a tolerant and humane Europe. In his pessimistic insistence on the hermetic nature of different cultures, Möllberg is the voice not of Frobenius, but of Spengler, the master. Edmond Vermeil, in the first sentence of his preface to *Le Destin des civilisations*, welcomed the French translation of this work, 'ne fût-ce que pour nous libérer, au moins partiellement, du fardeau qui fait encore peser sur nos esprits le souvenir récent d'Oswald Spengler et de ses deux épais

volumes *Le Déclin de l'Occident'*. Ever since Malraux had encountered
Spengler's work in the early 1920s, he had been preoccupied by the need to
refute his ideas. In 1942, he urged on Emmanuel Berl the need to 'régler
son compte à Spengler',(17) and in an interview published in *Fontaine* in
1945 in which he foresaw the rise of a new, American-based culture, he
still declared his anti-Spenglerian conviction: 'Je ne crois nullement à
une 'fatalité' des civilisations'.(18) Arguably the whole notion of
'metamorphosis', so central to his writings on art, was developed as an
antidote to Spengler's vision of the irrevocable decay and death of
cultures.(19) In this central chapter of *Les Noyers*, therefore, the
keystone in the arch of the novel, Malraux, having deliberately refused to
play the card of French nationalism, having stage-managed an idealised
setting in which the voices of France and Germany and all the cultures of
Europe are brought into free and open dialogue, constructs a symbol of the
defeat of German nationalism, and of the impotence of the would-be new
Reich of the spirit.

The next chapter finds Vincent Berger in the Intelligence section of
the German Army on the Russian Front in 1915: as an Alsatian he has
preferred to volunteer for service in the East rather than fight against
his other *'patrie'*, France. Here German brutality takes more concrete form:
he watches the interrogation of a suspected Russian woman spy, in which the
German officer uses a child reckoned to be that of the wanted person to try
to engineer her betrayal. Much worse is to follow, when Vincent Berger goes
to observe a gas attack, the first phosgene attack of the war, on
unprotected Russian troops across the valley. Malraux is here using an
historical event - such an attack did take place on the Vistula front on
the date he gives: 12 June 1915. In Malraux's narrative the attack is
organised by one Professor Hoffmann, and this character is arguably
Malraux's most virulently satirical creation, a chilling version of the now
familiar caricature of the mad German scientist with his eye on world
domination. Chemistry, declares Hoffmann, is 'l'arme définitive, l'arme
supérieure qui conférera aux peuples qui la manieront bien, - qui la
gouverneront - une suprématie mondiale. Peut-être même l'empire du
monde!...' (p. 177)(20) Malraux puts into Hoffmann's mouth statements of
splendid unconscious irony: 'Nous en sommes à la préhistoire dans la guerre
chimique!' (p. 176) A single sentence will serve to indicate the contrast
Malraux wishes to establish between Berger and the clinically single-minded
chemist: 'La voix du professeur énumérait les qualités et les défauts du
phosgène, et mon père ressentait la profondeur du monde slave jusqu'au
Pacifique.' (p. 175) Behind and beyond the brutalities in the foreground,
Vincent Berger has been increasingly aware of the presence of the
unchanging Russian landscape, its ancient villages and gilded domes and
peasant faces.(21) He had come to fight in Russia precisely because unlike
France and Germany 'la Russie lui était indifférente' (p. 158), but the
more he encounters it the more precious he feels it is. He experiences the
same sharp sense of an irreplaceable heritage vulnerable to brutality as
does his son in Chartres a quarter of a century later. It is possible to
argue too that Malraux wished to influence those of his readers for whom
'la Russie... était indifférente' to accept common cause not with the
Soviet Communist Party but with Mother Russia and her people. To drive home
with the utmost dramatic effect this notion of a common ground of humanity
between peoples, Malraux crucially alters the outcome of the gas attack. In
the real historical attack, the wind changed direction and blew the
gas-cloud back into the panic-stricken German lines: eventually after a

further veering of the wind, the Germans were able to advance 6 km., but at
the cost of 1,100 casualties, including 350 by gas. In Malraux's version,
the gas cloud moves over the Russian lines as planned, but the following
German infantry are so horrified at the sight of the gassed soldiers in the
Russian trenches that many of them try to carry one of the victims back to
safety and help in their own lines. It is now clear why Malraux chose as
his starting point a gas attack on the Eastern front: if he had
(mis)represented one of the similar attacks launched in the West, his
rewriting of history would have been flagrantly obvious to many readers,
and the moral of fundamental solidarity between French and German
combatants would have been too controversial. This might have obscured the
point of the episode, which is the implied, symbolic refutation of
Möllberg's pessimistic conclusions. Malraux wishes to suggest that at the
level of ordinary men even more than at that of the intellectuals, there is
a shared sense of basic humanity: the hopes, fears and superstitions
expressed by the German soldiers in the Eastern trenches in 1915 discreetly
echo those of the French prisoners at Chartres in 1940.

The final, 'epilogue' section is headed 'Camp de Chartres'(22) and
brings us back to the life of Berger *fils* in 1940. From the prison camp,
Berger recalls a tank advance in which he participated before his capture.
The placing of this episode at the end of the novel is crucial. If it were
read first, or in isolation, it could risk being seen as representing the
heroic struggle of an ordinary French tank crew against the unseen German
enemy. For a start, however, Malraux's narrative depersonalises the enemy;
the crew are gripped primarily by the fear of a tank trap or of mechanical
failure: 'L'ennemi n'est pas l'Allemand: c'est la rupture de chenille, la
mine et la fosse.' (p. 268) Tense with trepidation, they drive the tank on
towards enemy lines, and as they do so Berger imagines the equivalent
movement of German tanks towards him, and in them 'des hommes pareillement
crispés, pareillement distraits' (p. 271). The propaganda talk which the
crew had just had - 'la conférence où l'on nous avait envoyés par quatre
pour apprendre la nécessité de démembrer l'Allemagne' (p. 261) - has left
them unimpressed. The stolid peasant Pradé sums up his reaction: 'Ça me
plaît pas... qu'on me raconte des conneries. Je les connais les Fritz; moi
je les connais. Quand ils sont arrivés chez nous en '15, (...) y en a qui
nous ont foutu des calottes, y en a qui nous ont donné du pain. C'est comme
partout.' (p. 263) Here again on every level - in the narrative tone, in
the attitudes of the narrator or those of the average soldier - Malraux
makes no concessions to patriotic anti-German rhetoric.

The final pages confirm this emphasis, if confirmation were necessary.
After a tense ordeal when the tank seemed irrevocably trapped in a
defensive ditch, it extricates itself and they eventually arrive at dawn at
a village recently abandoned by the Germans. With the shadow of death
lifted from him Berger experiences that sense of 'retour sur la terre', of
the rediscovery of ordinary life which is a recurrent motif in Malraux's
writing. Finally the crew comes across an old peasant couple who have
declined to leave and who observe the passing spectacle of the war with
stoic, even ironic resignation. In accordance with a prevailing iconography
of the time this couple might have been presented as symbolising the
abiding tenacity of the French peasant, the 'terrien' virtues at the core
of the French nation. For Malraux however, nation is of no importance here:
the narrator's reaction echoes the similar response of Vincent Berger to
the Russian landscape and people, and the emphasis is placed on the notion
of 'la vieille race des hommes' (p. 288), as tough and as persistent a

species as the walnut trees of the title.

This rapid survey of some of the ideological elements implicit in the novel provides some answers to the questions raised at the beginning of this article. Has Malraux in this novel 'turned his back on current events', as Boak asserted? Certainly he did turn his back on political debate, a big change since *L'Espoir*: there is no mention of communism, or Nazism, nor any serious reference to current political figures. Nevertheless Malraux does implicitly project a clear and strong view of what the conflict is about. In particular, for Malraux, the war is not a war between nations - at every point the narrative excludes or condemns nationalism, whether French or German. It is not about politics or *patrie*: it is about the nature of man and of human civilisation. That is what is worth fighting for, and in that Malraux finds common cause with some Resistance writing. The identifiable 'enemies' in the text are not political leaders, or the SS - they are Möllberg and especially Hoffmann, German intellectuals who have placed their genius at the service of a science or a philosophy which devalues human life. Malraux implicitly draws a clear distinction between these monsters of the intellect and 'le peuple allemand'. He insistently suggests that the mass of ordinary Germans share with their French counterparts the same stock of fundamental emotions and attitudes. Even more clearly, in his fictional embellishment of the gas attack and its outcome, he sets out to construct an emotionally convincing manifestation of an unquenchable fraternity with the supposed enemy which transcends race and politics.

This solidarity of ordinary mankind appears to assume the function of the Communist myth of the international solidarity of the working class, but stripped of any explicitly ideological (let alone revolutionary) content. It leaves unsolved, however, the problem of whether a link exists, and can be defined, between the ordinary German and a Möllberg or a Hoffmann figure. In his rather crude dualism of the 'intellectual' and the 'fundamental', Malraux never confronts this problem clearly.

The conflict in *Les Noyers* is on two levels. There is the physical combat of war, waged by a mass of men who, whichever side they are on, share fundamental needs, attitudes and aspirations. The outcome of this combat is most often decided by technical factors, hence Malraux's insistence on 'l'aviation ou les tanks'. The other level of conflict is metaphysical and ideological; it is waged by the intellectuals, whose capacity for cultural analysis gives them an aura of shamanistic power. Here the battle-lines are drawn between those whose ideas tend to undermine the meaning of civilisation or the value of the human being - notably Möllberg-Spengler or Hoffmann - and those who, like the Bergers, seek to bring rational and irrational elements, theory and praxis together into a humane vision. When the text speaks of Vincent Berger's foreboding at the German public's reaction to Möllberg's ideas 'lorsqu'il (son système) atteindrait la culture génèrale et les passions qu'elle entraîne avec elle' (p. 109), it suggests Malraux's belief in the power the intellectual can wield over the mass. Such a belief in the charismatic shaper of ideas and aspirations prepares the ground for Malraux's enthusiasm for the populist aspect of post-war Gaullism.

In this text, however, Malraux is for the moment at a distinct distance from the fervent nationalism of de Gaulle. Vincent Berger, whose experience and personality strongly reflect Malraux's own, is a suspect figure in the eyes of the German authorities, a man 'dont le patriotisme n'était pas la vertu dominante' (p. 160). Malraux may have sensed that his own mistrust of patriotism, linked with his refusal to give priority to the violence of the present over his sense of the past and its abiding bequest, was not fully in the temper of the time, and was liable to be misinterpreted. This at least is one possible explanation for his apparent reluctance to give the work a wide circulation: it went through a short sequence of limited editions in Switzerland and, after the war, in France. It has not been republished for many years, although some sections have been reused in later books. (It will presumably figure in the new Pléiade edition of Malraux's works.) As a consequence it is, with *Le Temps du mépris*, Malraux's least well-known novel. To regard it however largely as a transitional text in Malraux's output is to do it less than justice, and to miss its historical specificity. The relationship of this text to the historical moment of its production is indirect, since it systematically subordinates the present to an infinitely larger perspective. Despite this, or perhaps because of this, it nevertheless articulates a challenging and powerfully individual response to the *débâcle* and its aftermath.

Notes

1. References will be to the 1948 Gallimard edition of the novel.
2. J. Hoffmann, *L'Humanisme de Malraux* (Paris, 1963), p. 261.
3. R. Caillois, 'Les Noyers de l'Altenburg de Malraux' in Pol Gaillard (ed.), *Les Critiques de notre temps et Malraux* Paris, 1970), pp. 92-96 (pp. 92-3). This review appeared earlier in *Circonstancielles* (Paris, 1946).
4. D. Boak, *André Malraux* (Oxford, 1968), p. 141.
5. The best biography of Malraux remains Jean Lacouture, *André Malraux. Une vie dans le siècle* (Paris, 1973). Particular light on this otherwise ill-documented wartime period of Malraux's life and on the genesis of *Les Noyers* is shed by Walter Langlois, 'André Malraux 1939-1942, d'après une correspondance inédite' in *André Malraux I: du farfelu aux Antimémoires* (Paris, Lettres Modernes, 1972), pp. 95-127.
6. Comments reported by Max Aub and Raymond Aron, quoted by Lacouture, pp. 276-277.
7. Lacouture, p. 271.
8. R. Stéphane, *André Malraux. Entretiens et précisions* (Paris, 1984), 114. Quoted also in the same author's *Fin d'une jeunesse* (Paris, 1954), p. 62.
9. Quoted in Lacouture, p. 277.
10. Quoted in Lacouture, p. 276.
11. This notion of framing is referred to, in rather different perspectives, by P.R. Côté, *Les Techniques picturales chez Malraux* (Paris, 1984), p.49, ·and by Susan M. McGrath, 'The Artist's (Auto)biography in Les Noyers de l'Altenburg', *André Malraux Review*, 18, No.2 (Fall 1986), pp. 124-134 (p. 129).
12. In *La Psychologie de l'art*, which he was working on alongside *Les Noyers*, Malraux sees the statues of Chartres as 'in dialogue' not only with those of Rheims and Amiens, but also with those of Bamberg, and with the paintings of Giotto. See *La Psychologie de l'art: la création artistique* (Geneva, 1948), p. 102.

13. L. Goldmann, *Pour une sociologie du roman*, rev. edn. (Paris, Gallimard (Idées), 1964), p. 255. Goldmann's view is contested by John Burt Foster, Jr., *Heirs to Dionysos. A Nietzschean current in literary modernism* (Princeton, 1981), p. 320.

14. The colloquia at Altenburg are clearly based on those at Pontigny which Malraux attended twice in the 1930s. Nicholas Hewitt has suggested a possible source for the name Altenburg: see his 'Malraux et Nietzsche: un rapport qu'il faut nuancer', *André Malraux III: influences et affinités* (Paris, Lettres modernes, 1975), pp. 135-160 (p. 137 n.4).

15. A. Hoog, 'Man, Möllberg and Frobenius' in R.W.B. Lewis (ed.), *Malraux: a collection of critical essays* (Englewood Cliffs, 1964), pp. 86-95. This article originally appeared in *Yale French Studies* 18 (1957), pp. 87-96.

16. *The Childhood of Man* (London, 1909), whose original German title was *Aus den Flegeljahren der Menschheit* (Hanover, 1901), was not apparently published in French. It therefore seems more probable that Malraux drew on the two translated works referred to here, which substantially use the same examples. Their original titles are *Kulturgeschichte Afrikas* (Zürich, 1933) and *Schicksalskunde im Sinne des Kulturwerdens* (Leipzig, 1932).

17. See E. Berl, *La Culture en péril* (Paris, 1948), p. 7, and Jean-René Bourrel, 'Emmanuel Berl et André Malraux: deux façons d'être dans l'histoire', *André Malraux V*, (Paris, Lettres modernes, 1982), pp. 57-75 (p.62). On Spengler's influence on Malraux, see J.-R. Bourrel, 'Malraux et la pensée allemande de 1921 à 1949', *André Malraux III*, pp. 103-134. Joseph Hoffmann (op. cit., pp. 263-264) notes the extent to which Möllberg reflects the ideas of Spengler rather than those of Frobenius.

18. *Fontaine*, 42 (mai 1945), pp. 293-296 (p. 294).

19. On metamorphosis as an anti-Spenglerian concept, see William Righter, *The Rhetorical Hero. An essay on the aesthetics of André Malraux* (London, 1964), p. 22.

20. One possible historical counterpart to the fictional Hoffmann is Fritz Haber, the director of the Kaiser Wilhelm Institute for Physical Chemistry, who was in charge of chemical warfare research and who visited the Vistula front in 1915. Another is Otto Hahn, one of Haber's collaborators, who actually observed the attack of 12th June. Haber has been described as 'the embodiment of the romantic, quasi-heroic aspect of German chemistry in which national pride commingled with the advancement of pure science and the utilitarian progress of technology'. Hahn 'witnessed many gas operations, although his autobiography deals with them as if they were scientific phenomena, and the effect on the enemy gets only the briefest of mentions'. See L.F. Haber, *The Poisonous Cloud. Chemical Warfare in the First World War* (Oxford, 1986), p. 2, pp. 36-37, pp. 236-237. Hoffmann can be seen as a caricatural mix of these elements of intense patriotism, total commitment to scientific and technological advancement and imperviousness to human consequences.

21. In Malraux's earlier novel *Le Temps du mépris* (Paris, 1935), Kassner, the Communist hero, evokes an image of 'l'église Saint-Basile avec ses oignons multicolores, (..)les coupoles toutes semées d'or d'un couvent forteresse (..); au-dessous, une ville contre-révolutionnaire pourrie d'ex-votos, de jouets et de pèlerinages, vieille Russie dont la mystique ensanglantée masque mal les corps des partisans pendus aux cloches.' (pp. 69-70) With the shift in historical circumstance and ideological orientation between the two books, the gilded domes of old Russia have, as it were, changed sides: from being the sinister symbols of reactionary oppression for Kassner, they have become for Berger the touchstone of a precious heritage, reassuring images of continuity.

22. Confusingly, 'Camp de Chartres' was the heading given (perhaps more appropriately) to the first 'prologue' section when it was published separately in *Fontaine* in 1943.

PREDICTIONS AND REACTIONS: FROM BERNANOS TO VERCORS

William Kidd

Recent historiography of the French experience during the Second World War has emphasised the complexities and ambiguities of a period which in many respects no longer appears amenable to the confident black-and-white distinctions of the 1950s and 1960s. It is true, and bears repetition, that in the last analysis Resistance and Collaboration involved moral and political choices which were diametrically opposed and often paid for in blood. But we now know that active Resistance, far from involving the majority of Frenchmen, was espoused by a minority whose heroism and self-sacrifice were in inverse proportion to their number. We know too that there were several 'resistances' and several 'collaborations' in time and space and, to use an analogy from Camus's *La Peste*, numerous 'cas douteux'. Awareness of such ambiguities has increasingly extended to the literature of the period, to the enrolment of criticism and culture by different groups, and to the ways in which 'écriture' in its Barthesian sense (fictional or non-fictional) transcends or subverts its author's intentions or its own historicity, the politico-philosophical context in which it appeared and for which it was deemed to provide intellectual justification.(1)

This approach has much to commend it to scholars in a 'deconstructionist' age in which 'history' is constantly collapsing into 'histoire' and didacticism into semiotics, though its inherent danger - the devaluation of the original experience in the name of an unstated revisionism - is obvious, and the basic perception scarcely new: the successive authorization and prohibition between November 1942 and February 1943 of Saint-Exupéry's *Pilote de guerre*,(2) and the suspicion in Free French circles, fuelled by an article by Ilya Ehrenbourg, that *Le Silence de la mer* might have emanated from the Propaganda Abteilung, are well-known examples of how individual works were construed differently at different times by the same groups, or at the same time by different groups.(3) And but for the historically sensitive nature of the period, it would have been trite to observe that writers who were on the same side politically speaking - Bernanos and Sartre, for example - had less in common thematically and stylistically than others (Drieu and Malraux) who belonged to opposite camps. Jean-Louis Curtis's *Les Forêts de la Nuit* was an early (1947) and remarkably frank portrayal of the complexities of the Occupation before the myth-making processes of 'résistancialisme (...) cette espèce de mythologie un peu tricolore, un peu paranoïaque sur l'occupation (...) dont on a encombré la littérature, le cinéma, les conversations de bistrot et les manuels d'histoire' inhibited serious discussion of the subject for two decades.(4) Times have changed. In 1986, Sartre's 'nazification' of the name Bras(z)illach in 'Qu'est-ce qu'un collaborateur?' prompted Russell Berman to observe that 'an antifascism that defines itself by insisting on the inviolability of the national community is evidently implicated in the same discursive structure it purports to oppose, producing the effect of a French *Volksgemeinschaft*.'(5) And Robert Pickering argues that in terms of the relationship between specific types of narrative and the reality they purport to represent,

> model Resistance texts can themselves be seen paradoxically to conform to certain criteria situated in an overarching propositional and counter-propositional dialectic with collaborationism, subversive as they may appear to be of officially promulgated doctrines.(6)

Pickering's awareness of the problem of referentiality, his avoidance of any influential, cause-and-effect, inference between the authors of the texts studied, and his subtle analyses of the relationship between the deviant ('against the grain') and the normative ('model Resistance texts'), make this an intereresting and challenging judgement, some of whose general methodological and evaluative implications I have explored elsewhere.(7) My present purpose in examining writing 'about' 1940 is to identify 'overarching' ideological, thematic and stylistic similarities which, independently of genre and across the hiatus of national defeat and humiliation, account for the remarkable homogeneity of the experience; and which, until the Resistance began systematically to subvert the discourse of collaborationism and invest it with alternative meanings, constituted a reservoir drawn upon by writers of different persuasions, creating the sense of complexity and ambiguity to which modern commentators have been so sensitive.

In this perspective, from Bernanos (1939) to Vercors (1942) will I hope seem less like a perilous dialectical leap into the void than an intertextual journey in language in which two other writers, Jean Schlumberger and Ramon Fernandez, provide intermediate 'gîtes d'étape'. Two of the texts chosen pre-date the 'débâcle' and two are posterior to it; it is in that sense that they may be considered 'predictive' and 'reactive', though the distinction demands qualification since imaginative writing, even about contemporary events, is necessarily regressive, and hindsight, with its attendant difficulties, the only kind of sight the historian ultimately has. By coincidence, three of the texts first appeared in the wartime *Nouvelle Revue Française* (hereafter *NRF*), and coincidence is also part of my sub-text.

During the 'jours noirs' of May 1940, Bernanos wrote to a Brazilian friend: 'Notre ligne forcée! Notre neuvième armée culbutée d'un seul coup! Notre neuvième armée - des garçons de la Touraine, du Berry, des gens de la Loire - vous ne savez pas ce que c'est pour moi!'.(8) Such sentiments were a natural reaction on the part of the writer, an émigré since 1938, and a poignant way of expressing solidarity with the stricken French forces, whom he evoked again a few days later, 'déchiré d'humiliations et d'angoisse' (*Corr II*, p. 324) as defeat loomed: 'Je vais et viens ici comme un fantôme, chaque jour nous apporte une nouvelle blessure; ah! que ne suis-je auprès de ceux de nos garçons qui se font tuer!'(ibid, p. 325). Natural too but more noteworthy, is the fact that in emphasising his compassionate identification with the 'garçons' of the quintessentially French 'pays de la Loire', he was referring indirectly to his maternal antecedents - his mother (d. 1930) was a Berrichonne, from Pellevoisin in the Indre; Bernanos is buried there - and not his equally patriotic but originally Spanish paternal lineage. Attachment to the 'Mother(-country)' is further expressed in the acknowledgement that his Brazilian interlocutor's 'passionate' love for France differs from that of Bernanos and his fellow-countrymen, '[qui] l'aimons comme des fils'(ibid, p. 322).

If therefore these letters were a prelude to Bernanos's career as a Resistance writer in exile until summoned home in July 1945 by De Gaulle's magisterial 'votre place est parmi nous',(9) they belong also to the retrospective inspiration which produced the work composed between September 1939 and April 1940, *Les Enfants humiliés*. Though sub-titled 'Journal 1939-40', this is a sombre account of the 'betrayal' by 'les Grands Citoyens de l'Arrière (du Derrière)'(10) of the combatants of 1918 and their descendants, the 'enfants humiliés' now called upon to fight again. Bernanos had served in the Great War and remained unforgiving towards politicians who in the name of 'la Démocratie Universelle', 'la déesse France et Saint Poilu'(11) had debased the language - 'les mots les plus sûrs étaient pipés' (ibid, p. 1040) - and had seduced 'la victoire', setting her up as a 'kept woman' (*EEC*, 779). Such genderizing is not unusual in the iconography of the 1920s and 1930s, and Bernanos was not alone in referring to 'la grande muette' (*EEC*, p. 1144), though the description of the soldiers' faithless conquest - 'quelle croupe! quel ventre! quels tétons!' (*EEC*, p. 778) - is unusually explicit, and suggests that the experience reflected in the work was emotionally powerful. Less banal and much more prescient is Bernanos's understanding of the linguistic appropriation of victory and his mythification of betrayal which, like all such myths, contains a partial truth: the Third Republic's failure either to secure a lasting peace with Germany when the auguries were best (before 1933) or seriously to prepare for a war it believed it could win. Early extracts of the manuscript brought to France by Henri Michaux in January 1940 appeared in the *NRF* on May I, ten days before the German onslaught in the West.(12)

The first paragraph reads as follows:

Nous retournons dans la guerre ainsi que dans la maison de notre jeunesse. Mais il n'y a plus de place pour nous. De la cave au grenier, toute grouillante, elle déborde de cris, de chansons, d'odeurs, de fumées. Ils ont vidé les armoires, jeté par les fenêtres nos souvenirs et nos morts, pêle-mêle, sans les reconnaître, et ils les brûlent en tas au milieu de la pelouse, sous la surveillance du service sanitaire. Une pluie fine tombe, mêlée de suie. Les premières fenêtres s'allument, la voiture de distribution, dans un grondement de tonnerre, jette son chargement de viande marquée du cachet de l'intendance. La cuisine ronfle et rougeoie comme une forge. Je me suis glissé dans l'escalier, mais il y avait vraiment trop de monde, le flot m'a repoussé dehors, sans me voir, dans un rire énorme qui n'en finissait pas, qui m'a poursuivi longtemps, qui m'arrivait encore à travers la brume, renvoyé d'une crête à l'autre, tandis que je regardais une dernière fois ma cruelle vieille maison, ma folle maison, tout éclatante d'une lueur furieuse, tirant sur sa chaîne et aboyant dans la nuit (*EEC*, p. 776).

There are several items of interest here besides the oft-quoted and justly famous first sentence. The evocation of the 'maison de notre jeunesse' conveys a desire to retreat from the present into a place (the house) and a time (the past) whose message is troubling and ambivalent. A full-scale party is going on; child-like, the author has sneaked into the stairs but is first ignored, then brushed helplessly aside by the adults and finally flees, pursued by the sounds of revelry, looking back from time to time at the house, lit up as if on fire, straining at its lead like a mad dog (by displacement: 'folle', 'furieuse', 'fou furieux'). By a coincidence which Bernanos could not have foreseen in September 1939 but came close to foreseeing in May 1940 (*Corr II*, p. 325-6), the house at Fressin (Pas-de-Calais) where he spent his adolescent summers and which he regarded truly as his 'vieille maison familiale' (*EEC*, p. 1038) was destroyed by fire during the hostilities, one extra-textual aspect of what, in its ambiguities and timing of publication, is a prophetic piece of writing. For who, after all, is burning the papers, the personal documents and memories? The unattributed 'ils' invites the question without providing an answer. On the one hand, the atmosphere of hurry and confusion and the 'surveillance' exercised over the operation suggests preparations for departure, for flight... On the other, the same military details (quartermastery, transport), and the fact that being burned are the belongings and symbols of legitimacy of the previous owners, suggest that the house has changed hands, has new occupants, occupiers...

The importance of 'la maison des vivants (...) et des morts' (*EEC*, p. 905) as a textual motif in *Les Enfants humiliés* is acknowledged in the German translation, entitled *Das Haus der Lebenden und der Toten*.(13) But there is a secondary metaphor here, a maritime one, in the 'grondement' of the lorry, the cargo off-loaded, cast up as if on the beach, the child pushed aside by the disdainful laughing 'flot', the sounds heard through the mist, from crest to crest, the dog pulling on its chain like a vessel dragging its anchor. Such imagery is a recognized feature of Bernanos's writing, including *Nouvelle Histoire de Mouchette* (1937) and *Monsieur Ouine* (completed May 1940), though attention has not hitherto been drawn to this passage. Behind the sound and fury of the house is a silent but tumultuous sea, 'une mer silencieuse'...

Written soon after the declaration of war but months before the battle for France, this passage reads therefore, with its sub-text of abandonment and occupation and its maternal/maritime overlay in the homophones 'mer/mère', like an anticipation of defeat. Lest it appear that I am making Bernanos's text 'say' more than might reasonably be asked of it, let me quote the short coda to this first section of the 'Journal': 'Le 3 septembre [= 1939], à cinq heures du matin, nous avons trouvé la maison vide. Elle [= la victoire] était partie sans rien dire, en emportant les meubles' (*EEC*, p. 779). When the call came, fickle victory was not at home, she was not, to paraphrase Bernanos's more suggestive language, 'fidèle au rendez-vous'.

A similar idea (turning up at the appointed hour) appears in another text published during the 'Phoney War', Schlumberger's January 1940 article 'Pour saluer l'année nouvelle' which begins thus:

> On voit surgir dans la nuit une grande forme hésitante. On ne distingue encore rien d'elle que sa stature inquiète et redressée. Elle est là, tout à coup, comme la proue d'un navire qui est entré dans le port tous feux éteints.(14)

Interestingly though coincidentally vis-à-vis the previous text, the new year is an animal before becoming a ghostly vessel, and contains a displacement of affect (the 'inquiétude') from the perceiver onto the perceived ('sa stature inquiète et redressée'). As with the Freudian phenomenon known variously as 'inquiétante étrangeté', the 'unheimlich', the unrecognizable and yet disturbingly familiar 'déja vu', the effect of these lines is to disorient, to prepare the reader for the unexpected. Will the fateful 'an quarante' be content to run its course prudently or, 'les flancs pleins d'événements à naître', prove to be 'une date illuminée par l'explosion d'un monde?' (ibid). The idea of birth, articulated by the metaphorical series ships/('flancs')/ animals, is developed in the new arrival's anxious thoughts as it turns for reassurance to the armies in position on the frontier:

> Elle n'a pas peur, mais l'air qu'inhalent ses premières respirations la suffoque un peu. Les relents de tout ce qui croupissait dans ce vieux pays ne sont pas encore partout balayés. Elle tend sa narine vers le souffle qui vient de la frontière. Son poumon s'en emplit, et déjà elle se rassure. Car elle a tout de suite reconnu cet air-là, rude et salubre, celui qui monte du vaste glacis peuplé seulement d'hommes sous le casque (p. 6).

Uncertain, the country does not know what to expect: death and destruction, or a long wait in 'la boue et l'ennui'. But if the writer predicts the

ultimate triumph of the helmeted legions 'sous le glacis', he remains alert
to the lingering presence of the unidentified 'relents' and the radiophonic
'ondes chargées de poisons' (p. 6) so deleterious to France's domestic and
international position in the 1930s, and his anticipation of victory is
stoic and voluntary rather than confident. Echoing a propaganda slogan the
régime came to regret, he writes that 'il ne se pourra pas qu'on ne soit
pas les plus forts' (p. 6); and a comment which Bernanos might have
endorsed that 'les cloches de l'armistice ne seront pas celles d'autrefois'
ushers in the following conclusion:

> Car il s'agira de refaire une autre France: la vieille, la
> poussiéreuse, ne pourra plus servir. Pour reprendre son rang
> devant le monde, il lui faudra autre chose qu'une sagesse de
> gagne-petit, devenue peu à peu sordide, d'autres charmes que
> ceux dont elle a brillé du temps d'Offenbach et de la Païva.
> Ses prestiges de luxe et d'esprit se sont étrangement fanés,
> depuis qu'ailleurs on est beaucoup plus riche qu'elle, et que
> des générations ont partout grandi qui ne savent plus sa
> langue. Il ne suffira plus d'être le pays de la vie facile,
> qui offre à l'étranger sa peinture et ses prostituées. C'est
> de fond en comble qu'il faudra tout rénover, tout dérouiller
> et rajeunir. Personne ne pourra rentrer dans ses vieux
> chaussons et regagner le coin de son feu en disant: Ce n'est
> pas mon affaire (pp. 6-7).

Schlumberger returned to the subject addressed in 'Pour saluer l'année
nouvelle' in an article in the conservative *Figaro* in April 1940 and
developed his diagnosis of France's longstanding decline in a series
written in the unoccupied zone in 1941, re-published under a 'Free French'
imprint in 1945.(15) The original was subsequently incorporated in the
Resistance anthology *La Patrie se fait tous les jours*,(16) acquiring its
final significance from post-Liberation hopes of a new social and national
order. But in January 1940, even taking the writer's age, background and
acknowledged moralism into account - he was born in 1877 of Protestant and
Alsatian extraction - his text is curiously regressive in its historical
reference - (Offenbach, the Second Empire), and its sub-text (the myth of
'foreign bodies' undermining a previous régime which succumbed to Germany).
For of the innumerable 'grandes horizontales' identified with national
decadence - Hortense Schneider, Cora Pearl, Lola Montez, Blanche d'Antigny,
Liane de Pougy, Emilienne d'Alençon - the choice of La Païva (Thérèse
Lachmann), a Russian émigrée whose lovers included a Bismarckian agent and
who was deported to Germany in 1879, is particularly apposite to the
circumstances of 1939-40, marked by lurking fears of a fascist 'fifth
column' and the Daladier government's rounding up of the Communists in the
aftermath of the Germano-Soviet Pact.

Schlumberger never of course subscribed to Maurras's 'anti-France',
nor did he endorse the repressive policies shortly to be pursued by Vichy
and the Nazi occupier. But his call for national regeneration ('refaire
une autre France') in the moral, cultural, intellectual and linguistic
fields ('on ne sait plus sa langue') is strikingly similar both in content
and tenor to those voiced by writers who did espouse collaborationism such
as Rebatet, Drieu la Rochelle or Chardonne. As the latter said of the
defeat, 'ce fut la fin de la France babillarde. Elle s'écroula au premier
choc, d'avance vidée par d'autres ennemis'.(17) The idea of the house
weakened from the inside before being occupied recalls Bernanos as well as
Schlumberger, whose comment on the 'relents de tout ce qui croupissait dans
ce vieux pays - pas encore balayés' might have emanated from any of the
writers mentioned above. Guy de Pourtalès wrote on 28 July 1940:

Avant de rebâtir sur l'emplacement d'une vieille maison
écroulée, il faut déblayer le terrain (...) Il sera nécessaire
de porter partout le fer et le feu (...) C'est cela que doit
se préparer la nation. A punir les responsables. A limoger les
incompétents. A vider les terrasses des cafés pour contraindre
les fainéants au travail.(17)

Similarly, just as critics of the Third Republic denounced the bankruptcy
of words and concepts, prostituted by politicians for their own purposes -
'c'est dans notre démocratie, pendant vingt ans, de Poincaré à Léon Blum,
c'est en Angleterre que l'on a discrédité les mots droit, justice, paix,
sociéte des nations, en les associant à la force ou aux débris de la force,
pour les employer enfin à cacher la débilité'(19) - so their opponents
attacked the appropriation of the language and its subordination to a
foreign ideology. Pierre Seghers's 'fausse parole' is perhaps the best
known example of this use of the same idea to convey a different
ideological message.(20)

It is true that it was chiefly Resistance writers who affirmed the
purifying imperative of 'silence' as the precondition of the reconquest of
the language and the culture. Or who, in 1942 and 1943, attacked what
Aragon called the 'mots démonétisés qu'on lit dans le journal',(21) the
devaluation of the linguistic and spiritual currency in a strange 'royaume'
where 'le Roi même faisait de la fausse monnaie'.(22) Since the Germans had
unilaterally devalued the franc after the armistice of June 1940, the
patriotic resonance of such allusions probably contributed to the
effectiveness of the subversive message. But it was the PPF's Ramon
Fernandez, in an article entitled 'Retour à Molière', who as early as
February 1941 produced the following:

En ces temps de gêne et d'ennui (comme disaient nos pères, qui
connaissaient le poids des mots, et non pas comme nous dirions
nous-mêmes, qui traitons les mots comme du papier d'échange),
la seule joie qui demeure est peut-être le retour aux trésors
spirituels de la nation. Leur éclat intact, la probité de
leurs alliages, la grâce sévère des plaisirs qu'ils dispensent
règnent tranquillement sur nos sursauts d'angoisse et de
désespoir. Des livres de nos bibliothèques émanent et
rayonnent des puissances messagères qu'aucune radio du monde
ne saurait égaler. Ces grands livres silencieux, droits comme
des tombes musulmanes, détiennent des secrets que nous
perdions en courant, le nez au vent, comme ces gens ahuris qui
n'ont jamais sur eux les papiers qu'il faudrait et que
pourtant ils possèdent, quelque part, ils ne savent plus où.
Au lieu de nous reconnaître pour les débiteurs d'un passé
illustre, nous étions devenus des camelots excités de
l'avenir, sans songer que l'avenir ne s'entrevoit seulement
que dans les reflets d'un grand passé. C'est par des retours
que doit se préparer et se calculer l'avance nécessaire qui
nous fera rattraper le temps perdu: retour à nos moralistes de
l'alliage d'un Vauvenargues, à nos épées spirituelles de la
trempe d'un d'Aubigné, à nos romanciers ardents de la chaleur
d'un Balzac.(23)

This text is a reaction to defeat, not an anticipation of conflict, and has
none of the affective imprint of *Les Enfants humiliés* or 'Pour saluer
l'année nouvelle'. Indeed despite the reference to 'nos sursauts d'angoisse
et de désespoir', Fernandez's tone is relatively measured - the passage
also appeared, without modification, in the Doriotist press,(24) so on this
occasion he was not using one language for the party readership and another

for the review - a trait which both distinguishes it from more predictably vitriolic diagnoses and makes it suspiciously complacent. It is a manifestly political piece, witness the coded reference to the BBC ('aucune radio au monde') and the suggestion that the country rectify past mistakes ('rattraper le temps perdu') by turning to authority-figures ('Nos pères ... connaissaient le poids des mots'), a doubly mythifying generalisation designed to support the devaluation of national calamity into 'gêne et ennui' and whose national and linguistic inclusiveness is undercut in Fernandez's own case by the Mexican nationality and early death of his father.

And yet if the 'unvoiced' message of the 'Retour à Molière' is the acceptance of defeat, its principal themes are common to collaborationist and Resistance writing alike: the need to restore the devalued currency of language ('du papier d'échange'), the emphasis on the purity of the past ('éclat intact', 'probité') compared to the doubtful alloys of the present, the importance of silence and reflexion ('tranquillement', 'grands livres silencieux', a future which is glimpsed - 'qui s'entrevoit'- not heard) in the period of repose which follows the storm. Nor can the authors mentioned be considered the automatic or exclusive patrimony of the fascist or Pétainist right; d'Aubigné, whose Protestant credentials made him a symbolic reference for the Resistance, is particularly noteworthy here - and all are martial or quasi-martial figures: d'Aubigné fought in the wars of religion, Vauvenargues soldiered before becoming a writer, Balzac's proclaimed ambition was to emulate with the pen what Napoleon had achieved by the sword. And if the return to the 'trésors spirituels de la nation' may be read as implying a political disengagement in the present - Fernandez's swordsmen are after all only 'plumitifs' and, like Molière himself, safely dead - that too arguably makes the piece more revealing than its place of publication (Drieu's new-look *NRF*) would suggest; for in January 1941 (when it was written) and February (when published), the wartime PPF was still in the doldrums, disenchanted with the Vichy régime but not yet wholly identified with the 'New European Order', a process marked by 'Operation Barbarossa' on 22 June 1941, the creation of the Légion des Volontaires Français contre le Bolchévisme (LVF) and German recognition of the party in October of the same year.

In stressing the need to rediscover the masterpieces of a more glorious past in the dark days of defeat, Fernandez was in fact expressing a reaction to events which was felt by a wider public in the first year of the occupation and a view held increasingly by intellectuals on either side of the ideological divide. This can be demonstrated by reference to numerous sources, among which and appropriate to the occasion is Ian Higgins's '"Assurer les relais": literary heritage in Resistance culture'.(25) The title borrows Seghers's declaration that 'certaines oeuvres brûlent comme des torches. Il faut assurer les relais',(26) a metaphor echoed by Fernandez's description of *Itinéraire Français*, in which material from the 'Retour à Molière' was incorporated in 1943 as an 'étude sur les grands esprits, de Descartes à Péguy, qui se sont transmis le flambeau de notre culture'.(27) However the consoling 'permanence' of the cultural inheritance found its most enduring expression and its most famous literary image in 1942, in the book-lined room in which the old man and his niece seek refuge from the elements and the invader in *Le Silence de la mer*. Their spatial retreat within the house mirrors the military and intellectual 'repli' of the country itself, but re-validates the present by calling up the spirits of the past immanent in her great works of literature:

Il était devant les rayons de la bibliothèque. Ses doigts
suivaient les reliures d'une caresse légère: '... Balzac,
Barrès, Baudelaire, Beaumarchais, Boileau, Buffon...
Chateaubriand, Corneille, Descartes, Fénelon, Flaubert... La
Fontaine, France, Gautier, Hugo... Quel appel!(...) Et je
n'en suis qu'à la lettre H!'(28)
In the same author's 'Désespoir est mort' (1943), which looks back to 1940,
the narrator explains how in defeat he rediscovered the 'courage désespéré'
and the 'opiniâtreté surhumaine' required of his predecessors 'pour se
passer de main en main un fragile flambeau pendant près de mille ans'.(29)
And he adds: 'Certes, je ne pensai pas précisément tout cela. Mais ce fut
comme lorsqu'on voit la reliure d'un livre qu'on connaît bien'(ibid).

Vercors's ideological purpose was of course wholly opposed to
Fernandez's, and it is a neat counterpoint to the latter that it should be
Von Ebrennac, the fictional German, cultured and Francophile, not the
Germanophile French intellectual, who informs us that 'cette maison a une
âme' (SM, p. 39) and who recites the litany of enduring authors who
characterise French civilisation. But the presence of the same idea in
texts of different genre (essential to an evaluation of Vercors's artistic
achievement) and different ideological intentionality further illustrates
the propositional/counterpropositional relationship between them. Le
Silence de la mer was a politically subversive work whose effectiveness
depended on its appearing to be aesthetically non-subversive, in its
event-transcending, tradition-reinforcing appeal to the thematics of myth,
fable and 'l'amour impossible' and in its characteristic narrative closure.
The 'Retour à Molière' appeals to tradition to reinforce the status quo,
and contains the embryo of a 'fiction' which received its final incarnation
in Itinéraire Français. Now however the almost liturgical rediscovery of
books is prefaced by the return of the 'soldat démobilisé' to the
'apartement silencieux où les meubles ne lui sont pas encore rendus', and
the casting aside of the external trappings of soldiery (the uniform, the
'musette'), becomes a 'bain exquis' in which the writer 'laisse remonter
vers lui la marée des idées qu'il n'apercevait plus qu'à la ligne de
l'horizon' (op. cit., pp. 7-8). The house, the silence, the sea.

Coincidence? very probably. Influence? just possibly. Given the
speculation in wartime literary circles about the authorship of Le Silence
de la mer, variously attributed to NRF writers whom Fernandez had known for
twenty years (Gide, Martin du Gard, Schlumberger himself), his continuing
links with Resistance figures such as Martin-Chauffier, and his agnosticism
about the 'mauvais maîtres' denounced by other apologists of
collaborationism, he could well have read Vercors; the converse is
unthinkable in the light of the stance adopted by the latter in December
1940 towards Chardonne and the NRF,(30) and in any case irrelevant here.
For where Fernandez's wartime writing is merely reactive, Vercors's is also
predictive. Indeed he claimed that a series of 'hasards' played a major
part in the events which made him a writer; these included artwork executed
in 1935 which prophesied the date of the invasion of France, 'à une semaine
près, (...) le 12 mai 1940'.(31) And on all the available evidence about
its conception, fundamental aspects of Le Silence de la mer pre-existed the
catalyst of defeat and occupation, and to that extent constituted a
'pre-text'. That being so, I conclude with two brief observations which
bring me back to my starting point. The first concerns the Shakespearian
dimensions of the story to which I drew attention in 1987, notably the
parallels with Hamlet which make Von Ebrennac a ghostly apparition, a
'revenant'.(32) The second concerns the view that Vercors displayed
considerable ingenuity - or considerable naïvety - in using a 'good German'

to embody and to condemn collaborationism. This antithesis is partly resolved if one accepts that Von Ebrennac is a projection of his creator, nostalgic for Franco-German reconciliation, and like the fictional father-figure (Von Ebrennac senior), bitter at the sins of omission and commission by the French right - 'vos Grands Bourgeois cruels (...) vos de Wendel, vos Henri Bordeaux et votre vieux Maréchal' (SM, p. 35) - which deflected France from the Briand-Stresemann vision of a lasting peace. It is this historic failure which in 1940 returns to 'haunt' the French couple in the person of their uninvited guest. The ghost is suddenly on the doorstep just as the ghostly vessel is suddenly alongside; the billeting orderlies have arrived, the house is about to be occupied, and the silent 'maritime' conflict of *Les Enfants humiliés* to be enacted by different protagonists and in different circumstances. It will not be possible, as Schlumberger predicted, [to] 'rentrer dans ses vieux chaussons et regagner le coin du feu en disant: 'Ce n'est pas mon affaire'. Vercor's *récit*, both by its message and its physical *décor*, recognizes that truth, and intra- as well as inter-textually reinstates, against the patriarchal ideology of the collaborationist 'Etat Français', the absent Mother-figure.

Notes

1. Highly representative of this trend is R. Kedward and R. Austin (eds), *Vichy France and the Resistance: Culture and Ideology*, (London: Croom Helm, 1985), 293 pp.

2. See S.Beynon John, 'Saint-Exupéry's *Pilote de Guerre: Testimony, Art and Ideology*', in Kedward and Austin, op. cit., pp. 91-105, p. 95.

3. Sartre's comments on *Le Silence de la mer* in *Qu'est-ce que la littérature?* are perhaps the best-known expression of this differential perception (Paris: Gallimard, coll. 'Idées', 1948), pp. 92-96.

4. André Harris, quoted in Alan Morris, 'Attacks on the Gaullist myth in French Resistance Literature since 1969' in Ian Higgins (ed), *The Second World War in Literature* (Edinburgh: Scottish Academic Press, 1986), pp. 71-83, p. 75.

5. 'The Wandering Z', Foreword to Alice Yaeger Kaplan, *Reproductions of Banality. Fascism, literature and French intellectual life* (Minneapolis: University of Minnesota Press, 1986), pp. xi-xii.

6. 'Writing against the grain: some French literary responses during the Second World War', University of Cork Inaugural Lecture Series, No 3, Cork University Press, 1986, p. 13.

7. 'Resistance and collaborationist writing: discourse analysis or value judgement?', unpublished paper delivered at the Conference of University French departments, The Burn, 27-29 October 1989.

8. In *Combat pour la Liberté* (1934-1948), *Correspondance*, vol. II, (Paris: Plon, 1971), p. 321; hereafter Corr II.

9. See Joseph Jurt, 'Bernanos et la Guerre', in *Revue des Sciences Humaines* 1986-4 No 204, pp. 75-87.

10. In *Essais et Ecrits de Combat* (Paris: Gallimard, Bibliothèque de la Pléiade, 1971), pp. 773-905. pp. 778-779. Hereafter *EEC*.

11. See 'Interview par Frédéric Lefèvre' and 'Lettre à Frédéric Lefèvre' (both 1926) in *EEC*, pp. 1038-1055, p. 1049.

12. Vol. LII (janvier-juin 1940), pp. 577-598. On minor variants between the *NRF* text and final mss, see William Bush, '*Les Enfants humiliés*. Composition, thèmes et titre', in *Etudes bernanosiennes* 14, 1973, pp. 7-24, p. 8.
13. Dusseldorff, Schwann, 1951.
14. *NRF* Vol. LII, pp. 5-7, p. 5.
15. *Jalons* (Marseille: Editions du Sagittaire, 1941; Londres: Editions Penguin, 1945, 122 p.). See in particular 'Le gentil art de vivre' (refers to 'Pour saluer l'année nouvelle'), 'Pour rester grande nation pensante', 'Un peuple ne vit pas de ses rayons', and 'La réforme intellectuelle et morale' (contemporarises Renan's post 1870 work of that name); loc. cit. pp. 38-39, 45-47, 90-92 and 113-4.
16. Edited by Jean Paulhan and Dominique Aury (Paris: Les Editions de Minuit, 1947), pp. 45-47.
17. *Chronique privée de l'An quarante* (Paris: Stock, 1941), p.90.
18. Quoted by Wolfgang Babilas, 'La querelle des mauvais maîtres', in *La Littérature française sous l'Occupation*, Actes du colloque de Reims, Ier et 2 octobre 1981 (Presses Universitaires de Reims, 1989), p. 200.
19. Chardonne, op. cit. 1941, p. 106.
20. 'Octobre 1941' in Ian Higgins, *Anthology of Second World War French Poetry* (London: Methuen, coll. Twentieth Century Texts, 1982), p. 160. Cf introduction, pp. 18-19.
21. 'Le Musée Grévin' (1943), quoted in Seghers, *La Résistance et ses poètes. France 1940-45* (Paris: Pierre Seghers, 1974 [2nd edition]), p. 276.
22. 'Absent de Paris', published in *Poésie 42*, No 9 (Mai-juin 1942), quoted in Seghers. op. cit., 1974, p. 406.
23. *NRF* Vol. LIV (janvier-juin 1941), pp. 356-360, p. 356.
24. *L'Emancipation Nationale*, 8 March 1941, pp. 1/10.
25. *Forum for Modern Language Studies*, Vol. XXI, No 4, October 1985, pp. 274-290.
26. Seghers, in *Poésie 41*, No 4, quoted in Higgins, art. cit., p. 278.
27. Paris, Editions du Pavois, 1943, pp. 7-9. The description was used for pre-publication purposes in *La Révolution nationale*, *France-Europe*, and *Panorama* in August-September 1943.
28. In Vercors, *Le Silence de la Mer et autres récits* (Paris: Le Livre de Poche, 1979), pp. 23-77, p.39. Hereafter SM.
29. Published clandestinely in *Chroniques Interdites*, in SM, pp. 7-20, p. 19.
30. See Vercors's letter to Lucien Scheler in my 'French Literature and World War II: Vercors and Chardonne', *Forum for Modern Language Studies*, Vol. XXIII, No 1, January 1987, pp. 38-47, p. 46. Like Chardonne, Fernandez was known to Vercors (Jean Bruller) before the war; in 1934-35 he was a prominent anti-fascist and 'fellow-traveller,' though contrary to the latter's assertion, not a member of the PCF before joining Doriot in 1937; see Vercors, *Les Occasions perdues: l'après- Briand*, 1932-1942, 'Cent ans d'histoire de France', t II (Paris: Plon, 1982), pp. 90/132. Hereafter OP.
31. *La Bataille du Silence* (Paris: Presses de la Cité, 1967), p. 17; see also pp. 67, 105 and 113; and OP, pp. 181, 202).
32. 'Von Ebrennac Prince of Denmark? *French Studies Bulletin* No 22, Spring 1987, pp. 17-19.

'LES HYPOCRITES, NOUS TOUS': MARCEL AYME AND THE 1940s

Christopher Lloyd

'Une tête de collaborateur'?

> Ayant instauré la terreur et élevé la délation à la dignité
> d'une vertu (souvenons-nous des affiches invitant les
> Parisiens à dénoncer leurs voisins et connaissances), le
> gouvernement [...] chercha un moyen de confier au pur
> arbitraire l'apparence de la légalité. [...] On créa donc une
> loi réprimant le délit d'opinion, mais une loi *à effet
> rétroactif.* Ce monument de barbarie, de cynisme d'hypocrisie,
> ce crime crapuleux contre l'humanité fut alors unanimement
> approuvé par tous ceux qui avaient l'autorisation d'écrire
> dans les journaux. [...] les juges, ayant prêté serment au
> Maréchal, tremblaient de peur dans leurs robes et n'avaient en
> tête que leur sécurité et leur avancement. Ces misérables
> auraient pu se contenter d'être les fonctionnaires de
> l'injustice, mais non. Au lieu d'appliquer la loi avec
> modération, ils firent infliger les peines les plus dures et
> rivalisèrent de lâcheté, de cruauté, de bassesse.

These are the words of Marcel Aymé, writing in 1950 about the experience of
Frenchmen in the Second World War. But the government to which he refers as
raising a monument to cruelty and ignominy is not, as one might suppose,
that of Marshal Pétain and the Vichy régime, but that of General de Gaulle
in the months following the liberation of France in 1944.(1)

For Marcel Aymé, France's fall from grace seems to have occurred not
so much in June 1940 as in August 1944. This is certainly the thesis one
could derive from his novel *Uranus* (1948), an account of life in a
provincial town in the final weeks of the War in spring 1945. Much of the
town is in ruins, thanks to the Allies' bombs which failed to hit any
military targets and killed 300 civilians. The atrocities described are
committed not by Germans but members of the French Communist Party against
minor collaborators. While ordinary citizens who try to resist the brutal
and petty-minded power of the communists are arrested, a collaborator who
has made millions on the black market goes unscathed. Satirising human
foibles and showing how ideologies are constantly subject to the arbitrary
influence of temperament and circumstances: these are constant features of
Aymé's writing, but never before had he presented them with such truculent
force as in the books he wrote immediately after the Liberation, or
suggested such deep offence at the spirit of the age.

Aymé was an extremely private writer, both in the sense that he
refused to engage in public intellectual posturing and that his fiction is
curiously impenetrable to (auto)biographical probing. 'Il n'y a pas de
rapport entre ma vie privée et ce que j'écris', he remarked.(2) One could
however hazard a guess that at least some of the bitter and angry
perception of injustice and savagery which is such a striking feature of
the immediate post-War novels *Le Chemin des écoliers* (1946) and *Uranus* (and
which recurs in less vitriolic form in the essay *Le Confort intellectuel* of
1949 or a play like *La Tête des autres* in 1952) is a direct cause of the
mauling which Aymé received, or thought he received, in the period
immediately following the Liberation. In the issue of *Crapouillot* which

contains his denunciation of de Gaulle, Aymé is presented as a 'véhément défenseur des maréchalistes et des collaborationnistes sincères'. The word 'sincères' should be noted: Aymé was never an apologist for fascism or the Vichy régime, but would rather have liked to see himself as the champion of freedom of expression and the individual (however misguided the expression and eccentric the individual) in their constant struggle against the totalitarian forces of the state, the Church, political parties or other oppressive groups and institutions.

Thus he was actively involved in the unsuccessful campaign to save Robert Brasillach from the death sentence passed on him in January 1945. Three years later he protested again when Brasillach's brother-in-law Maurice Bardèche was sentenced to a year's imprisonment for questioning the Allies' right to condemn their defeated opponents as war criminals in his book *Nuremberg ou la terre promise*. The moral was a simple one, Aymé suggested: 'Mettons-nous bien dans la tête que la liberté de l'écrivain finit là où commencent à s'affirmer certaines susceptibilités politiques. Là où elle vient à heurter certains thèmes de propaganda qui ne font, d'ailleurs, plus illusion à personne.'(3) Political power groups, it would seem, have no hesitation in squashing the independent writer (Bardèche was first acquitted and convicted only on appeal), even if the unwelcome truth he affirms is a generally recognised one.

The issues, of course, are rather more complicated than Aymé makes out in these polemical journalistic pieces. In the essay *Le Confort intellectuel* he remarks again that 'Il est devenu moins dangereux d'assommer une rentière que d'exprimer une opinion' (ch. 6). The book takes the form of a dialogue about the nature of poetic language, held mainly between two rather shifty characters, neither of whose views can be taken at face value. The first-person narrator is a comically fearful figure who has gone into hiding in December 1944 because he is suspected of committing murder. The general atmosphere is one of denunciation and mutual suspicion: he is finally evicted from his hotel because the other clients 'trouvaient que j'avais une tête de collaborateur' (ch. 12). His interlocutor, M. Lepage, appears at first sight to be a reactionary bourgeois philistine who engages in an amusingly wrong-headed denunciation of the supposed obscurities of Baudelaire's sonnet 'La Beauté'. But as he observes, 'on ne se méfiera jamais assez de la poésie' (ch. 2): artistic revolutions allow the possibility of social revolutions; poetry subverts the lucidity of language and hence the possibility of rational thought; words and reality come to bear little relationship to one another; 'le vrai péril [...] est dans la confusion du langage' (ch. 4).

The argument is pointedly illustrated by reference to a certain type of resistance poetry published in 1943 which is of such obscurity that it reveals only 'une grande maîtrise dans l'art de l'insignifiance mystérieuse' (ch. 7), and stands more generally for 'Le gâtisme révolutionnaire de nos élites dorées' (ch. 10). By deriding spurious resistance and creating a central character who is cast as a collaborator largely on the basis of physiognomical prejudice, Aymé is partly defending and also concealing his own position, which in some ways was a weak one. Supporting Brasillach might suggest sympathy for the underdog and loyalty to a friend (Aymé's friendships crossed political boundaries and included both the anti-Semite Céline and the communist film-maker Louis Daquin); on the other hand, Brasillach as an avowed fascist and editor of the collaborationist weekly *Je suis partout* (1941-43) was hardly an innocent victim of circumstances. Suppressing writers for reasons of political expediency may not be justifiable, but this was hardly an invention of General de Gaulle. Moreover, the whole issue of the responsibility of the writer himself as a public figure is one which Aymé seems to overlook, either ingenuously or disingenuously.

Apparently at Brasillach's urging, Aymé himself contributed articles to *Je suis partout*, each issue of which sold some 300,000 copies by the end of the Occupation.(4)   The novel *Travelingue* (1941) was serialised between 20 September 1941 and 17 January 1942 in this paper,while *La Vouivre* (1943) was serialised in the pro-Vichy weekly *La Gerbe* from 22 July to 9 December 1943, along with other stories by Aymé. Michel Lecureur, the author of two recent books on Aymé, has made a thorough study of the writer's journalistic output during the War years and demonstrated convincingly that it is absurd to consider him in any way to have been an active collaborator. Admittedly Aymé commented in *Je suis partout* on 28 November 1943 'Je me fous du socialisme et de ses cabotineries',(5) and in *Travelingue* mockingly portrayed the Popular Front government of 1936 as being run by a barber in his spare time. Such satirical jibes hardly constitute enthusiastic support for the Nazi jackboot, however.

On the other hand, associating one's name with journals that were unequivocally pro-German surely implies either wilful ignorance or tacit approval for their cause. Is a position of studied neutrality acceptable or even possible in a situation of extreme social and political crisis? Critics of Aymé have frequently debated his supposed position on the political arc, without arriving at very fruitful conclusions. Lecureur reminds us that Aymé was brought up in an anti-clerical, republican household in the Jura and was unlikely to have sympathised with the 'vieille France' rhetoric of Vichy, still less with the racist mysticism and boy-scout pageantry of fascism. He also abhorred cruelty and the victimisation of the weak, whether they were Jews, Arabs, children, women or animals. As Lecureur remarks, a commentator like Pascal Ory writing as late as 1977 offers a regrettable distortion of Aymé's fiction when he accuses him of producing an anti-Semitic stereotype in the character Lina Lebon in *Le Chemin des écoliers*.(6)

Jean-Louis Bory produces an equally contorted argument, however, when he asserts that not only Aymé but also Céline, by virtue of their non-conformism, are 'des tempéraments de gauche': 'Le conformisme, par essence, est de droite. Un conformiste "de gauche", du moment qu'il est conformiste, est de droite.'(7)   This sounds rather like Ionesco's proof that a dog is a cat in *Rhinocéros*. Aymé's dislike of socialism and communism has already been noted; in fact he distanced himself from the Left as early as 1935 by signing a right-wing manifesto in support of the Italian invasion of Abyssinia. In 1938 he remarked teasingly 'On ne sait sans doute jamais sûrement si l'on est à droite ou si l'on est à gauche'.(8)   By temperament, Aymé was probably a conservative individualist with a liking for order. He insists for example rather oddly on the illegality of the régime that followed the Liberation, compared with the legitimate nature of the Pétain government. Though this view is strictly speaking correct,(9) in a wider context it seems rather trivial: Hitler's rise to power in 1933 was after all legitimised by substantial electoral support.

In any case, the key question is not that of Aymé's political affiliations, or lack of them, or even of his personal motivation and grievances for implicitly or accidentally assisting the wrong side during the Occupation. (In 1946, he was condemned to 'un blâme sans affichage pour

avoir favorisé les desseins de l'ennemi' by the Préfecture de la Seine. His
offence was to have sold a script to Continental Films, a German-backed
company. His sense of injustice at this rebuke was strong enough for him to
refuse the Légion d'honneur when it was offered as a sort of compensation
three years later in 1949. The film in question was an innocent farce
starring Fernandel, *Le Club des soupirants*).

Le Chemin des écoliers

Questions of farce, with their undertones of tragedy and grotesquery, seem
indeed to be a lot more central. 'Vous êtes un farceur, dans le fond',
Bérenger is told, and later finds he is unable to become a rhinoceros and
join the herd. Like Ionesco, Aymé is a great comic writer. His
confrontation with the horrors of war and its aftermath granted him moments
of Voltairean savagery in the novels *Le Chemin des écoliers* and *Uranus*.
Both texts deal with the different ways in which various individuals come
to terms with the extreme situations of occupation and liberation. At first
sight, both novels appear very much as conventional third-person
narratives, transparent referential texts written in order to bear witness
to the social history of France in the mid-twentieth century. More careful
study reveals a considerable amount of speculation about the moral and
aesthetic function of the novel. If Aymé avoids the overtly self-reflexive
markers of pretentious, highbrow fiction (he is a popular and a populist
writer), he also eschews the fantastical elements which make some of the
stories about the Occupation in *Le Passe-Muraille* (1943) so delightfully
appealing but which also perhaps tend to demote them to the level of safer
entertainments.

How does the individual retain his identity, or his life, in the face
of intolerable social pressure? The problem can be perceived farcically. In
his pre-war novels, Aymé treated the issue of commitment to a cause and the
double standards and hypocrisies this can produce in a fairly light-hearted
manner. M. Berthaud in *Le Boeuf clandestin* (1939) is an ostentatious
vegetarian, but proves to be a secret meat eater; his life is based on a
facade of lies. His son Maurice has changed his allegiances with such
dizzying rapidity that he is little more than a comical cipher:

> On l'avait connu Jeunesse patriote, blumiste,
> surréaliste, freudien, moscoutaire, nudiste, trotskiste,
> nietzschéen, comtiste, monarchiste, antisémite,
> philosémite, tout pour le peuple, à bas le peuple, tout me
> fait suer, vienne la guerre, je crois en Dieu,
> successivement ou en même temps avec des retours et des
> revenez-y. (ch. 15)

Aymé's positive characters invariably recoil from the abject or ridiculous
surrender of personal integrity which submission to an external
organisation like the Church or Communist Party involves. These positive
figures are rarely heroic or worldly, but like Chauvieux in *Travelingue* are
'plus attentifs aux individus qu'aux catégories' (ch. 3). In the novels
about the War, they become helpless but decent witnesses of terrible events
and acute dilemmas. Chauvieux tries to assuage the militaristic, paranoic
fantasies of his former comrade-in-arms Malinier (while simultaneously
conducting an affair with the latter's young wife) by persuading him to
masquerade as a communist and thus behave in a slightly more normal
fashion.

In *Le Chemin des écoliers*, set in the spring of 1942 six years after the events of *Travelingue*, Malinier reappears in a minor role. 'Les malheurs de la France lui étaient toujours présents' (ch. 6). He oscillates between hatred of Germany and admiration for Nazi 'discipline'. Finally he resolves his patriotic dilemma by joining the Légion des Volontaires Français and leaving to fight on the Russian front. Unlike most of the other characters, Malinier's concern for the fate of his country does genuinely override selfish personal interests; in this sense he is honest and sympathetic and his example tempts the adventurous schoolboy Paul Tiercelin to consider whether joining the Resistance or the L.V.F. might be preferable to continuing his studies (the juxtaposition of these alternatives was doubtless more provocative in 1946 than it is now, when the theme of the essential arbitrariness of such choices has become a familiar one). But Malinier's choice of action is nonetheless shown to be misguided, and his conceptions of fascist ideology are rather comically primitive: his hate figures include Jews, communists, cubist painters, and Racine.

Later in the novel he is persuaded to impersonate a German officer in order to intimidate Antoine Michaud's family and deter them from enquiring too closely into their son's dubious activities (they do in fact assume erroneously that he must have joined the Resistance). The narrator remarks that with his long green raincoat Malinier looks more like a gas man than a Nazi, although his shiny boots have an air of authority. He laughs involuntarily at his attempt to speak in broken French, an effect which the family find to be particularly sinister. But Malinier pays a high price for his shift of identity: in one of a series of twenty footnotes which are inserted throughout the novel, the narrator informs us that at the end of the War he is captured by the Americans, handed over to the French authorities, imprisoned, tortured repeatedly along with the other prisoners, both male and female, tried, and finally sentenced to death in December 1945, his defence of true patriotism having particularly offended the court (ch. 9).

These footnotes merit attention, for a variety of reasons. Most obviously, they clearly move us on to another plane from Aymé's wryly comic and vastly entertaining account of life under the Occupation and the strange bedfellows it brought together. Aymé had occasionally added footnotes to earlier novels and stories, as a jokey way of providing supplementary information, but the systematic use of the device is peculiar to *Le Chemin des écoliers*. In 1948 he said that 'Les faits qu'elles rapportent sont tous exacts; c'est pourquoi je les ai placés en notes.'(10)

Strictly speaking, this cannot be literally true. Nearly all the notes are anticipatory, looking forward in time to record the fate of a given character after the events recounted in the novel are over. Sometimes, this serves mainly to provide a tidy conclusion to the narrator's fiction. Thus in the last chapter the narrator tells us what eventually becomes of the relationship between the flirtatious secretary Solange and the dim-witted office boy, and how the central characters Michaud and Lolivier turn to blackmarketeering and become extremely rich but not especially happy. The fact that the office boy takes sick for frustrated love and dies in a sanatorium seems to reflect a rather macabre authorial caprice. Here Aymé is drawing attention to the essential arbitrariness of his fictional inventions, as he does in chapter ten when he reminds us we are reading a novel with the phrase 'Bientôt, la dispute dépassa en violence celle qu'ils avaient eue à la fin du chapitre II'.

Such self-reflexive gestures tend to reinforce rather than to subvert our faith in the author as storyteller, however, for they effectively add another dimension to the narration. Moreover, Aymé is not simply drawing gratuitous attention to the controlling function of the narrator. The office boy's grimly arbitrary fate forms part of a wider thematic preoccupation both with the fortunes of war and with the nature of writing: most of the footnotes in *Le Chemin des écoliers* connect story to history. Many of the notes are laconic, matter-of-fact accounts of atrocities inflicted on minor characters in the novel. In fact, these victims are often not functional characters in the plot itself: they are extras who appear for the express purpose of allowing Aymé to prolong his fiction into an extra-textual footnote which records the barbarities of his age, sometimes attributing them to 'witnesses' in order to assert their authenticity. For instance, the first footnote follows up four German soldiers who pass Michaud in the street. One is killed on the Russian front. A second loses his legs, returns home, and is poisoned by his wife. The third is a P.O.W. in Belgium. The death of the fourth occurs during the insurrection in Paris in August 1944 and is reported to the narrator by a cobbler who witnesses it: separated from his unit and the worse for drink, he is attacked by a ravenous mob which tears his body apart, so that within a few moments all that remains of him is a few bloody traces on the road. Aymé was insistent that this was a true story. Later in the novel itself, Lolivier's son Tony, a brutish psychopath, graduates from torturing animals to murder and cannibalism.

A similar footnote in chapter four focuses on an attractive blonde whom Michaud glimpses passing in a lift. In December 1943, an agent of the French Gestapo attempts to pick her up in a shop but she rejects his advances. He has her arrested, steals her jewels, and for a month she is raped by the agent and his subordinates who then murder her and dispose of her body in the Seine, first cutting it into separate pieces 'pour la commodité du transport'. Such deadpan, anecdotal accounts of savagery are quite out of tone with anything Aymé had written before. (The two novels which precede *Le Chemin des écoliers* and which he published during the Occupation, *La Belle Image* (1941) and *La Vouivre* (1943), resolutely turn away from the horrors of contemporary history towards charming escapist fantasy.) These *faits divers* serve a moral purpose, which their very gratuitousness illustrates: to warn the reader that the evils of war strike entirely at random, and to supply a more public context for the private dramas which obsess the fictional characters. It will be noted that the atrocities recounted are committed by Frenchmen as often as by Germans. When Michaud is told about the systematic extermination of Jews in Poland by the émigrée Lina Lebon, he prefers to disbelieve her. The footnotes have a concrete immediacy and apparent veracity which give them a force and credibility which exceed the usual impact of fiction and the more abstract retailing of the statistics of death in history books. The moral point is precisely that one does not really know how to react to them, other than with fascinated revulsion.

Aymé also somewhat jokingly raises the issue of the specific moral responsibility of the writer on several occasions both in *Le Chemin des écoliers* and in *Uranus*. In *Uranus* the collaborator Maxime Loin ironically finds himself whiling away the time in his hide-out by reading a caricatural Resistance novel, in which 'la mâle beauté des résistants' is set against 'l'immonde personnage' of a black-market dealer. Loin's revenge is to think that 'le trafiquant n'avait rien perdu à la victoire gaulliste' (ch. 13). The reader is clearly invited to interpret Aymé's own text as a less simplistic and one-sided version of affairs. Certainly in *Uranus*, all parties are presented with a degree of sympathy and have their motivation examined in a rather more sophisticated manner. That said, it is also fairly obvious that Aymé is presenting an early 'revisionist' account of the Liberation, which is seen to have a destructive and disruptive influence on the lives of respectable and neutral citizens like the engineer Archambaud, the teacher Watrin, or the café owner Léopold. Those who thrive or achieve influence are disreputable characters like the black marketeer Monglat or bullying members of the Communist Party. The 'resisters' who appear are usually thugs, like Monglat's son or the youths from the F.F.I. who hold Archambaud up at gunpoint: 'Ceux-là n'étaient pas des hypocrites. Ils laissaient paraître leurs instincts', as he observes (ch. 3). Alternatively, they are represented by a sadistic coward like the communist Rochard, who achieved notoriety by gouging out the eyes of a *milicien* before his execution by the liberators, or 'libératueurs', as they were called by the editorial team of *Je suis partout*.

As Margaret Atack observes, *Uranus* is as partisan as any pro-Resistance novel, however appealing its ambiguities.(11) We can do no more than attempt to construct or reconstruct our own version of the truth from such fictions. The character Archambaud considers novels directly responsible for the defeat of 1940: experiencing life vicariously through literature turns us into impotent spectators of events (ch. 13). In a similar way, Michaud in *Le Chemin des écoliers* remarks that 'Ecrire, c'est se ratatiner, c'est user la vie et l'avenir' (ch. 8). In a self-directed jibe, Aymé presents the case of a retired cavalry colonel M. de Monboquin who has published a book on archeology 'sous la botte gemanique'. Taking a high moral tone, Michaud agrees with the Colonel's wife that he should refuse an invitation to the Institut allemand: however innocent the subject, such collaboration involves 'un certain coefficient de propagande, qui jouera pour la cause hitlérienne' (ch. 4). Later Michaud decides that his arguments are idiotic, but the Colonel complies, and deprived of an outlet for his interests actually dies.

Aymé's examples are telling, but what do they tell us? That there are no straightforward answers: writing or not writing can be equally detrimental. 'Au lieu de s'expliquer à tout prix, on ferait mieux de rester sur un certain sentiment des choses' is Michaud's conclusion (ch. 4). The title *Le Chemin des écoliers* with its pedagogic implications offers a sort of message. The schoolboys' path is a roundabout one, undertaken for the journey rather than to arrive at a specific goal. Unlike the adults in the novel, the schoolboys are less constrained to indulge in hypocritical moralising: the sixteen-year-old Antoine makes his family's fortune by black-market dealing: 'le patriotisme' était à ses yeux qu'un résidu sentimental de l'histoire' (ch. 7). In fact his behaviour is considerably more ethical than this statement might suggest. He eventually abandons his whorish mistress Yvette and returns to his parents, to a revised and revived family unit which has survived the horrors of war. This unit is sharply contrasted with Lolivier's hellish household: his only source of affection is a white mouse he rescued from his son Tony, who was preparing to burn its eyes out. Lolivier's bitter personal experiences allow him to deflate some of Michaud's more sentimental notions about patriotism and human solidarity. Michaud may not be able to stand the sight of German officers, but he didn't like French officers any better, Lolivier reminds him (ch. 5). Intense personal suffering of the kind he himself experiences isolates him from the rest of humanity and the public events that preoccupy most people: 'Les grandes dates fatales de ces dernières années ne seront pas pour moi celles des autres' (ch. 12).

Uranus

Uranus is a giant gas planet completely covered in cloud and situated in the outer solar system. It was first observed in 1781 by William Herschel. In Marcel Aymé's novel, the maths teacher Watrin happened to be reading a book about Uranus on the night when the Allies bombed Blémont. His wife and her lover were killed during the bombing. He was left suspended in his bed on the second floor of the ruins of his house. Each night since he has had an oppressive vision of the dead planet and each day has enjoyed a reawakening to the Earth, which in comparison seems a rather appealing environment, even when overrun by Nazis and communists. Margaret Atack descries an 'essentialist, absurdist pessimism' in works like *Uranus* and suggests that Watrin's 'zoological vision of the planet excludes a moral attitude to social, political and moral conflicts which are inscribed within the natural order of things'.(12) It would be fairer to say that Watrin has redefined his morality in a wider context, as a remedy to despair and as a means of restoring a more optimistic view of the world. He is 'un homme sans parti' (ch. 11) and a tolerant materialist: 'acceptant avec optimisme les évidences les plus désobligeantes pour l'éspèce humaine, il aimait la vie et les hommes pour ce qu'ils étaient sans éprouver le besoin de les transfigurer et il ne méprisait rien ni personne' (ch. 16). His pantheistic serenity does at times suggest someone not fully in tune with the realities of life (his smile is 'un peu comme celui qu'on voit si souvent aux visages des morts' (ch. 6)). On the other hand, his behaviour compares favourably with that of the other characters. Ideologues like the fascist Maxime Loin and the communist teacher Jourdain are equated and implicitly condemned as men 'chez lesquels une idée ou une doctrine tient plus de place que la vie' (ch. 18). Politically neutral characters, who live comfortably under the Pétain régime, now find themselves to be guilty of collaboration and hypocrisy to be a universal necessity. As Watrin observes to one: 'Vous avez peur avec trente-neuf millions de Français' (ch. 16). Solidarity too often takes a purely negative form. In one key scene, a crowd which has assembled to welcome returning prisoners of war witnesses the beating of a renegade communist by his party comrades. Typically, only Watrin has the courage to intervene to assist the victim. The rest pretend nothing has happened; Archambaud, to his self-disgust, finds he has become a molecule in the organism of the crowd, unable to escape its cowardly complicity.

As such examples suggest, *Uranus* is a sombre and rather stirring novel. Aymé's barbs had never been sharper or his humour blacker. When the town brothel is destroyed in the bombing, all that remains of the *notaire* is his testicles on the turntable of the record-player; his wife identifies them the next day (ch. 11). The café owner Léopold, an alcoholic giant, is inspired by the school lessons now held in his café to try his hand at writing verse: he tries to create a role for himself in Racine's *Andromaque* as rescuer of the heroine, and over a period of weeks finally produces six alexandrines before he is shot by the gendarmes who come to arrest him for insulting the Communist Party. The parallel with *Andromaque* and its world of fallen heroes, betrayed by war and passion, is not as comically inappropriate as it may at first appear.

Aymé writes as a social chronicler and deliverer of home truths, as a *moraliste* rather than as a moraliser. In the wider context of all his writing, the label 'essentialist, absurdist pessimist' does not fit very comfortably on to his customary fictional garb. Jean Cathelin suggests that his fiction is written to overcome the temptation of the absurd: Aymé 'renoue sans gêne le lien avec le cosmos après avoir perçu le divorce avec le social: c'est l'étranger réintégré'.(13) His most endearing works are about peasants and children, and include a strong dose of the fantastic (*La Jument verte, La Vouivre, Les Contes du chat perché*). He might be compared to Jean Giono, whose pacifistic non-conformism also made him unpopular after 1944, although his lyricism is more contained and less poetic than Giono's. Aymé had no truck with politicians or political theorising, yet his best novels from *La Jument verte* (1933) to *Uranus* are very much about the politics of the everyday, the rise and fall of the Third Republic, if ones takes politics to mean power relationships, the conflict between individual and group, male and female, adults and children, as well as social classes.

In a famous paradox uttered in the aftermath of the Liberation, Sartre remarked 'Jamais nous n'avons été plus libres que sous l'occupation allemande'.(14) The daily confrontation with oppression gave every thought or action heightened meaning as an expression of submission or independence. Aymé's writing suggests that for most people, on the contrary, Occupation epitomised bad faith (business as usual, only obeying orders, wait and see), and furthermore that such high-flown rhetoric is itself a good example of the bad faith of sham heroics: we ought at least to be honest about our hypocrisies. M. de Monboquin observes dolefully of the Germans, 'Mais tout ce que nous faisons: manger, dormir, circuler, ce n'est autant qu'ils le veulent bien' (*Le Chemin des écoliers*, ch. 4). In a later article written in 1945, Sartre offered a modified view which is considerably closer to Aymé's: 'dans cette situation ambiguë nous ne pouvions vraiment ni *agir*, ni même *penser*'.(15) Aymé's heroes, or rather his protagonists, are not locked in a determinist essentialism in the fashion of a naturalist novel by Zola. In fact he seems much closer to Sartre in his recognition of how both behaviour and the interpretation of events are fluid and provisional, and of how historical or psychological truth is constantly redefined. Thus the ruin of Blémont is officially due to German bombs; only 'les mauvais patriotes' attribute it to the Allies; but later the communists find it convenient to blame the Americans openly for this catastrophe (*Uranus*, ch. 5). Even displaying flags at a window becomes problematic: the French flag alone now no longer signals patriotism but collaboration and requires the addition of an allied flag to make it respectable (ch. 19). In the story 'Traversée de Paris', a superbly atmospheric evocation of double-dealing in occupied Paris, the central character is himself revealed to have a double identity, part gangster, part artist; characters can be indeterminate. 'Ce sont les mous qui font les durs', as he says.(16)

Circumstances often offer Aymé's characters the unexpected chance of redefining the image which they and others have of them. The novel *La Belle Image* (1941) exemplifies this, when the hero undergoes a physical metamorphosis. But he prefers to return to a banal, unheroic norm, coming full circle, as the title of an earlier novel, *Aller retour* (1927), suggests. Marcel Aymé remarked in 1957 that 'L'écrivain devrait être non plus le témoin, mais la conscience de son temps' and consequently refuse ephemeral and quixotic commitments.(17) His own conscience may not have been entirely easy after 1944. In an odd essay called 'Le Trou de la serrure', written in 1946, he observed that the discovery of the extermination camps meant that novelists ought to do more than peep at humanity through a keyhole. But then again, the limited vision offered by the keyhole might be infinitely preferable. Having tellingly portrayed the bad conscience of his defeated nation in *Le Chemin des écoliers* and *Uranus*, Aymé virtually abandoned the novel for the remainder of his writing career. These two books thus remain as partial but powerful memorials to an epoch which many of us must be glad we did not live through ourselves and which we can enjoy, rather uncomfortably perhaps, as literature.

Notes

1.   Aymé, 'L'Epuration ou le délit d'opinion', *Crapouillot*, 11, (1950) pp. 77-79, (p. 77).
2.   Quoted by Pierre Hahn, 'Marcel Aymé: j'écris pour me faire plaisir', *Paris-Théâtre*, p. 185 (1962).
3.   Quoted in Georges Robert and André Lioret, *Marcel Aymé insolite* (Editions de la Revue indépendante, 1958), p. 107.
4.   'Le nom de *Je suis partout* est resté le symbole de la trahison intellectuelle dans la France occupée par les Allemands entre 1940 et 1944.' Pierre-Marie Dioudonnat, *Je suis partout* (La Table ronde, 1973).
5.   Quoted by M. Lecureur, 'Les Articles de Marcel Aymé pendant l'occupation', *Littératures*, 8 (1983), 97-105 (p. 101).
6.   M. Lecureur, 'Un prétendu coupable: Marcel Aymé', in *La Littérature française sous l'occupation* (Presses universitaires de Reims, 1989), pp. 5-13.
7.   Jean-Louis Bory, 'Le Pays derrière l'arbre', *Magazine littéraire*, 124 (1977), p. 30.
8.   *Silhouette du scandale* (Grasset, 1973), p. 138 (first published in 1938).
9.   See e.g. Hilary Footit and John Simmonds, *France, 1943-1945* (Leicester University Press, 1988).
10. Quoted in M. Lecureur, *La Comédie humaine de Marcel Aymé* (Lyon, La Manufacture, 1985), p. 144.
11. M. Atack, *Literature and the French Resistance* (Manchester University Press, 1989), p. 235.
12. Atack, p. 235, p. 217.
13. Jean Cathelin, *Marcel Aymé ou le paysan de Paris* (Nouvelles Editions Debresse, 1958), p. 151.
14. 'La République du silence', *Situations III* (Gallimard, 1949), p. 11.
15. 'Paris sous l'Occupation', *Situations III*, p. 42.
16. *Le Vin de Paris* (Gallimard, 1947), p. 70.
17. Quoted in Lecureur (1985), p. 305.

GERMAN OFFICERS AND JEWISH CHILDREN IN THE HAUTE-LOIRE*

Richard Maber

In the aftermath of the 1989 San Francisco earthquake, *Newsweek* magazine published an article about the acts of altruistic heroism that had been reported. It included the following comment:

> But even the most prolonged nightmares spawn astonishing acts of benevolence. A Dutch civilian named Miep Gies risked her life daily for more than two years to feed and shelter the Frank family during the Nazi Holocaust. The 3,000 peasants of Le Chambon, a Huguenot village in south-central France, took similar risks to help Jewish refugees flee the occupation.(1)

To this one can add a 1988 quotation from the Toronto journal *Lifestyles*:

> It has been said that there were three 'sparks' of goodness among the evil of the Holocaust: that of an individual, of a community, and of a country. The individual was Raoul Wallenberg, the country was Denmark, and the community was Le Chambon, France.(2)

Now Anne Frank and Raoul Wallenberg are thoroughly familiar as individuals and as symbols, but what is this about Le Chambon? As the *Lifestyles* article goes on to say, 'While many know the stories of Wallenberg and the Danes, few are familiar with Le Chambon. In many ways it is the most remarkable story of all...'

I am not primarily concerned to relate in detail the story of Le Chambon-sur-Lignon during the Occupation, extraordinary though it is, and tempting as it would be to concentrate simply on that. My main subject is what has happened to this story over the past ten years: how the local history of a small community has acquired the symbolic value of that *Newsweek* reference; the different interpretations placed on, and messages drawn from, the events of Le Chambon; and in addition, the way in which they have been drawn into the great revisionism debate. This process of the 'creation' of history, of shaping and interpreting a highly complex pattern, is still very far from complete. In studying one case in detail we can gain insight into the problems attendant on all discussions of the Occupation period, whether local history or broad general synthesis.

But first, one must say something about the rather unusual background of Le Chambon-sur-Lignon itself.(3) The village is situated in wild and beautiful country at the very northern end of the Cévennes, 3,000 feet up on the high plateau to the north of the Mont Mézenc (the 'plateau Vivarais-Lignon'). As a boy in Le Chambon in the 1950s, I felt that the horizons of this world were quite clearly delimited: it extended from Le Puy in the west to Valence in the east, and from the Mont Mézenc and the Gerbier de Jonc in the south to Saint-Etienne in the north. The distant great city was Lyon.

Since the sixteenth century the plateau has been an enclave with a substantial Huguenot population in an otherwise Catholic region: the ancestral legends, folk-songs, experience of persecution and tradition of resistance of the region are immensely important in understanding the events of the Occupation.(4) Some idea of this historical continuity can perhaps be given by statistics: in 1626, according to the Bishop of Le Puy, Le Chambon contained 2,000 Protestants and 150 Catholics; while in 1936, the census recorded 2,600 Protestants and 121 Catholics. In Le Chambon's sister village of Le Mazet it used to be an article of faith that it was the only commune in France to be 100% Protestant, and that it

had been 100% Protestant since the sixteenth century. Although no longer
entirely accurate, such a tradition conveys a good idea of the strong
sense of local identity and distinctiveness.

Le Chambon had been used to receiving considerable numbers of summer
visitors since the nineteenth century, including, notably, organized
charitable summer holidays: for poor children from Saint-Etienne, young
workers from other industrial towns, church children's organizations,
Salvation Army mission camps, and so on. It had developed an appropriate
infrastructure: hostels were founded, and the peasants took in visitors on
their farms. The village became known as a place that welcomed those in
trouble: after the Spanish Civil War many Republican refugees arrived,
followed in 1940 by refugees from the German invasion, Alsatians,
Parisians, and French and foreign Jews. All of this provides part of the
essential background for subsequent events.

The other determining element was more individual. In 1938 the village
pastor, André Trocmé, had founded a school run on extremely advanced and
idealistic lines, to provide free education for Plateau children supported
by fee-paying children of the better-off (the Collège Cévenol, now a
celebrated independent Protestant educational institution). Its first
headmaster was another pastor, Edouard Theis. These two men were both
Christian pacifists with very strong personalities and great personal
bravery. When the rounding-up of foreign Jews in France began in the
winter of 1940-41, Pastor Trocmé set about mobilizing the village's
resources to help the persecuted. It began with children extracted from
French concentration camps by American Quakers; and then became a flood of
Jewish refugees of all kinds and all ages as the scale of persecution
increased (from foreign Jews to French Jews in the Occupied Zone; then the
arrest of foreign Jews in Vichy France under Laval from Summer 1942; and
finally general anti-Semitic measures after the German occupation of the
South of France in Autumn 1942). Escape routes were set up to get adults
and families to Switzerland; and, most remarkably of all, large numbers of
Jews, particularly children, were concealed in the homes and farms of the
Chambon region until the Liberation.(5)

The cards were not all stacked against the Chambonnais. They benefited
from well-placed French sympathisers, such as the gendarmes in the small
town of Tence, the nearest police-station. When in 1942 these gendarmes
were ordered to arrest all foreign Jews in Le Chambon, they contacted
Pastor Trocmé the day before to ask for his help; needless to say, when
they came they found no-one. (The 'brigadier de la gendarmerie' at Tence
later joined the Resistance himself.)

The Chambonnais also had well-organized hiding-places and escape
routes. After the failure of the Tence gendarmes, a convoy of cars and
buses came up from Le Puy with some 60 gendarmes, who saturated the
village for three weeks and carried out searches: but in all that time
they found just one person, an Austrian gentleman, who turned out to be
only half-Jewish and was subsequently released. After this second, massive
failure by the gendarmerie the Vichy authorities left the village in
relative peace for a while. Subsequent visits from the gendarmerie had
little better success. On one raid they arrested a Jewess called Mme
Bormann, who had not hidden because she said she was a second cousin of
Martin Bormann and so no-one would dare to trouble her. (So far as I know,
this remarkable claim has never been pursued.) She was arrested all the
same, but the resourceful lady feigned a fit and was released on medical
grounds. The real problems did not begin until 1943, when the German
forces in Le Puy were well established.

Another great asset of the Chambonnais was the clandestine presence of

a master-forger, a young Jewish refugee called Oscar Rosowsky (alias Jean-Claude Plunne). His first feat had been to forge documents to get his mother released from a concentration camp; and on the Plateau between 1942 and 1944 he successfully forged papers for some 5,000 people.(6)
But there were some disasters. By 1943 the general level of danger had increased immensely. The worst incident occurred on 29 June 1943, when the Gestapo raided a student hostel - acting either on information received through Vichy after the hostel's registration, or else, it is thought, from an infiltrated informer - and arrested about twenty young men. These were mainly Jews, but also Spanish Republicans and French Protestants. Many were sent to German concentration camps, including the man who ran the hostel, Daniel Trocmé (a cousin of the Pastor), who died in the extermination camp at Maidenik. The appalling potential risks involved in sheltering the refugees could hardly have been more clearly demonstrated.
The provision of a refuge for the Jews around Le Chambon became a community effort of astonishing dimensions: it has been suggested that during the course of the war up to 5,000 Jews in all were taken in by a local population itself of about 5,000 people, although estimates of the number of refugees vary greatly.(7) It was also an effort of a very unusual kind. Although there was some initial central co-ordination in the village, this was soon overwhelmed by events, and the local people acted as individuals in sheltering the fugitives. Obviously, they acted in conditions of the utmost secrecy, out of sheer self-preservation. Equally important, though, is the type of people they were; one can hardly overestimate the effect of the individualistic, self-contained, privacy-respecting social attitudes of the Huguenot farmers and villagers of the Plateau. To offer a refuge to the oppressed was so much a natural and unquestioned part of their tradition that many hundreds of individuals, acting quite independently, made the identical choice. None, of course, would have dreamt of accepting any payment. To quote from a chronicler of the episode, Pierre Sauvage (about whom more later in this paper):
Nowhere do we have a parallel to such a story. No one was turned away. No one was betrayed. No conversion was imposed. There was a need, and the 5,000 people of the area became - no one had any idea of it at the time - Occupied Europe's most determined and most persistent haven of refuge for the Jews ... And all this under Vichy's nose, within striking distance of the SS, with convalescing German soldiers walking the streets of Le Chambon during the final year ... The people of the area are still amazed at how widespread the perilous hospitality was, are still surprised to learn that such-and-such a neighbour had also sheltered Jews.(8)
Le Chambon is clearly a very powerful latent symbol. But of what exactly? We must now consider the subsequent recording and transmission of these events.
In fact, the story remained very little known for thirty-five years after the Liberation, and it is only in the last ten years that it has attained any wide currency. There have been two major presentations of the story, a book and a film, both originating outside France; and also one minor contribution which, although slight in itself, is the source of much of the current controversy.(9)
The first widely-diffused account of what happened in Le Chambon was published in 1979 by an American, Philip Hallie (Griffin Professor of philosophy and humanities at Wesleyan University in Connecticut), under the title *Lest Innocent Blood be Shed* (in the French translation: *Le Sang*

des innocents).(10) The subtitle is: 'The story of the village of Le Chambon, and how goodness happened there', which one might feel immediately rings alarm bells. However, Hallie had interviewed a large number of survivors of all kinds, and the book has some value, despite being written in a rather sentimental and dramatic manner, full of imaginatively recreated conversations and novelistic narrative devices. It presents an easily-assimilable picture of heroism and simple Christian goodness, and enjoyed considerable success. There is one serious drawback in Hallie's method: the starring roles are inevitably given to those who most liked to talk about themselves (i.e. who are often untypical rather than the reverse), and the reticent are relegated to the sidelines. There was a serious plan to produce a major film based on this book, to be directed by Carl Foreman, and financed apparently by American Mennonite sources; but Foreman pulled out because of the lack of a dramatic enough story-line, and the reluctance of survivors to let him invent one.

The second major presentation of the events in Le Chambon is a documentary film, completed in 1987, called *Weapons of the Spirit* (in French: *Les Armes de l'Esprit*). This was made by a Hollywood-based producer called Pierre Sauvage, whose interest in the story could hardly have been more personal: he was himself born in Le Chambon in 1944, to Jewish refugee parents given sanctuary on a farm. The film, which makes extensive use of interviews with survivors in reconstructing the story, is not yet on general release; but it has been shown at major film festivals, received enthusiastic reviews, and won a number of prizes.

So far, so good. But while Sauvage was making his film an explosive new ingredient was added by Philip Hallie. Depressed (as he tells us) by his failure to comprehend the heroism and moral purity that he had found in Le Chambon, he had decided that the explanation for the whole affair was that the Jews in general, and the village in particular, must have been protected by the German commander in Le Puy. This man, Major Julius Schmähling, now becomes for Hallie the true hero of the Haute-Loire: a secular, compromised, flawed, but humanly noble figure. Hallie expressed his new beliefs in a lecture delivered in October 1986 at Quinnipac College (and I believe repeated elsewhere), which was published by the College under the title 'Tainted Decency, Goodness, and a Nazi Officer in France'. To give the flavour of this paper, it begins:

> I want to tell you about a certain German army officer who, while being dutiful, and even efficient, in Hitler's military managed to save the lives of many people in the mountains of southern France. He was a good man who was part of an evil cause, and so his story is paradoxical at its very center.

And it ends:

> This was Major Julius Schmähling, who in the midst of battle made room for thoughts and acts of love unconsoled, unsupported by religion or by ethical or political principles. In studying him and in learning to admire him, I have learned much about respecting myself and others in a maculate world. I have learned that ethics is not simply a matter of good and evil, true north and true south. It is a matter of mixtures, like most of the other points on the compass, and like the lives of most of us. We are not all called upon to be perfect, but we can make a little, real difference in a mainly cold and indifferent world. We can celebrate human life in a local, intimate celebration, even with the coldness not far away.

I must say, in passing, that in its cavalier treatment of the evidence I find his paper a quite astounding mixture of wishful thinking, selective quotation, and factual error; but that is not the main point here. The most intense concern was aroused by Hallie's announcement that he was working on a new historical book, a pendant to his book on Le Chambon, which would revolve around a justification of its central figure of Schmähling.

It will scarcely come as a surprise to learn that Hallie's claims have stirred up a hornets' nest. A furious controversy has ensued, involving survivors and descendants of the Chambon refuge, Resistance leaders, and French historians. In large part this has been led and co-ordinated by Oscar Rosowsky, the young master-forger of the war years, and now a distinguished doctor in Paris. Protests and denunciations have been published in Le Monde,(11) in Jewish periodicals, and in passionate private letters released for general circulation. In an open letter (over a number of signatures, but bearing the stamp of Rosowsky's authorship) published in the intellectual periodical Le Monde Juif, Hallie's claims are vigorously called 'un tissu quasi délirant de contre-vérités assenées avec aplomb dans le plus pur style des spécialistes du revisionnisme historique'.(12) And in that word 'revisionnisme', of course, we have the key to the outrage. Further, the same open letter notes the Mennonite sources of finance for the projected film of Hallie's book, and reminds readers of the role of Mennonite communities in South America in organizing a refuge for Nazi war criminals, including Dr Mengele. Much of this has been dismissed by opponents as wild rantings, but rightly or wrongly we are suddenly in very deep and murky waters.

The attack on Hallie was also extended to include Sauvage's film. For a preliminary draft version, shown in Le Chambon, a certain amount of use was made of the suggestion that the Germans might have turned a blind eye to what was going on; and although much was subsequently cut, the final version does still raise this as a question. Rosowsky, who has a good line in polemic, wrote in a letter to Le Monde that it was 'L'Histoire revue et corrigée par Walt Disney dont le public est friand', and elsewhere writes of a 'réduction de vérités européennes à des stéréotypes marchands américains et de falsifications historiques'. However, Sauvage has riposted as vigorously as he was attacked - justifying a certain sympathy towards Schmähling, but claiming that this has only the most minor and incidental role in the film - and the controversy looks as though it still has some way to go.

What can one say about Schmähling? At first sight, he looks unpromising material as a prospective 'good German', given that he was an old friend of Sepp Dietrich, the chief of the Waffen-SS. But he was hardly a militaristic fanatic. A schoolteacher in civilian life, he was 58 when he arrived in Le Puy in December 1942 with the first German troops, and his past military record was less than glorious (in the First World War he was taken prisoner in August 1914, and sat out almost the entire war). He was replaced as commander in Le Puy in May 1944 by a much harder man, a career officer (Oberst Metger), but he remained there until the end.

Some evidence can be claimed in his favour. Chiefly, this consists of his own manuscript memoirs, written for his children, and not unnaturally primarily self-justifying. His own self-image is of a good-humoured, easy-going, art-loving francophile doing his best in a difficult situation. But also, there is a general tendency of people in the Haute-Loire to talk of him in terms of qualified approval; and various Vichy officials in Le Puy speak well of him, although this might be considered rather ambiguous support.

As regards his attitude to Le Chambon, this depends almost entirely on the testimony of one Roger Bonfils, the propriétaire of the Hôtel du

72   FRANCE 1940

Lignon in Le Chambon, where convalescent German troops were quartered. Bonfils has stated that Schmähling came to Le Chambon several times, that he knew perfectly well what was going on, and that in May 1943 he had an interview in the Hôtel du Lignon with Pastor Trocmé - at which Bonfils was the only other person present - in which he let it be known that he would protect Trocmé's activities. It is also claimed that Schmähling should be exonerated of responsibility for the raid on the hostel in 1943 - that was a Gestapo affair, and Schmähling was in the Wehrmacht. And finally, if it was not protected, given the massive and constant provocation going on, how did Le Chambon escape the fate of Oradour-sur-Glane? (a question seriously asked by both Hallie and Sauvage).

But there is also much to be said on the other side. The statistics are difficult to interpret, but there seems to have been no significant shortage of arrests and deportations in Haute-Loire under Schmähling's control; and in his memoirs he writes of the vicious Vichy *milice* - who could compete with the Gestapo in sheer human nastiness - as 'les meilleurs enfants de la France'.(13) Above all, the testimony of Roger Bonfils is considered worse than suspect by everyone who was in Le Chambon during the war. Bonfils was not a Chambonnais, and was universally regarded as the leading local informer and collaborator.(14) Far from Schmähling being a frequent visitor to the village, so far as I know nobody else ever seems to have seen him there. And as for the all-important interview with Pastor Trocmé, presided over by the hotel-keeper, there is no mention of it in either Schmähling's or Trocmé's unpublished memoirs, and good evidence that the two men never met until the last days of the Occupation.(15) Worse still for the theory of the German protector of the village, Le Chambon is not even mentioned in Schmähling's self-justifying memoirs; and when the Major was captured and interrogated by the Resistance forces who liberated Le Puy, he again made no mention of what, if it had been true, would have been such an obvious and vital point in his defence. I find this fact very difficult to explain away.

The most controversial episode in which Schmähling was involved occurred in the last days of the German occupation of Le Puy. On 5 August 1944 the Le Chambon doctor, Roger Le Forestier, a man of considerable personal charisma, was driving to Le Puy and gave a lift to two young maquisards who told him, wrongly, that they were unarmed. They apparently lost their nerve, and without his knowing hid their two revolvers under the back cushions of his car. Later, in Le Puy, Le Forestier's car was searched and the revolvers discovered; he was arrested and tried under martial law, and of course condemned to death. Schmähling presided over the court-martial. Le Forestier's young wife pleaded with Schmähling, who subsequently told her that he had intervened on her husband's behalf with the other two senior German officers (Metger and Rittmeister Coelle). He claimed that he had arranged for the doctor to work in a hospital in Germany. Le Forestier was indeed sent away, on the very last convoy to leave Le Puy. He was sent, not to Germany, but to Klaus Barbie's men at the Fort Montluc in Lyon, where he was tortured and eventually shot. It is impossible that Schmähling should not have known that the liberation of Le Puy was imminent. Had Schmähling kept Le Forestier in prison in Le Puy for just a few days more, he would have been freed by the maquisards.

Now this episode has been seen as evidence of Schmähling's honour and goodness, cruelly let down by events and his fellow-Germans (and in old age he was wont to weep publicly and sentimentalize self-pityingly about the beautiful young widow who had trusted him). Others have taken a less charitable view.

As always with the past, one can never fully know what really happened: the very phrase 'what really happened' instantly invites challenge as meaningless. And the recent past has the particular inconvenience for the historian that survivors can rise up and dispute what they are told is the truth about their own experiences. This does not necessarily mean that the historian is wrong, often quite the contrary; but history is so much more manageable when all the participants are safely dead. One can only speculate as to what will happen to the history of Le Chambon in a couple of decades time.

No competent historian nowadays needs instruction on the problems and dangers associated with the testimony of those actively involved in any sequence of events, let alone events so laden with moral significance as these. Consciously or unconsciously such testimonies select, they re-interpret, they aggrandize, they diminish (and historians do the same). Old men forget: they also invent. Witnesses are modest or vain; they may seek to enhance their own role, or to conceal it; they may be committed to a personal cause or faith or interpretation of events. The same individual may be regarded as a convincing witness, or as a self-preserving fantasist (as seen in the case of Roger Bonfils). What to one society, and one generation, seems normal, to another, in different circumstances, can seem frankly incredible; and then a different explanation must be sought in accord with the mental clichés of a new age.

The same process can happen in reverse, and commentators can hopelessly confuse what is plausible conjecture and what is not. An example might be the unexpected conclusion Hallie draws from Schmähling's friendship with General Sepp Dietrich of the Waffen-SS - the architect of the Night of the Long Knives, who gave the orders for the massacre of civilians and prisoners-of-war at Malmédy in the Ardennes in December 1944. Hallie believes that this friendship 'had much to do with Schmähling's power to protect the region from Klaus Barbie and other Gestapo chiefs in the south ... A word from Dietrich on the telephone could, and I am convinced, *did* prevent Gestapo raids in the Haute-Loire'. One feels that Sepp Dietrich might have had more pressing concerns in 1943-44 than telephoning Klaus Barbie to protect Jews from the Gestapo.

One of the strongest impressions left by a study of Le Chambon during the Occupation is the complexity of a picture that at first looks relatively simple. It is a common mistake, for example, to attribute near-omniscient and above all near-omnipotent power to a monolithic enemy bloc, which was in reality divided between SS, Gestapo, and Wehrmacht, and also between the Vichy authorities, the milice, and the gendarmerie; the situation was further complicated in this region by the presence of six companies (1200 men) of the Volga Tartar Legion, who arrived in Le Puy in 1944 and, under the command of Rittmeister Coelle, soon gained an unsavoury reputation. Indeed the exact division of responsibility between these different elements, and their relative involvement in individual episodes, is often a stumbling-block to clear understanding.

Equally, the forces generally grouped under the label of Resistance defy any neat generalizations. Around Le Chambon, quite apart from the community effort of concealing Jewish children, there was the civilian Resistance; active armed groups, disciplined and well-led; a loose maquis of escapers from the STO (the Service de Travail Obligatoire, in Germany), mainly from cities like Saint-Etienne, who gradually got absorbed and organized, but could cause considerable problems; the Communist FTP (Francs-Tireurs Partisans) a little further away, in the Ardèche; and an important element of Jewish resistance. The Scouts, organized by one of the leaders of local Resistance, played an important role as couriers, guides, and in liaison within the network of contacts; while the Girl Guides developed escape routes locally. Finally, large numbers of Vichy officials played a double game, some out of conviction and some for self-preservation, especially once it appeared that the Reich might after all lose the war.

Two examples will illustrate the paradoxical situations that could arise. Le Chambon was used as a convalescence station for injured German soldiers from the Russian Front. In the summer of 1943 some maquis enthusiasts formed a plan to surprise a large number of German soldiers while they were bathing in the Lignon, and shoot them all. Word of this reached the local civil Resistance leader, Léon Eyraud, who was horrified: not only would it entail murderous reprisals, but very probably the destruction of the village and everything that it was doing (of which the maquis hotheads were largely unaware). The action was forbidden, but the maquis operators were not reliably under control; to make quite sure, the Resistance leader and his son-in-law Adolphe Caritey spent all day patrolling the woods opposite the bathing-place, protecting the Wehrmacht from any harm.(16)

The second concerns two Vichy officials whose ambiguous roles have been much debated, and interpreted in very different ways. The incident happened to Lesley Maber, who organized the Girl Guides. Among many other activities, she had taught at the Collège Cévenol since its foundation, and with a partner ran a pension that was often more than half-full of Jewish children during these years. In February 1943 she and another teacher were arrested. Passing through Le Puy on the way to a concentration camp at Bagnères-de-Bigorre in the Pyrenees she was summoned before the préfet of the Haute-Loire, who ascertained that in the 1930s she had brought up two abandoned children, and said that this provided grounds for her release. She went on, with other detainees, towards the camp. The order for her release reached their train at La Bourboule, beyond Clermont-Ferrand, and she and the other teacher were able to return to Le Chambon. The train itself never reached Bagnères: it was stopped by the occupying forces at Tulle, not much further on, and diverted straight to Germany; not one person on board returned. Now both the beginning and end of this story contain surprises. Lesley Maber was apparently denounced by an 'inspecteur de police de Vichy' stationed in Le Chambon, Inspecteur Praly, who was not altogether an enemy of the community - when two Gestapo killers got drunk in the village once and boasted of the men they had come to kill, he had them recalled in disgrace. Both Hallie and Sauvage have made efforts to rehabilitate him. Yet a little later, in August 1943, he was gunned down in cold blood by the Resistance. And Préfet Robert Bach, who saved Lesley Maber's life, was regarded as a contemptible collaborator. Only when he was put on trial after the Liberation did the extent of the good that he had done become clear, and he was acquitted to general acclaim.

Very little in this world of the Haute-Loire was quite what it seemed to be on the surface. But as we saw with the initial quotation from *Newsweek*, the sense of the uniqueness of the phenomenon of Le Chambon (which itself may be exaggerated) invites mythification, the retrospective reduction of its complexity to a simple symbolic value. The process is familiar enough: historical events have become an ideological shorthand, which works as an instantly recognizable trigger for a simple and predictable response. It is particularly interesting to see how different commentators have extracted quite different messages from Le Chambon. The two most important of these by far might be characterized as 1) the Brave Christian Peasants, and 2) the Good German; these two are not necessarily mutually exclusive.

Most often, obviously, Le Chambon is hailed as a rare communal example of true Christian love and self-sacrifice in action. This approach is taken to the edge of sentimental implausibility in Hallie's book, and inspires attitudes of semi-incomprehending adulation in many reviews of Sauvage's film. On the other hand, as we have seen, the story of Le Chambon later came to provide for Hallie a quite different message: an alternative, secular, humanist hero in what he calls the 'tainted goodness' of the compromised but admirable German officer; and thereby it was ineluctably drawn into the revisionism debate. But other messages have been found, from other perspectives. Jewish writers, particularly after Pierre Sauvage's film, have seen it above all in the light of the intense intellectual debate about the Holocaust, and found in Le Chambon an argument for optimism against what have been called 'the professional Holocaust pessimists offering convoluted excuses for mass murder cloaked in pseudoreligious academic jargon'.(17) In France, on the other hand, it has been taken as a valuable and necessary corrective to excessive simplification of the experience of Occupation: for the critic of Le Monde, Jean-Louis Mingalon, Sauvage's film offered '[des] Images bouleversantes d'une France méconnue'.(18)

In conclusion, I should perhaps say something about my own views on the questions raised in this paper. Firstly, I think that one should be wary of one's natural instincts in such matters: just because an explanation is attractive and sympathetic, and one would very much wish it to be true, it does not necessarily follow that it must be false.

I do believe in the exceptional and perhaps eccentric goodness of a considerable number of dominant characters in Le Chambon, and that this was crucially supported by the basic, unquestioning attitudes of the overwhelming majority of the native population of the Plateau. I do not find these attitudes, the so-called 'choice for good' of the Chambonnais, incredible or incomprehensible or beyond normal experience, as some (particularly trans-Atlantic) commentators have done, although they are admirable and humbling: I think that a community of Cornish Methodists, for example, would have reacted in exactly the same way.

The very cliché 'choice for good' invites the outsider to get things wrong, and to expect the Protestant plateau-dwellers to be quite other than they are. Like any remote community in France (and doubtless elsewhere), Le Chambon during the war had its share of feuds and jealousies. If one expects everything to be sweetness and light, and the Chambonnais all to have loving smiles and warm outgoing personalities to strangers, then one is going to be sadly disappointed.

Above all, though, I do not find it incredible or incomprehensible that so many Jewish children should have been concealed without trace. For someone who does not know the area well, a short visit to Le Chambon can be misleading. The Plateau of the 1970s and 1980s is, superficially at least, a very different place from that of· the early 1950s, when I first knew it, let alone ten years earlier under wartime conditions. Given the very poor communications of those years, the vast spaces, the remote farms and hamlets, and the tight yet individualistic community all make such a successful concealment entirely plausible. I can believe the well-attested story of the hamlet of Villelonge, which consists of six or seven farms. Each one of these sheltered at least one or two Jews; and yet not one family knew until after the Liberation that the others were doing the same thing. If one starts by disbelieving the possibility of such total concealment it becomes increasingly difficult to make sense of what happened. Incidentally, Albert Camus stayed for some time just outside Le

Chambon in 1943, while writing *La Peste*, and was to be met with walking in the woods. One would not normally attribute to him obtuseness or lack of perception, but he clearly had not the faintest suspicion of what was going on all around him.

There is no need whatever to suppose the necessity for a secret German protector of the village. But on the other hand Le Chambon was used for convalescent German troops from the Russian Front, and I can imagine that Schmähling was not going to go out of his way to look for trouble himself so long as things remained quiet. That, however, is perhaps as far as one can go.

The question raised by a voice-over in Sauvage's film is entirely legitimate: 'Se pourrait-il que [Schmähling] aussi savait bien que Le Chambon était plein de Juifs, mais évita de le signaler à ses collègues?' I can understand that this, following after Hallie's more provocative and far less defensible claims, should have touched on an acutely raw nerve in those particularly sensitive to the outrage of extreme revisionist theories. However, in the present state of knowledge I think that the answer to Sauvage's question must be 'Non'.

Many details of Le Chambon during the war years will never be definitively established. The whole episode seems certain to be the subject of continuing debate, as the numbers of those with first-hand experience of events inevitably diminish, and the evidence with all its ambiguities is reconsidered by new generations of historians. Fortunately there can be no dispute about the only fact that really matters: the remarkable, sustained collective enterprise on the Plateau of providing safe refuge for the victims of persecution.

Notes

*   This paper owes an immense debt to my aunt, Dr Lesley Maber, who lived in Le Chambon-sur-Lignon for more than forty years, including all the war years, and was actively involved in the events described. She generously put at my disposal her unpublished memoirs *The Bundle of the Living*, as well as her invaluable dossier of correspondence and other first-hand material relating to the Chambon refuge. All expressions of opinion are, of course, entirely my own.

1.   Geoffrey Cowley, 'A Disaster Brings out the Best in People. Why?', *Newsweek*, no. 45, 6 November 1989, 39-40.
2.   Quoted in the newsletter 'Friends of Le Chambon', published by Pierre Sauvage, Los Angeles, 1988.
3.   Le Chambon-sur-Lignon is not to be confused with the much larger town of Le Chambon-Feugerolles, very close to Saint-Etienne.
4.   According to the 1936 census there were 8,268 Protestants out of a total Plateau population of 18,457, or 33% of the total; but they were (and are) heavily concentrated in a relatively small number of the 17 communes, above all in the neighbouring communes of Le Chambon (95% Protestant) and Le Mazet-Saint-Voy, whose population of 2,221 was 96% Protestant.
5.   The terrible fate that befell thousands of French Jewish children has recently been exposed by an investigative report in *L'Express*: Eric Conan, 'Enquête sur un crime oublié', *L'Express*, no. 2025, 4 May 1990, 22-31. This profoundly

disturbing article serves as a reminder of the realities of occupied France beyond the Chambon refuge.

6. There were of course other groups and individuals engaged in forging documents of all kinds, including ration books to feed the refugees.

7. Precise estimates of numbers are quite impossible, and have been the subject of some recent controversy. No individual involved had more than a very partial view of what was going on, and secrecy, concealment, and the absence of records were the very essence of the operation. Above all the situation was complex, with several different groups involved, and never static: many refugees were helped on their way to Switzerland or Spain, while many others (particularly children, and sometimes entire families) remained concealed for long periods of time. The figure most frequently given is of 5,000 refugees, but estimates have been as high as 8,000. At the other extreme, in search of an absolute and verifiable minimum, a figure of 500 Jews has been proposed, based on the lists of 'israélites français et étrangers' kept in the Vichy departmental archives (François Boulet, 'Quelques éléments statistiques', Colloque du Chambon, October 1990: see below, note 9). Yet the assumptions behind this figure are highly questionable: it goes without saying that the overwhelming majority of the refugees were trying their utmost *not* to be recorded on the Vichy lists, and most of them undoubtedly succeeded in keeping their presence secret. The very idea of finding objective confirmation of any figure should probably be abandoned. Considering all the evidence, one might very tentatively suggest a total of 2,000-3,000 Jewish refugees who were helped to escape or concealed on the Plateau; but this might well be an under-estimate.

8. Preface to the unpublished memoirs of Lesley Maber, *The Bundle of the Living*.

9. Most recently, a very important collection of papers on all aspects of the subject was presented at a conference in Le Chambon in October 1990: 'Le Plateau Vivarais-Lignon: Acceuil et Résistance, 1939-1944. Colloque du 12, 13, 14 octobre 1990, Le Chambon-sur-Lignon, Haute Loire'. This is hereafter referred to as 'Colloque du Chambon, 1990'. See also *Cévennes, terre de refuge: textes et documents*, edited by Patrick Cabanel, Philippe Joutard, and Jacques Poujol (Montpellier, Presses du Languedoc, 1988), and Sabine Zeitoun, *Ces enfants qu'il fallait sauver* (Paris, Albin Michel, 1989), pp. 213-240: 'Le Chambon-sur-Lignon ou "l'autre France"'.

10. Philip P. Hallie, *Lest Innocent Blood be Shed* (New York, Harper & Row, 1979); translated into French by Magali Berger as *Le Sang des innocents* (Paris, Stock, 1980).

11. *Le Monde*, 4 June 1987.

12. 'Le mythe du commandant SS protecteur des Juifs: un texte de Magda Trocmé, Madeleine Barot, Pierre Fayol et O. Rosowsky; une lettre de Raymond Aubrac, Philippe Boegner, Oscar Rosowsky, Pierre Vidal-Naquet et Georges Wellers; et une lettre de Georges Bollon', *Le Monde Juif*, no. 130 (1988), 61-69 (p. 66).

13. Schmähling's unpublished memoirs are quoted extensively in Lucien Volle, *Des maquis de la Haute-Loire jusqu'au bord du*

Rhin: la singulière épopée du 'Groupe Lafayette' (Le Puy, Imprimerie Jeanne-d'Arc, 1987; second edition 1988), passim, and 'Annexe', pp. 340-49.

14. Bonfils was not only not a Chambonnais, but half-German and a Catholic. He was a fairly recent arrival in Le Chambon when the war started, and left the village after the Liberation.

15. Confirmed in a letter to Lesley Maber, 7 April 1988, by Pierre Fayol, second-in-command of the Resistance forces in the Haute-Loire, who interviewed Schmähling on 22 August 1944 after his capture. On Trocmé's memoirs, letter to Lesley Maber from Pierre Sauvage, 24 April 1988; on Schmähling's memoirs, letter to Pierre Sauvage from Lucien Volle, 27 December 1988.

16. See Aline Caritey, 'Un chef local: Léon Eyraud' (Colloque du Chambon, 1990).

17. Laurence Jarvik, 'The Banality of Good' [review-article on the film *Weapons of the Spirit*], *Tikkun*, March/April 1988, 1-3 (p. 3).

18. Review written when the film was shown at the Cannes film festival in 1987.

1940 VU PAR UN ALLEMAND: ERNST JUNGER

JARDINS ET ROUTES (GARTEN UND STRASSEN, 1942)

Daniel Madelénat

En 1940, lorsqu'il prend part à la campagne de France, Ernst Jünger est un écrivain célèbre; héros de la première guerre, figure de proue de la droite nationaliste dans les années vingt, suspect au Troisième Reich dont il refuse les avances, il vient de publier - grâce à l'intervention personnelle du Führer qui l'admire - *Sur les Falaises de marbre* (*Auf den Marmorklippen*, 1939), roman allégorique où l'extermination, intemporalisée, déploie ses abattoirs et ses charniers. En France, *Orages d'acier* (*In Stahlgewittern*, 1920), traduit en 1930, fut un des témoignages les plus remarqués sur la vie dans les tranchées.

L'émigré de l'intérieur, ennemi secret de l'idéologie officielle, imprégné de culture française, va devenir une personnalité du Paris de l'occupation, et la traduction de *Jardins et Routes, pages de journal 1939-1940*, chez Plon, en 1942 (par Maurice Betz, le traducteur de Rainer Maria Rilke), s'insère, objectivement, dans la stratégie politique et culturelle allemande de réconciliation et de séduction (comme la parution chez Gallimard, en 1942, de *Sur les Falaises de marbre*, *Le Coeur aventureux* et *Jeux africains*).(1) Néanmoins, c'est un périlleux exercice de virtuosité qui doit rappeler des jours douloureux sans rouvrir de blessures ni réveiller de cruels souvenirs; ménager l'honneur des vaincus sans amoindrir la gloire des vainqueurs (dont la police surveille le virtuel rebelle à l'*'ordre nouveau'*).(2)

Pour accomplir ce tour de force, Jünger choisit la forme du journal: il la pratique depuis longtemps et elle ne surprendra pas son lecteur. Mais à l'intérieur de ce cadre familier, le thème se module: jadis glorieuse, pleine de sang et de fureur, l'expérience de la guerre au limite à l'arrière, à l'après, et aux coulisses du théâtre; mais elle garde une signification existentielle et ontologique pour l'officier qui, à la faveur de l'événement, découvre le nouveau visage du monde, et l'orientation nouvelle de son propre destin.

1. Le Journal: Forme et Sens

Réduit à un acte élémentaire de communication, le journal se caractérise par une énonciation à destination réflexive (de soi à soi) et à fonction principale mnémonique (garder une trace des jours qui s'écoulent). Cela génère un texte que ne spécifient aucun thème précis, mais certaines caractéristiques: absence de la deuxième personne, structure discontinue avec indication de dates, mélange (en proportions variables) de description et de réflexion, de vision et de commentaire. Quand interviennent un second destinataire, une promesse de publication plus ou moins prompte, de nouvelle conventions s'ajoutent aux premières: règles du genre, souplement fixées par une époque et une tradition (ce qu'il faut dire - et ne pas dire - comment le dire et l'adapter à des publics différenciés, etc.).

Essayiste brillant et militant, Jünger, dès *Le Travailleur (Der Arbeiter*, 1932), adopte l'arme péremptoire du fragment (poursuivant une tradition qui remonte à l'esthétique romantique): l'affirmation se pose, les raisons viennent après, l'Idée bouscule et réordonne les données obscures de l'expérience immédiate; ainsi la *figure* du Travailleur - forme titanesque de la Volonté de Puissance - doit se lire clairement dans l'affrontement des peuples et dans les incertitudes désenchantées qui suivent 1918. Le genre confidentiel, intime, du *journal*, peut, dans une certaine mesure, intégrer cette violence incisive qui refuse d'argumenter: quand les choses sont vues de haut 'l'expression et l'énoncé même ont un caractère métallique; la langue décrit la création frappée dans l'airain avec une densité et une netteté suprêmes' (p. 86, à propos du *Bouclier d'Hercule* d'Hésiode). Mais le demi-jour de l'intimité livre surtout des aperçus, des intuitions, des 'ébauches de pensées' qui ne se figent pas en discours organisé: 'Il semble que la substance des pensées soit précédée d'une autre substance, plus subtile, qui attaque en quelque sorte la matière par érosion et la rend divisible d'une façon particulière. L'esprit, rêvant à moitié, joue ainsi avec les choses en les touchant, sans les distinguer encore, comme avec des antennes. L'obscurité précède la lumière' (p. 234-235).

Carnets, notes de combattants, plus ou moins transformés en mémoires, abondent dès les campagnes napoléoniennes et se multiplient après la guerre, déjà très médiatisée, de 1870-1871. Jünger fonde *Orages d'acier* sur son journal de guerre, source primordiale du récit;(3) il adopte même la forme diariste dans le chapitre 'Chronique quotidienne de la guerre de tranchées' (p. 87-111), dans l'ensemble du *Boqueteau 125* (*Das Wäldchen 125: Eine Chronik aus den Grabenkämpfen 1918*, 1925), et, bien sûr, dans *Feu et Sang* (*Feuer und Blut (...)*, 1925), consacré à une seule journée, mais en remaniant et en regroupant les faits (les adaptations sont avouées dans l'avant-propos du *Boqueteau 125*: 'Bien que, pour éviter des répétitions constantes, j'aie dû modifier quelque peu l'ordre de succession des événements, j'ai conservé la forme extérieure du journal qui est, après la lettre, la plus apte à traiter sans effort un sujet aussi complexe'.(4) La méditation de la guerre - intense en ces années où se publient *Feu et mouvement* (*Feuer und Bewegung*, 1930), *La Mobilisation totale* (*Die totale Mobilmachung*, 1930), *La Guerre notre mère* (*Der Kampf als inneres Erlebnis*, 1932) - impose une réinterprétation expressive et, pour ainsi dire, pédagogique.

Fidèle à l'expérience immédiate, le 'petit cahier' de guerre est un témoignage émouvant, une déposition pour l'histoire, une discipline qui oblige l'auteur 'à tirer la quintessence de chaque événement relaté, à s'élever par la méditation (...) au-dessus de son entourage habituel' (*Le Boqueteau 125*, p. 70-71). L'opacité du vécu se traduit dans le morcellement, aux antipodes du cours de stratégie ou du traité. La focalisation restreinte prend sur le fait de leur émergence les situations nouvelles, les grandes fractures des mentalités: quand Jünger lit le journal d'un capitaine français, il saisit dans la matérialité même de l'écriture le passage de la sécurité à l'angoisse (p. 183). La souplesse modulable de la structure additive n'exclut pas le commentaire, implicite ou explicite: la distance entre le narrateur et l'action varie selon le recul de la réminiscence; les divers rythmes de la vie s'entrelacent, se juxtaposent, se relativisent (le temps de la nature, de l'histoire générale, de l'histoire locale - le secteur du front -, de la vie quotidienne, de la microsociété, de la vie mentale profonde ...).

Mais la fragmentation heurte la grande tradition épique du récit de guerre, celle qui va de Tolstoi à Soljenitsyne (*Août*), en passant par Zola ou Jules Romains; elle s'adapte mal au *Blitzkrieg*, coulée continue de l'invasion: son polythématisme estompe les lignes de force et disperse les effets; son hyperindividualisme ne correspond guère à la massivité

collective de l'action. Loin d'une représentation rationalisée, d'une
narration logique qui hiérarchise les plans et démêle les causes, le
journal entre dans une stratégie d'élucidation: l'événement dispersé,
atomisé au fil des jours, décentré, élude, même, se cosmicise, se réfracte
en images superposées, se répercute en symboles, secrète sa propre
herméneutique; soustrait aux formes militaires et sociales, il concentre en
lui les surgissements du vouloir-vivre, le rayonnement de la *figura*
(l'archétype intemporel qui génère le bouillonnement du temps). Dans
l'écriture du journal, comme dans le travail du souvenir, 'les faits
viennent à nous à l'état brut et par fragments (...). L'esprit, en
réfléchissant, essaie de saisir l'ensemble qui est enfermé dans les
détails, de voir la figure pleine de sens. C'est possible par abréviation;
le hasard est retiré du creuset comme une écume. Mais il arrive aussi que
des additions précisent l'image, de même que des anecdotes d'une invention
heureuse sont des ébauches de récit' (p. 241). La factualité est une
condition nécessaire, mais l'auteur doit 'élever les données de
l'expérience individuelle au niveau d'une signification plus large',(5) les
spiritualiser pour libérer l'universel qui en est la substance. Mircea
Eliade nomme 'méthode Jünger' la sélection de l'essentiel, la discipline du
regard, le style d'une vision (qu'il oppose à la 'méthode Léautaud',
spontanéité du premier jet sans correction): l'attention lit la forme et
l'idée dans l'anecdote; le 'vécu' devient alors une révélation éclatée, une
épiphanie multiple; à l'ordinaire *dianoia* - médiation par la logique - se
substitue une *noèse* 'asystématique'.(6)

2. Une Expérience Déceptive

Le guerrier de légende, engagé à dix-huit ans dans la Légion étrangère (il
a raconté cette équipée dans *Jeux africains* (*Afrikanische Spiele*, 1936)),
quatorze fois blessée, décoré en 1918 de la croix 'Pour le mérite', le
théoricien du conflit total, le romancier critique des *Falaises de marbre*,
aborde, quand il est mobilisé en août 1939, une expérience cruciale:
comment se répètera la tragédie? en farce (pour reprendre l'expression de
Marx), en fade *remake*? L'homme qui approche des quarante-cinq ans
retrouvera-t-il l'état de grâce, la consonance avec l'heure? L'enthousiasme
de 1914, en tout cas, cède la place à l'inquiétude, à l'angoisse et à un
certain scepticisme.(7)
    Jünger pressent que la guerre se gagnera à l'ouest; les combats de
Pologne, écrit-il le 31 décembre 1939, 'm'ont toujours semblé de moindre
importance historique, comme s'ils se déroulaient en des pays brumeux où
les contours s'effacent' (p. 80). Quand il apprend, en mai 1940, les
bombardements sur l'Allemagne, il voit pointer 'la guerre totale, qui nous
menace en tous les points de l'existence à la fois' (p. 146). Il sent
l'appel du destin: sa promotion au grade de capitaine le 30 août 1939,
signe de la 'faveur' d'Arès (p. 53), son rêve d'escadres aériennes qui
coïncide avec l'offensive et le tournant du 10 mai 1940 (p. 134-135). Comme
en 1914, il voit dans le combat le creuset où se forment les gemmes, où
s'exaltent les énergies: 'Cette haute chevalerie qu'a produite la première
grande guerre. C'est seulement après que la braise est refroidie, que les
diamants se détachent du noir flux charbonneux' (p. 116).(8) L'ancienne
fraternité d'armes, Jünger est anxieux de la retrouver: 'Je suis presque
dans le même état d'esprit qu'en 1914, lorsque je craignais surtout de ne
pas avoir ma part de bataille' (p. 139).(8)

Au regard de ces espérances, la déception sera lourde. Après les longs mois de faction immobile, Jünger comprend que les succès rapides de la cavalerie et de l'aviation creusent un gouffre entre l'ancienne guerre de position et la nouvelle prédominance du mouvement: 'Je fus particulièrement surpris, moi pour qui la résistance extraordinairement tenace des fronts était devenue, après des centaines d'expériences, une sorte de dogme' (p. 143; voir encore p. 158).(9) La compagnie de fantassins court derrière une guerre introuvable; 'ça viendra, ça viendra. Vers Saint-Quentin' (p. 152), lance le général, le 27 mai; la ligne, cependant, s'éloigne sans cesse sous la pression des chars (p. 160, 163, 164). Le contact qui semblait enfin s'offrir se dérobe (p. 168): le bataillon est cantonné à Laon; Jünger conclut le 21 juin: 'Il semble peu probable maintenant que nous soyons engagés dans des combats violents au cours de cette campagne, et si je le regrette en tant que soldat, j'en suis heureux pour ceux qui souffrent' (p. 198). Au plus proche, il n'aura subi qu'une attaque aérienne (pp. 181-182). Il évoque avec nostalgie la situation limite par excellence, le dialogue de feu au-delà de la raison et de la parole (pp. 166-167): 'Alors s'élèvent ces voix d'airain et de feu, faites pour inspirer la peur, - et vraiment les coeurs sont éprouvés jusqu'à leur tréfonds' (p. 167).(10)

Les travaux et les jours se réduisent donc aux heures mornes de la 'drôle de guerre': tranchées et fortifications face au Rhin, coups de feu des Français sur un mannequin au masque de Chamberlain (p. 83), rafales sporadiques (p. 93), cérémonie d'anniversaire et fête du 13 mai pour la compagnie (p. 116, 136), manoeuvres (p. 134). Pour évoquer ces temps d'ennui, Jünger recourt à des procédés éprouvés: raconter, du matin au soir, une journée comme les autres avec ses inspections, ses promenades, ses rencontres et ses lectures (pp. 97-104. Voir *Le Boqueteau 125*, pp. 44-52); développer un exploit qui tranche sur la grisaille: après la fusillade du 29 mars, la récupération d'un cadavre sous le tir français (pp. 116-117. Voir dans *Le Boqueteau 125* (pp. 108-109) l'expédition à découvert en direction des lignes anglaises). Quand se déclenche la guerre de mouvement, elle réserve au fantassin des épreuves monotones: marches pénibles, étapes sans confort, ordres et contre-ordres qui assimilent la progression à une errance ...

L'esprit libéré de l'urgence guerrière, Jünger observe la vie naturelle: plantes, animaux (ce sont les 'chasses subtiles' de l'entomologiste), variations saisonnières des paysages. Dominant, l'espace (vu à grande ou à petite échelle) élimine les informations techniques sur la stratégie et la tactique, et surtout le temps historique majeur (réduit à quelques cursives indications: la proposition d'un armistice apprise aux prisonniers français, p. 190; le champagne pour la signature, p. 206). La durée vécue - celle du régiment, voire de la compagnie - baigne dans les rigueurs de l'hiver ou les fleurs bourdonnantes de l'été: le conflit se noie dans cette naturalité envahissante. Les promenades militaires, d'abord cantonnées au pays de Bade (Greffern et sa 'hutte aux roseaux' jusqu'au 23 février; Karlsruhe, Iffezheim, puis Friedrichstal jusqu'au 15 mai) se transforment en un grand cercle derrière le front (Monts du Hardt, frontière luxembourgeoise, Neufchâteau et Bouillon en Belgique, Sedan, Laon, du 15 mai au 7 juin; séjour à Laon du 7 au 15 juin; Soissons, Château-Thierry, Montmirail, Bourges, du 16 au 22 juin; séjour à Bourges du 22 juin au 2 juillet; mouvement de retour par Bonny, Troyes, Château-Salins, Adelange, Wadgassen en Allemagne, du 3 au 24 juillet).

Les routes prodiguent vues et aperçus qu'évoque un dessinateur et un coloriste précis: l'hiver sur le Rhin, l'opulence de Friedrichstal, le pays

romain de la rive gauche de fleuve, l''antique solitude des forêts' (p.
133) dans le Hardt, les grasses beautés de la Picardie ('On sent ici de
façon toute élémentaire que l'on est en France, c'est pourquoi vallées et
coteaux ne peuvent jamais être perdus pour la patrie', p. 162), les lignes
parfaites de la Champagne (p. 191), la géographie sacrée et tellurique de
Laon, limite symbolique du Nord (p. 165), le 'bain tiède' des vacances à
Bourges, avec la quête des insectes dans les jardins (p. 206), les fermes
ancestrales du Berry (p. 217), les tristes terres de la Haute-Marne
('Pauvreté, fermes abandonnées, saleté', p. 231), la décrépitude et
l'atmosphère 'hors du temps' des villages lorrains (p. 238). Dans ces
terroirs, à la faveur des circonstances, Jünger, tel le diable boîteux,
soulève le toit des maisons: 'Les cantonnements sont un peu pour moi une
quête d'hommes' (p. 230); il connaît tout le spectre des logeurs: la
vieille dame courtoise (p. 160-161), les enfants que le visiteur choye pour
'faire jaillir les sources de l'abondance' (p. 221), l'hôtesse aguicheuse
(pp. 224-225), le digne maire, le bon curé qui sait plaisanter (pp.
226-227), l'aubergiste à la fois joviale et dure (pp. 233-234). Les grands
dérangements de la guerre élargissent le cercle des relations: 'Les
rapports de l'hôte avec le soldat sont particuliers en ce que, à l'instar
du droit sacré s'asile, ils relèvent encore des formes de l'antique
hospitalité que l'on accordait sans considération de personnes' (p. 144).
    Un officier d'Etat-Major confesse sa frustration: 'il avait été
condamné à occuper un poste d'où l'on ne voyait la guerre que du côté de
l'ombre' (p. 204). Cette grisaille taciturne échoit aussi à Jünger: partout
'le palais de la Belle au bois dormant' (p. 152), l'absence, l'immobile
silence après l'exode, 'un immense foyer de mort' (p. 153), les pénates et
les dieux lares abandonnés; le cauchemar d'un monde déserté s'accomplit (p.
153) et invite les soldats à une régression anarchique: 'Restons des
gentilshommes' (p. 147) dit le commandant à ses hommes troublés par les
maisons ouvertes, les tables mises pour des fantômes, les animaux
domestiques qui errent, les troupes de civils en fuite, et, bientôt, les
flux pitoyables de prisonniers.
    Si les destructions ne s'occultent pas, leur vision est oblique et
décalée: après, de loin, par l'intermédiaire de récits, Jünger prend
conscience, à mesure qu'il s'enfonce en territoire ennemi, des
bombardements et des paniques (pp. 144-145, 151, 227-228, 231 ...). Une
femme pathétique qui veut déterrer son mari tombé dans les ultimes combats
lui montre 'les effets indirects des projectiles' (p. 239); les munitions
abandonnées qui explosent attestent qu''Arès a semé à chaque pas ses jouets
sanglants' (p. 243). Un processus de déplacement transfère la mort aux
animaux: le premier corps est celui d'un cheval (p. 138); un bouc est le
'dernier des innombrables cadavres que nous ayons vus, - tout desséché,
avec des trous dans la peau, par lesquels on voyait les côtes ainsi que les
barreaux d'une cage. Il montrait les dents comme s'il eût souri en signe
d'adieu' (p. 244).
    L'ellipse de la guerre va encore plus loin: dans la page de titre
ornée d'un bouquet de fleurs imprimé en vert; dans la titularisation même
qui articule les charmes sédentaires de la paix avec l'élément dynamique,
mais euphémisé, de l'offensive; dans la chronologie large qui décentre la
violence (du 3 avril 1939 au 24 juillet 1940); dans l'*incipit* et l'*explicit*
qui évoquent la maison de Kirchhorst et, à Wadgassen en Sarre, 'les
premiers habitants qui reprenaient possession de leurs maisons et de leurs
jardins' (p. 244); dans les signes et les images multipliés du retour au
labeur et au chez soi: les paysans sont au travail dès le 25 mai malgré les

bombes et les mines (p. 147), les transactions commerciales se renouent (p. 199), les champs revivent, puis le négoce et les métiers, 'l'homme se remet à jouer' (p. 233), le lavoir retentit à nouveau du babil des femmes (p. 236).

Dans cet intervalle entre guerre et paix, Jünger ordonne l'incertitude et régule l'anarchie des flux humains. Il préserve villes, édifices (Laon où il organise inventaire et sauvegarde des monuments, p. 169; Essômes, Montmirail, pp. 186-188) et hommes, qu'ils soient réfugiés ou prisonniers (pp. 176, 203, 205 ...). Puissance tutélaire, il pare aux maux les plus urgents: 'Il est des situations où la simple présence d'une force autoritaire est déjà un remède. Grâce à sa seule existence, des blessures se referment par où s'échappait l'aveugle substance élémentaire. Ce sont des instants où le mystère propre à toute fonction se révèle' (p. 199).

Lors de ce rendez-vous manqué, Jünger se découvre lui-même à travers la déception: 'A certains carrefours de notre jeunesse, Bellone et Athéné pourraient nous apparaître: l'une avec la promesse de nous enseigner l'art de conduire vingt régiments au combat, de telle sorte qu'ils soient tous présents à la bataille, tandis que l'autre nous promettrait le don d'assembler vingt mots de façon à former une phrase parfaite. Il est possible que nous choisissions le second de ces lauriers, qui fleurit, plus rare et plus discret, sur le versant rocheux' (p. 179). Le héros, devenu auteur au sens plein du terme (11), abandonne à ses cadets le vif de la lutte; décoré pour l'épisode d'Iffezheim il médite sur ce 'tempora mutantur et nos mutamur in illis': 'Cet événement me fit mesurer combien cette guerre était pour moi différente de la précédente. Jadis, les plus hautes décorations pour avoir abattu des adversaires; aujourd'hui un petit ruban pour un acte de sauvetage. Etrange aussi que je sois resté si loin du feu. Héraclite a raison: nul ne traverse deux fois le même fleuve'. Le sujet et l'objet s'interprètent l'un l'autre dans cette confrontation existentielle: 'Les choses sont attirées et élues par notre être: le monde est ce que nous sommes' (p. 204). Le cosmos ne connaît pas le hasard: 'Chacun trouve dans la vie la place qui lui revient' (p. 206). Si l'absence, le non-engagement, la randonnée dans la diversité remplacent l'ivresse de tuer et les éclairs du feu, ils s'alourdissent d'une signification ontologique.

3. Une ascese hermeneutique

Déception et frustration: les pressentiments initiaux sur l'"annus mirabilis' que le froid 'annonce extraordinaire même au point de vue purement élémentaire' (p. 88) furent-ils un leurre? Quand Jünger croit s'"acheminer vers des événements exceptionnels, proches et inconnus, qu'aucune imagination ne peut deviner', il ne trouvera pas, comme en 1918, 'les repaires brûlants de l'épouvante' (*Orages d'acier*, p. 419) mais il parviendra, une fois de plus, aux confins où le mythe 'frappe' le temps, aux portes de l'absolu, une fois déchiffrés les signes disséminés au long du chemin. Le destin lui offre, en retrait de l'immédiat engagement une distance propice à la contemplation et à la *représentation* (puisqu'en termes schopenhauériens il participe moins de la *Volonté*): déjà une dissidence qui annonce celle du *Waldgänger*, voire de l'*anarque* d'*Eumeswil* (1977).

Dès septembre 1939, l'attente - 'le loisir ressemble ici à celui d'une araignée dans son filet' (p. 104) - implique une réceptivité douloureuse:

'La guerre des nerfs met les hommes dans un état très proche de la captivité, où le simple écoulement du temps est déjà ressenti comme une souffrance' (p. 102). L'équipée, ensuite, s'accompagne d'émotions propices à une lucidité supérieure: 'Un étrange sentiment d'enivrement. Je suis plein d'images comme un vase qui déborde. Elles découlent de moi' (p. 186). Les éléments désaccordés d'un monde défamiliarisé agissent sur les sens comme des drogues: 'l'irritation caractéristique provoquée par la vue d'un mort' (p. 120), la vue des maisons désertes, 'd'abord excitante, puis lassante, enfin angoissante' (p. 175). Les spectacles sont oniropoétiques: 'La nuit, beaucoup de rêves, comme si des sujets nouveaux avaient tissé leur toile dans les maisons abandonnées, où la végétation des songes commençait à foisonner. Il me semblait voir le noyau ou le squelette de cette guerre' (p. 158).(12)

Cette transfiguration de l'existence qui élonge la banalité, le *grégaire* nietzschéen, en disloquant les formes accoutumées, ouvre sur une vision stellaire, lointaine et précise à la fois: elle enregistre des images 'qui, par un processus mystérieux, ne sont en quelque sorte développées qu'après des minutes ou des heures' (p. 186). L'arrière se fait surplomb, l'inconfort des fortifications, prélude. 'Un ascétisme même inférieur procure de l'espace aux hommes. Lorsque nous vivons en saints, l'infini nous tient compagnie' (p. 90). L'autre face des choses, l'illimité du vouloir-vivre transparaît: 'Il est des points dans l'univers d'où l'harmonie des mondes doit être visible dans son ordonnance suprême' (pp. 93-94).

Les apparences, fissurées par le séisme physique et moral de la guerre, laissent d'abord entrevoir le *type*, hypostase du vouloir-vivre, figure qui régit le devenir. Le regard de l'interprète discrimine le superficiel et le profond, discerne les formes de la volonté de puissance en opposant, par exemple, le dressage et l'énergie interne: 'Il y a deux sortes de disciplines: l'une qui agit du dehors comme une substance caustique et qui durcit l'homme; une autre qui rayonne d'un noyau vers l'extérieur ainsi qu'une lumière, et qui, sans rien lui retirer de sa douceur, rend l'homme intrépide et sans crainte. Pour obtenir la première nous avons toujours besoin de maîtres, mais la seconde naît souvent en nous comme une semence' (p. 85). L'archétype du *Travailleur* s'imprime dans le béton, l'acier (p. 81) et l'habileté technique: 'Les hommes sont d'une intrépidité imperturbable, d'étranges centaures, esprits non historiques, mais doués d'une grande force pour le siècle dans lequel ils sont nés' (p. 200).(13)

Fidèle à une herméneutique de l'histoire fondée sur cette figure du *Travailleur*, Jünger, contrairement à Bernanos, ne condamne pas le machinisme: à la recherche d'un nouvel équilibre, 'la souffrance elle-même crée des forces supérieures de guérison' (p. 173); à des officiers français qui attribuent leur défaite aux bombardiers en piqué, il répond que la 'victoire de l'ouvrier' se doit aux leçons de l'humiliation 'façonnées comme en des creusets brûlants' (p. 190). Celui qui, bientôt, reviendra aux forêts peut bien goûter la légèreté des petits abris façonnés de roseaux (pp. 80, 94-95, 98 ...), l'odeur des rondins qui brûlent, l'intimité du refuge loin des blockhaus qui attirent le feu (p. 128); il attribue l'effondrement de l'adversaire à un renoncement ontologique, à un consentement résigné. L'abandon du patrimoine signale un affaissement moral radical (p. 178); l'abattement des prisonniers montre que 'toute reddition des armes implique un acte irrévocable qui atteint le combattant à la source même de sa force' (p. 177); les captifs, obsédés de nourriture et de paix, ont 'l'allure mécanique et irrésistible qui est propre aux catastrophes'; ils sont 'une image du flot sombre de la destinée elle-même' (p. 189); les malheurs de la patrie découvrent 'la source la plus profonde de la souffrance' (p. 211). La soif de bien-être, les craintes pacifistes de l'avant-guerre ont préparé le cataclysme: 'Lorsqu'on veut mener si bonne vie, il faut renoncer aux armes' (p. 231). L'analyse éthique rejoint ici l'idéologie du régime de Vichy qui incrimine le mensonge et l'esprit de jouissance.(14)

Les figures de l'ouvrier vainqueur, du jouisseur vaincu s'inscrivent encore dans le tissu du temps; la répétition hante la route de l'invasion qui rappelle 1815, 1870, 1914 (pp. 151, 155, 163, 180, 195), s'intériorise dans un rêve qui se situe à trois époques différentes ('Je regardais comme à travers un verre où trois couleurs se rencontrent', p. 141) et amène le contemplateur aux portes de la temporalité: l'affrontement évoque la lutte des Grecs et des Perses (p. 222); l'idéal de la chevalerie (p. 92) s'incarne en Moltke (p. 115); Falstaff revient d'âge en âge: 'C'est un type que les guerres produiront toujours et les mêmes apparitions l'entourent: serviteurs roués et voleurs, oies grasses, filles légères, beuveries et jeux de cartes' (p. 85). L'espace des monuments où se condensent les aspirations du passé signifie cette permanence du même: au sommet de la cathédrale de Laon, devant le spectacle des trains et des avions, 'je sentis, écrit Jünger, l'accord entre ce temps passé et notre époque. Je sentis surtout que le passé ne doit pas m'échapper et je me fis le serment de ne plus jamais oublier désormais ce que je dois aux aïeux' (p. 170).

Mais les formes architecturales entraînent aussi vers l'anhistorique: cônes tronqués, ouvrages militaires, *magie* qui manifeste 'la proximité immédiate de la puissance'; tours élancées où s'exprime l'aspiration *mystique* à l'idéal (pp. 122-123). Les 'figures martiales' des conducteurs de char montrent 'Vulcain et son sens du travail' (p. 187); des visions ou des rêves tératologiques assument la passion haineuse de la lutte: un rat à tête et à queue de serpent incarne 'le caractère répugnant des inimitiés' inhérentes à la vie (p. 91. Voir pp. 107-108 le même type de rêverie devant un chiffon de laine); un chat qui s'enfuit au crépuscule avec un pigeon dont battent les ailes est 'une de ces images énigmatiques (...) où le plaisir et la douleur s'inscrivent ensemble de façon presque inextricable' (p. 235); un gnôme ivre, en fureur contre la volaille, caricature l'instinct de mort (p. 194); l'épidémie de violence rappelle la peste (pp. 88-89); la mort multipliée, une macabre pompe baroque (pp. 239-240); la cosmicité du combat, les primitives théomachies transmises par Hésiode (p. 82) ou le grouillement d'animaux et de démons qui peuple la cathédrale de Laon (p. 170). Ces réverbérations mythiques, symboliques ou légendaires participent d'une stratégie d'ellipse déjà soulignée; elles désintègrent le sens littéral de l'événement, transfigurent, naturalisent et infinitisent le microcosme local; en un saut ontologique, elles bondissent de l'*étant* à l'*être*.

Le rythme de la nature, basse continue, image de l'éternel retour du même, invite sans cesse à cette 'épistrophe': 'L'univers est réellement, dans une de ses perspectives, organisé dans un sens purement pédagogique' (p. 113); les coquillages fossiles préfigurent les oeuvres de l'homme, et notre vie 'est réussie, même si nous ne faisons ou ne laissons que pressentir la part d'éternité qui repose en elle' (p. 237); la contemplation des trésors que dénudent les cratères des bombes nous métamorphose: nous parvenons 'à un état apparié à la richesse de la terre, et dans lequel se change en or tout ce qu'effleure notre main' (p. 194). La nuit de pleine lune et ses formes spiritualisées nous approchent de l'absolu immanent: 'Si une formule magique était prononcée à cette minute, nous resterions irrévocablement prisonniers de la matière' (pp. 130-131). Même les rites ou les spectacles sociaux renvoient à ces configurations intemporelles: témoin dans un procès militaire, Jünger, 'à la fois attentif et profondément enfoncé dans le rêve de la vie', voit la texture secrète de la socialité: 'Ce caractère immuable, qui tient de la vie des insectes, me donnait un peu de confiance et de sérénité en me faisant penser ceci: il y a malgré tout là-dessous une loi plus profonde que les cultures, et quand même celles-ci s'évanouiraient, le tissu se reformerait' (p. 124); lors de la cérémonie à la cathédrale de Bourges, les constellations que forment les hommes laissent deviner les fils du jeu de marionnettes qui mènent de l'éphémère à l'absolu (p. 212).

L'expérience de la guerre, proche de la mort et des morts, nous affronte plus que toute autre à l'inconnaissable: 'La vie et les choses recèlent des vertus que le cours ordinaire ne nous dévoile pas, mais qui se révèlent à l'instant où nous nous élevons d'un degré ou accédons à un temps nouveau'. Comme le printemps ou l'amour contiennent des puissances inconnues, 'l'homme cache des vertus que la mort seulement déploiera' (p. 121), en une suprême aventure, rencontre sous le signe de l'invariance: 'La distance absolue qui nous sépare de la mort demeure éternellement la même' (p. 168) quels que soient les mirages qui encombrent la route. Les multiples cadavres composent une 'image très sombre, comme issue des pensées nocturnes d'un esprit extraordinairement puissant' (p. 197), qui s'éclaircit parfois: le spectacle d'un animal mort, les embryons qu'il portait projetés autour de lui, inscrit 'la volonté de la grande mère immanente', et 'le livre de l'univers devient un peu plus lisible' (p. 182); ailleurs, devant des cadavres, le filtre de la temporalité s'efface, l'image sort 'du cadre de l'histoire': 'je sentis la présence de puissances dont nous ne connaissons plus depuis longtemps que les noms abstraits' (p. 209).

Après avoir lu les *Consolations* de Boèce, et médité sur la double instance du temps, lieu du libre arbitre, et de l'éternité, siège de la providence, sur l'immanence de l'intemporel au moindre de nos actes, Jünger conclut: 'Il faut que nous éprouvions la souffrance jusqu'au bout. Mais tandis que, dans les régions inférieures de la vie, son pouvoir s'exerce de façon chaotique, le contact avec la grandeur et avec la noblesse lui impose une forme. La consolation l'introduit dans une cage dorée, ou mieux dans un autel dont la valeur est plus haute que tous les dommages que peut subir par son fait une vie d'homme' (p. 105). Là est la véritable tâche de l'écriture, devant les opacités du devenir: mettre en dialogue les aléas de l'événementiel et la psyché profonde; intérioriser, interpréter la guerre en lui impostant les figures du rêve, ce *perpetuum mobile* de l'esprit (pp. 192, 196). Les mots font advenir les formes et les idées sous-jacentes aux péripéties anecdotiques: non pas alchimie ou charme, mais ailes qui transportent 'jusque dans la zone d'un éther sans pesanteur où l'on n'a plus besoin d'ailes. Ces voiles multicolores, nous finissons par les rejeter, eux aussi' (p. 226).

Plongé dans la pulvérulence factuelle, aspirant à l'illimité de l'Etre, le diariste rachète et sauve: sa lecture métaphysique de la guerre l'amène à éteindre dans des moments d'intuition presque extatique les souffrances et les angoisses du vouloir-vivre. Sans doute ne perçoit-il pas encore clairement, en cette heure médiane de la vie, la crise morale qu'il traversera au début de l'occupation, ni la mutation de sa pensée dont témoignera *La Paix* (*Der Friede*, 1945). Mais la méditation des traces et des signes - ascèse qui succède à la prouesse - ressemble à un adieu aux armes, et contient promesse d'une ère nouvelle: 'Le langage secret des modèles d'après lesquels nous commençons aujourd'hui à construire, annonce des époques longues et égales, qui suivront les périodes de désordre' (p. 238).

Notes

1. Voir sur cette politique de l'Allemagne le best-seller d'Henri Amouroux, *La Grande histoire des Francais sous l'occupation*, t. III, *Les Beaux jours des collabos*, R. Laffont, 1978, pp. 197-524. On rapellera le rôle de l'ambassadeur Otto Abetz, du directeur de l'Institut allemand Karl Epting, du sculpteur Arno Breker (avec sa fameuse exposition de mai 1942), les amitiés, les protections, les voyages "organisés" en Allemagne...

2. Comme toute récente mise au point sur la réception et la situation de Jünger en France, on consultera Julien Hervier, "Ernst Jünger, un francophile vu de France", *Revue de Littérature comparée*, 1989, no.1, pp. 87-97.

3. Par exemple dans *Orages d'acier*, Christian Bourgois, 1970, p. 22: "Je retrouve même dans mon journal, à la date du 6 janvier, cette observation furibonde: (...)". Jünger conserve encore aujourd'hui ses carnets de notes de guerre, quatorze volumes (J. Hervier, *Entretiens avec Ernst Jünger*, Gallimard, 1986, p. 25), et il a sous-titré *Orages d'acier Aus dem Tagebuch eines Stosstruppführers* (tiré du journal d'un chef de groupe d'assaut).

4. *Le Boqueteau 125*, éd. du Porte-Glaive, 1986, p. 12.

5. J. Hervier, *Entretiens* (...), p. 112.

6. Mircea Eliade, *Briser le toit de la maison*, Gallimard, 1986, pp. 245-250, "Notes sur le Journal d'Ernst Jünger". L'écrivain revoit ses oeuvres: en 1950 *Jardins et routes*, en 1949 et 1960 *Sur les Falaises de marbre*. La présente étude se fonde, naturellement, sur l'oeuvre telle qu'elle parut en 1942.

7. Voir J. Hervier, *Entretiens* (...), pp. 28-29, et, sur le thème de la guerre en général chez Jünger, J. Hervier, *Deux individus contre l'histoire, Drieu La Rochelle, Ernst Jünger*, Klincksieck, 1978, pp. 13 à 89.

8. La lutte sculpte un noble type humain; Jünger cite la lettre d'une amie: "La guerre n'est pas belle, mais nous aimons les hommes qui la font, tandis que les pacifistes sont affreux" (p. 120).

9. L'aveu surprend chez un des théoriciens du mouvement (*Feuer und Bewegung*, 1930).

10. Jünger revient sur cette campagne dans J. Hervier, *Entretiens* (...), p. 31: "Nous courions derrière les chars de Guderian. Notre avant-garde a été un peu au feu, mais de façon très minime". Jünger escomptait alors, dit-il, une paix rapide avec l'Angleterre.

11. Celui qui est développé dans *L'Auteur et l'Ecriture*, Christian Bourgois, 1982, trad. de l'allemand.

12. On rapprochera cet "étrangement" de l'expérience de la drogue qui plonge la conscience dans le monde nocturne de l'intuition (*Drogues, approches, ivresses, Annäherungen. Drogen und Rausch*, Klett, 1970).

13. Cette prédominance de la figure est rappelée en 1986: "La seule chose qui survive, c'est la figure mythique du travailleur. Elle traverse les défaites, les guerres civiles, le feu et le sang, et se renforce à travers eux" (J. Hervier, *Entretiens* (...), p. 36).

14. Et aussi l'analyse de Marc Bloch, en 1940, qui souligne la défaite de l'imagination et l'effondrement du moral: les 'défaillances de caractère' chez les chefs, 'le mol affaissement des syndicats', la 'faiblesse collective' (*L'Etrange défaite*, Société des Editions Franc-Tireur, 1946, pp. 132, 158, 151).

A CHEVAL SUR LA FICTION ET L'HISTOIRE:

CLAUDE SIMON EN L'AN QUARANTE.

Anthony Cheal Pugh

> *Cette période 1940 a engendrée une littérature profuse. Le traumatisme qu'elle a provoqué a fait d'elle un creuset générationnel pour ceux, quel que soit leur âge, qui l'ont vécue: on ne s'étonnera donc pas qu'elle soit demeurée un enjeu de mémoire de première grandeur.*
>
> Jean-Pierre Azéma(1).

Dans *La Route des Flandres*, *Histoire* et *Les Géorgiques*,(2) les romans les plus connus de Claude Simon, un narrateur angoissé par la paradoxale présence simultanée d'images mentales remémorées et d'impressions toutes récentes s'interroge sur sa façon de vivre son époque, passant à la loupe les épisodes les plus marquants de sa vie. Le fascinent, surtout, les souvenirs qui correspondent aux divers 'rites de passages' de la vie: l'enfance, l'adolescence, l'initiation à la sexualité, et, finalement, la guerre et la mort. Avant toute autre chose, l'expérience de la déroute de mai 1940 semble l'avoir marqué de façon indélébile et il ne cesse de la revivre en mémoire.

Pourquoi Claude Simon continue-t-il, encore aujourd'hui, à réécrire sous forme de fictions ses souvenirs de la défaite? Qu'espère-t-il découvrir en revenant sur des lieux devenus à présent une série de *topoi* immédiatement reconnaissables? C'est *L'Acacia*(3) qui fournit les éléments d'une réponse à ces questions, confirmant par ailleurs ce que les lecteurs de Simon ont ressenti depuis longtemps: que tous les romans racontent, d'une manière ou d'une autre, la *même* histoire, celle de la quête d'un lieu à la fois géographique et symbolique: la tombe du père de l'écrivain, qui disparut en août 1914 au cours d'une des premières offensives allemandes. Dans les premières pages de *l'Acacia*, sur un rythme lent et funéraire, l'auteur évoque les recherches futiles de la mère, parmi les charniers de la grande guerre, en vue d'identifier le lieu exact où gît son mari. Avec ce roman, qui fait pendant à *Histoire*, il semble donc que Claude Simon rend hommage à ses parents: à un père purement mythique, connu à travers portraits, photos et anecdotes; à une mère digne et dévote qui assume presque trop naturellement le rôle de la veuve éplorée avant de devenir, peu après, une mourante méconnaissable au visage de Polichinelle.(4) Ces portraits, fidèles, romancés ou fantasmés, sont forts ambivalents, et c'est en regardant de plus près la façon dont les textes insistent sur le rapport d'homologie apparente entre le destin du père et l'histoire du fils, dans le contexte des deux guerres mondiales, que je vais interroger de nouveau, ici, quelques aspects de la *confusion volontaire* de l'histoire et de la fiction si caractéristique des romans de Simon.

Analysant certains effets de *la mémoire textuelle* chez cet auteur, j'ai décrit ailleurs la nature des conflits psychologiques chez l'enfant explorés dans certaines des plus belles pages d'*Histoire*,(5) mais il faudrait répéter, ici, que le but de ce travail n'était pas une *psycholecture réductive* des romans de Claude Simon. Au mieux, L'emploi d'une grille psychoanalytique permet d'émettre des hypothèses concernant une infime proportion des *transitions*(6) et des *coupures*(7) qui permettent à ce que l'écrivain a souvent décrit comme 'un magma' de souvenirs et d'impressions de devenir un *texte*, c'est-à-dire une séquence *composée*, plus ou moins *lisible*. M'intéressent en particulier, par conséquent, les moments où la difficulté 'technique' (continuer d'écrire, tout simplement) paraît surdéterminée: où 'ça bloque', pour ainsi dire. Ce moment est admirablement décrit dans *Les Géorgiques,* lorsque le scripteur, décrivant une ambuscade sur 'la route des Flandres', lève la main, incapable de faire la part de l'histoire et de la fiction, incapable de décider si la vérité (ce qu'il *sait*, ce dont il *se souvient*) est plus 'fidèlement' représenté, pour le lecteur, dans un récit autobiographique, fictionnel ou historique.(8)

Maintes fois débattu, le problème 'générique' (littéraire, philosophique, institutionnel) en recèle un autre pourtant, cette fois *générationnel*, qui me paraît central ici. Les romans de Simon y reviennent constamment, par toutes sortes de biais, et parfois d'une façon très directe. Il s'agit du rapport entre le sujet écrivant et le sujet écrit, donc du niveau de la personnalité artistique où le *moi* se trouve confronté à son *autre*, et où se révèle, périodiquement, la crise d'identité à l'origine l'activité créatrice, car créer, c'est chercher à se donner une identité à part soi, autonome, indépendant. La question de la place du sujet dans la lignée familiale, à commencer, bien entendu, par son rapport aux géniteurs, est donc capitale. Pour qui écrit-on, au fond? Lorsque le narrateur des *Géorgiques* pose la question de *l'adresse* de son texte, la question du rôle du lecteur empirique est en fait secondaire: tels 'bloquages' et la répétition/réécriture de scènes de guerre sont liés non seulement parce que le destinataire du texte, comme tout lecteur, est *absent*, mais parce qu'il est *mort. Mort sans sépulture,* en plus. Voilà pourquoi je me propose d'examiner le thème de la défaite par rapport au thème de la mort du père et de la survie du fils. L'hypothèse de travail est simple, impossible à prouver, mais tout à fait compatible avec les autres lectures produites par une oeuvre si riche. Elle consiste à dire que les grands romans de Simon illustrent le lent cheminement d'un voeu inconscient exprimé en fragments dispersés à travers le travail d'un demi-siècle et que son travail a entraîné la reconnaissance graduelle et sans doute pénible d'une dette filiale d'abord déniée mais finalement reconnue(9).

Telle dette ne peut jamais se solder, même symboliquement, cependant. D'où, peut-être, chez Simon, ce complexe de *répétition*: la part de l'imaginaire qui, ne pouvant pas accepter que le père ait disparu sans traces, continue de réécrire la mort de ce double incestueux de l'auteur, (double par la ressemblance - la coïncidence historique qui fait du fils un 'guerrier' 'comme son père' - et double par le travail de l'écriture qui le fait revivre de façon posthume). Ainsi - et c'est ce qui est inconcevable et inacceptable pour l'*ego* - l'auteur devient-il l'auteur de son auteur, ou, symboliquement, son propre géniteur.(10) Son travail se nourrit de la liberté et de l'indépendance financière qui résultèrent de cette mort, mais au prix de la répéter en l'imaginant.

L'hommage rendu au père dans *L'Acacia* paraît ainsi témoigner de la nécessité d'un travail de deuil tardif, conduit par le moyen de la reconstruction de la vie, de la mort et de la gloire posthume du père et de son régiment décimé. Juxtaposées aux scènes de la défaite de 1940 et de l'humiliation du fils qui, contre toute attente, ne meurt pas, les pages où est imaginée la mort du père constituent un arrière-fond sombre et émouvant au roman et, peut-être, une clef permettant de comprendre pourquoi le récit se construit dans un mouvement d'aller et retour du passé (du passé du présent de la représentation) au futur imaginé (dans le passé représenté) par le guerrier-narrateur: ce futur dans le passé, c'est sa mort certaine. C'est comme si le scripteur ne pouvait toujours pas comprendre pourquoi il a survécu, repassant dans sa tête le film de ses expériences de l'an quarante, revenant sur ses écrits antérieurs pour en remplir les blancs et en boucher les trous. L'écriture essaie de réaliser l'impossible: représenter les *transitions* constantes entre mémoire, imagination et perception présente et comprendre les *coupures* (opérations d'oubli et de censure) qui en rompent la texture continue. Le scripteur sait qu'il n'arrivera jamais à faire correspondre le passé tel qu'il l'a vécu (vu, senti) et sa re-présentation en mots, mais continue quand même - au prix de faire de la répétition l'une des caractéristiques les plus problématiques de son travail. Reconnaissant le problème dans *Les Géorgiques* (c'est l'une des signification des passages décrivant le mouvement de l'ombre de la main du scripteur sur son manuscrit(11)), Simon semble l'avoir assumé dans *L'Acacia*, soulignant les allers et retours dans le passé en donnant pour titre à chaque chapitre une date: 1919, le 17 mai 1940, le 27 août 1914, et ainsi de suite.

Le rôle de la mère - sans parler des soeurs du mari - est sans doute crucial dans *L'Acacia*, mais tout en soulignant, de nouveau, l'importance du 'versant maternel' des romans de Simon,(12) je me contenterai ici de noter que le récit des voyages réels effectués par la mère, à la recherche de la tombe du père, constitue l'arrière-fond essentiel aux récits, fragmentés, indirects, disseminés, *alterbiographiques*, où le fils se représente comme un jeune bourgeois révolté en train de se faire une nouvelle identité, d'abord par la peinture, ensuite par l'écriture. Malgré tant de récits où narrateurs et personnages tâchent de se libérer de leur passé (*Le Tricheur, Le Sacre du printemps, La Route des Flandres*), l'édifice littéraire crée par Claude Simon est manifestment hanté par quantité de figures parentales (souvent composites, superposées) et de ces portraits d'ancêtres qui ouvrent la voie à la construction de généalogies imaginaires. Symboliquement, c'est un *tombeau* (au sens poétique et musical): un lieu symbolique à la fois privé et public, un domaine où mythe et destin personnel coïncident et où le moi peut entretenir des rapports conviviaux avec ses autres au lieu de se battre avec eux, car il s'agit de soigner ses blessures narcissiques en les présentant comme appartenant à *autrui*: pas moi, *lui*, le narrateur-personnage à la tierce personne, ou 'le brigadier'.

En dépit de thèses et de théories, et à l'encontre du dogme central du *nouveau roman*, les romans de Claude Simon racontent ainsi quelque chose qui est de l'ordre du vécu (mais seulement à base de vécu), car l'ordre désiré par le scripteur est toujours *à construire* ou *à refaire*, d'où la nécessité d'un constant mouvement de *retour* dans le passé. Le 'référent' (autobiographique, historique), c'est ce que le texte *semble ramener*, mais abolit du même coup, laissant dans son sillage des *traces référentielles* étoilées de *références*. A la différence des 'référents', les *références* sont vérifiables: elles constituent autant de relais à une histoire collective encore en train de se faire, se défaire et se refaire.

Un exemple suffira pour montrer comment, malgré les efforts des puristes pour garder l'oeuvre de Simon à l'écart de l'histoire en marche, celle-ci (présentée dans *Les Géorgiques* sous les traits d'un dieu farceur)(13) a de nouveau démontré son étonnante capacité de rebondissement. Anecdotique, certes, cet épisode n'en est pas moins significatif: à la suite de la publication d'un article dans *Le Figaro* sur la campagne de mai '40 telle qu'il l'a vécue et où Claude Simon a décrit à nouveau la mort du chef de son escadron, brandissant son sabre contre l'adversaire invisible qui l'abat, l'écrivain a été menacé de poursuites par la fille du même colonel Ray qui fut le modèle du capitaine de Reixach de *La Route des Flandres*: l'écrivain aurait porté atteinte à l'honneur d'un soldat mort pour la patrie. Selon sa fille, Ray serait en fait mort ailleurs, et différemment. La mort du fictif capitaine de Reixach ne serait donc pas 'fidèle' au réel? Qu'importe? - c'est un *personnage de roman* qui raconte ses souvenirs et pose la question de leur 'fidelité' au vécu, non pas le romancier 'lui-même'.(14) Malheureusement, bon nombre de déclarations de l'auteur à l'intention de journalistes et un grand public incapable de comprendre de telles nuances ont systématiquement brouillé la distinction, cruciale, entre la fiabilité de la mémoire et la véracité de récits qui se servent de souvenirs, référents et références comme *point de départ* à un travail d'imagination et de 'bricolage'. *Le point d'arrivée* ne peut être que le lecteur, et celui-ci, pour qu'il soit relativement averti, ne s'intéresse pas du tout au réel, sachant que l'histoire et la fiction s'en réclament toujours, mais ne s'y rattachent que par le truchement de *présupposés de référence* qui, pendant l'acte de lire, permettent à l'imagination du lecteur de se brancher sur tel ou tel réseau de connaissances ou tel ou tel réservoir d'images, de souvenirs ou de fantasmes.

Ce à quoi notre lecteur aura affaire, chez Simon, n'a rien à voir, en tout cas, avec l'histoire en tant que *genre littéraire* ou *science humaine*, car le phénomène de *mémoire textuelle* que j'ai décrit dépend d'une expérience de lecture tout à fait particulière, où la répétition joue un rôle essentiel. Constamment, le lecteur simonien se trouve dans un *terrain familier*, mais s'il croit reconnaître telle province (les Flandres, le Jura, le Roussillon), telle ville ou même tel village, ce sera comme dans un rêve, car il s'agit de ce que l'on pourrait appeler les 'lieux communs' de la *mémoire textuelle*. Ce que le lecteur ressent, c'est le *déja lu*. De même, il reconnaîtra, ou croira reconnaître, des *présences familières*. Celles-ci, cependant, sujettes au travail de l'écriture, ne seront jamais *identiques*. Même les membres de la famille - la mère, le père, l'oncle, les tantes, cousins et cousines, etc. - connaissent d'étranges mutations, assimilations et reduplications. Si vérité autobiographique il y a dans les romans de Simon, ce n'est donc pas au niveau de la représentation d'un 'famille réelle', mais au niveau de la réalité du souvenir et du fantasme, où dates, identités et faits se brouillent (sont brouillés?) dans un étonnant *simulacre* de la mémoire du sujet écrivant. Le 'réel' auquel ce simulacre sera rattaché, enrichi de reflets et de reliefs imprévisibles, ne peut jamais être autre que celui *du lecteur*, et ce réel comprendra forcément un savoir, même des plus fragmentaires, situé dans un de ces *cadres contextuels* (culturels, historiques, biographiques) qui permettent de relier le particulier au général, et le privé au public.

Par le moyen de l'*alterbiographie*, Claude Simon a donc réussi cette gageure: rendre presque tangible, et terriblement convaincant, ce qu'il a vécu en mai '40. 'Illusion référentielle', diront les puristes - mais aucune pirouette théorique ne fera en sorte que les impressions et les fantasmes du lecteur ne se rapportent pas, de loin en loin, à travers ces relais complexes que sont un *contexte*,(15) à cet événement public que fut la défaite de '40. En lisant un récit d'histoire nous imaginons les événements en opérant des *présupposés de référence* correspondant aux conventions épistémologiques du moment; il en est de même des conventions de tout 'réalisme' littéraire. Ni fiction 'pure' ni histoire tout court, le récit simonien est à cheval sur tous les types de récit, du mythe au reportage. Pour narrateurs et personnages, le passé est présent mais insaisissable; pour le narratologue, le récit simonien est par définition aporétique(16): il n'arrivera jamais à son but. Aussitôt qu'ils commencent à se souvenir, à imaginer (et à écrire), le sujet écrivant et ses narrateurs et personnages se retrouvent à la dérive dans une zone temporelle où toutes les époques peuvent se superposer les unes aux autres. Inutile de dire que le lecteur ressent tout aussi fortement cette *confusion*. Légendes familiales, images remémorées, perceptions présentes - tout se présente *en même temps*. Il n'y a donc pas de commune mesure entre ce temps - celui de l'écriture - et celui de ce que nous appellons 'l'histoire'. Et cependant, celle-ci existe, si ce n'est que sous les traits de morts qui ne veulent pas se tenir tranquilles (ou d'une progéniture soucieuse de maintenir la réputation du clan et de la classe). L'histoire est aussi une question de *générations*, donc de choix: pour ou contre les parents, la famille, la patrie.

C'est pourquoi, tout en évoquant la débâcle de mai '40, il est nécessaire, s'agissant des romans de Claude Simon, de rester attentif à cette zone floue où mythe et réel se confondent et histoire et fiction se chevauchent. J'irais même jusqu'à dire que l'un des *plaisirs* spécifiques qu'offrent à leurs lecteurs les récits simoniens réside dans le statut souvent *ambigu* (et donc dangereux) du domaine référentiel qu'ils évoquent: en imaginant l'histoire de la déroute à l'aide des fictions, l'on retrouve, par exemple, tous les clichés habituels concernant une armée française incapable de résister au choc du *blitzkrieg*; la fiction confirme l'histoire et leur relation incestueuse (ou interdépendante) s'en trouve réconfortée. Lisant la fiction à la lumière des livres d'histoire militaire, par contre, l'on se rend compte très vite des dangers de mythification courus par tout récit, quel que soit le *genre* ou la *discipline* auquel il semble appartenir. Or, tout nous porte à croire que lorsqu'il écrivait *La Route des Flandres*, Claude Simon se fichait bien de l'histoire des historiens. Depuis, et peut-être à cause des activités des critiques (dont moi-même, qui lui ai demandé force précisions sur la campagne de mai '40), l'auteur a certainement lu ou relu des livres d'histoire militaire. Il fut très surpris et assez impressionné, lorsque je lui ai révélé, il y a quelques années, lorsqu'il travaillait au roman qui est devenu *L'Acacia*, que son escadron en retraite avait suivi l'avancée des panzers de Rommel, un général quasi inconnu avant 1940. Une page de *L'Acacia* est même la conséquence directe de ce renseignement (très) rétrospectif: un portrait du guerrier debout dans son char, imaginé sans doute à partir de photos et de reportages filmés qui, maintentant, appartiennent à notre mémoire collective de la guerre de '39-'45: 'le menton haut, rasé de près, droit comme un mannequin, avec son oeil d'oiseau de proie, son visage de cuir (...)'(*L'Acacia*, 329). Le stimulus initial qui a déclenché le processus d'écriture et qui nous a donné ce portrait (caricature?) de Rommel, fut néanmoins un *texte*: les photocopies d'extraits du livre de Liddel Hart que j'avais communiquées à l'écrivain.(17) A se demander par conséquent si, dans l'affaire du général (Rommel) et du colonel (Ray, sa fille), le romancier n'a pas perdu cet équilibre si délicat qu'il décrit dans son premier livre, *La Corde raide*,(18) dont il sera question tout à l'heure. Ce qui est sûr, c'est qu'en mai '40 Claude Simon ne savait pas qu'il marchait (chevauchait) sur les traces d'un géant - mais comme chacun le sait, impossible de contredire le type d'*histoire* qui se construit à rebours et se fige en *légende*. Pour les lecteurs de l'interview du *Figaro*, en effet, nul indice n'indique la route que j'ai suivie avant d'offrir à l'auteur ce *détail*, ce fragment d'un *cadre contextuel* incomplet du fait de la disparition ou du silence de tant de témoins.(19)

Et c'est pour ces raisons qu'il faut revenir à ce qui fait que la mémoire humaine et l'histoire des particuliers, des généraux et des colonels posent tant de problèmes, en interrogeant, un petit instant, le grand récit mythique qui sous-tend *Les Géorgiques*, le roman où Claude Simon a 'tout remis en question'.(20) Mes anecdotes le démontrent très clairement: on ne *se souvient* que parce qu'on *oublie*, parce que l'on a des blancs, des trous de mémoire, et parce que la vie mémorielle - selon la doctrine neo-freudienne, du moins - est entièrement soumise à l'influence de zones *interdites* ou *innommables*. Dans *Les Géorgiques*, Claude Simon a joué à un jeu un peu dangereux: réécrire le récit, qu'il considérait mensonger, d'un *autre* (Orwell). Mais il a également raconté un mythe très personnel (la recherche d'une morte dans l'espace infernal de l'inconscient) à travers l'histoire d'un personnage plus évidemment mythique: Orphée. De ces deux *alter ego* en OR, le deuxième est de loin le plus significatif pour le travail de l'écrivain et les problèmes que ses textes posent à une critique anxieuse de tout savoir, car l'histoire d'Orphée explique la nécessité de l'échec symbolique ou bloquage affectif initial qui est au coeur du désir de créer - et ce bloquage masque souvent une blessure plus ancienne. Les allusions à Glück et Virgile dans *Les Géorgiques* sont nombreuses et évidentes: le titre du roman invite même à une sorte d'assimilation du poème latin au texte moderne qui *emprunte* son titre. Le titre du roman constitue ainsi un *alibi*; ce qui est vrai, ou 'fidèle' peut également être faux. Quant au mythe plus ancien qui porterait la marque d'une 'blessure plus ancienne' et qui raconterait une histoire plus vieille que celle d'Orphée et de sa bien-aimée, c'est bien sûr celui qui raconte une autre descente aux enfers où un homme part à la recherche de son père et de l'origine de sa race. D'une part, c'est le désir de reconstituer une lignée, de sentir une appartenance à quelque chose. En même temps, c'est le désir tout à fait contradictoire de s'affranchir, devenir l'auteur de soi-même. Le scripteur est fait et défait par le texte, et celui-ci, le fruit de son labeur, *s'autogénère*.

Enée, aîné, né avant. On veut savoir 'comment c'était' pour l'*autre*; en l'occurrence, celui qui vous a fait, mais que vous ne pouvez connaître, *sauf à répéter l'histoire*. On peut jouer avec le nom d'Enée, mais c'est dans le Nom du Père que (le) *Ça* (se) joue. La coïncidence ORwell/ORphée résume aussi un conflit entre deux types de savoir, et deux types d'histoire. Dans le premier, le sujet *sait* qu'il n'y a pas de retour (mais beaucoup de possibilités de répétition). Il se retourne, et perd celle qu'il aimait. Dans le deuxième il retourne au passé, et retrouve son père (son aîné), et donc lui-même - et, partant, son autonomie de créateur. Le même gagne, en quelque sorte, contre l'autre; et le *daemon* de la création artistique l'emporte sur le reportage romancé, avec ses truquages, ses embellissements, ses censures.(21) Ainsi, chez Claude Simon, mythe, récit classique virgilien, paradigme inconscient universel et une histoire réelle (plusieurs) se superposent; on ne lit pas *La Route des Flandres*, *Les Géorgiques* ou *L'Acacia* pour en savoir plus long sur la déroute, mais pour faire dérouter son savoir.(22) C'est pourquoi, dans *L'Acacia*, il semble au jeune homme qui essaie de vivre *sa* vie entre deux guerres mondiales que l'on ne fait qu'attendre de lui qu'il solde la dette encourue: sa génération n'a grandi que pour mourir à son tour (*L'Acacia* 165, 190). Orphée, Enée - et (partout) Oedipe. Le thème de la quête du père se voit d'ailleurs doublé, comme dans *Histoire*, par des images de la mère mourante et des évocations, bien plus précises qu'auparavant, de la jeune femme dont le suicide inexpliqué hantait déjà le narrateur du roman de 1967; peut-être devons nous ajouter Ophélie à la liste des modèles, car l'inconscient parle très fort dans l'oeuvre de Claude Simon, à travers allusions et assimilations, métaphores et métonymies, censures et silences.

C'ainsi (très schématiquement) que se développe et s'enrichit, de roman en roman, le fil 'alterbiographique' de l'oeuvre.(23) Et s'il est évident, avec *L'Acacia*, que la tombe introuvable du père en forme le centre mythique, c'est parce que la quête de ce *topos* innommable et intouchable explique également la *mise en abyme* répétée des générations, la confusion et le téléscopage des géniteurs et génitrices. Cet abîme, c'est la mémoire elle-même, dans la mesure où l'écriture ne cesse de faire des plongées dans l'inconscient: un espace intemporel où les sons, le couleurs, les goûts, les mots et les noms se confondent. Il n'y a pas d'ordre ici, outre celui qu'imposent les écrits successifs et le travail de rationalisation de la critique (quelle est la critique qui n'essaie pas de trouver *l'ordre* secret de l'oeuvre?). C'est pourquoi nous allons suggérer, dans la seconde partie de ce travail volontairement *spéculatif* - c'est-à-dire attentif aux effets de miroir produits par le jeu du même et de l'autre, effets particulièrement puissants dans les textes simoniens - que cet 'ordre' est en fait celui que dicte le corps de l'écrivant. Si l'écriture simonienne marque une convergence croissante, depuis quelques années, entre récit *alterbiographique* et récit *autobiographique*, ce serait donc parce que cet ordre, celui du *corps*, relayé (et même étayé) par celui du *corpus* accumulé, obéit à une sorte de loi ou de pulsion immuable: la recherche de l'unité impossible d'un *moi* et des *doubles* produits par récits, représentations, reflets et répétitions.(24)

Les romans de Claude Simon sont réputés difficiles, mais dans *L'Acacia*, de loin le plus ouvertement autobiographique de ses romans, Claude Simon aide son lecteur (ses nouveaux lecteurs surtout) à débrouiller les identités et à identifier les époques en ajoutant des dates aux divers épisodes racontés. Autoritaire et mécanique, le temps du calendrier et des annales a de nouveau, et très littéralement, voix au chapitre. Comme si le roman simonien commençait à faire des concessions à un *ordre* qui ne serait pas purement esthétique. Cependant, reliées ainsi aux tables de l'histoire, personnes et voix perdent un peu du charme ambigu qu'ils exerçaient auparavant, et les fouilles entreprises dans l'imaginaire familial se transforment, petit à petit, en récit autobiographique plus conventionnel, comme si l'auteur cherchait finalement à 'restituer' le portrait de famille lacunaire des ouvrages antérieurs, comblant certains des trous les plus évidents dans le tissu de mots discontinu mais remarquablement cohérent que l'écrivain a 'bricolé' depuis *Le Tricheur*. Archive labyrinthique de souvenirs personnels, picturaux, littéraires et historiques, le roman simonien raconte un drame à la fois banal et monumental: celui de la constitution d'une personnalité d'artiste dans le contexte d'une inextricable confusion entre conflits personnels et publics (militaires, idéologiques, théoriques), conflits que résument et amplifient les incessants *retours* des textes vers cet événement crucial qui fut la déroute: la fin d'une vie d'un soldat destiné à mourir comme son père (*L'Acacia*, p.190), et le début d'une (vraie) vie de créateur.

*

C'est donc cette mort imaginée du sujet-narrateur, faisant écho à la mort du père réel, qui fait que l'expérience de la défaite militaire de la France constitue aussi une déconstruction du moi écrivant, expliquant ainsi pourquoi l'histoire de la débâcle constitue une pièce maîtresse dans l'édifice instable et mouvant du souvenir simonien et pourquoi les textes successifs y reviennent tout le temps. Et c'est pour cette raison qu'il faut regarder aussi du côté du sujet *ontologique* de ces fictions de plus en plus autobiographiques, car le dernier produit de ce lent travail dans les archives de l'imaginaire, *L'Acacia*, représente en fait un retour au point de départ: *Le Tricheur*, le premier roman publié par

Claude Simon, et *La Corde raide* (1947),(25) un curieux recueil de
'souvenirs' plus ou moins désavoué par son auteur. Cet ouvrage contient déjà
l'essentiel, cependant - à part un style capable de représenter les
opérations de la mémoire: c'est le début d'un travail de longue haleine,
puisqu'il s'agit de transformer une énergie créatrice bouillonnante, une
'vision simultanée' de l'oeuvre en procédures concrètes, en discipline
quotidienne et, au besoin, en procédés techniques. D'où une longue période
d'expérimentation compositionnelle et de raffinement stylistique, de 1947 à
1989, pendant laquelle l'évolution vers l'oeuvre future est toujours doublée
par un mouvement de recul et de rétrospection.

Les premiers romans après *Le Tricheur*, *Gulliver* (1952) et *Le Sacre du
printemps* (1954)(26) sont moins 'râtés' que l'on ne le dit, mais c'est avec
Le Vent (1957) et *L'Herbe* (1958) que Simon développe une technique narrative
et descriptive et un appareil linguistique capables de provoquer l'illusion
d'une conscience aux prises avec son passé. Une fois cette technique
acquise, avec tous les procédés caractérisitiques de cette période - une
abondance de participes présents, de parenthèses, de parenthèses à
l'intérieur de parenthèses - Simon pouvait abandonner définitivement et
chronologie romanesque traditionnelle et personnages unitaires. Après *La
Bataille de Pharsale* (1969), et jusqu'aux *Géorgiques* (1981), il semblait
avoir réglé son compte avec son passé, et donc avec la défaite de 1940.
L'écrivain ne semble plus porter son regard en arrière vers quelque
Eurydice, et l'ombre des ancêtres semblent peser moins moins lourd
qu'auparavant.

La préoccupation avec les qualités sensibles ou formelles du texte en
tant qu'objet esthétique ne fait qu'augmenter, cependant, l'écart entre le
présent de l'énonciation et ce que le sujet essaie d'énoncer ou de faire
dire au texte. Dans *Les Corps conducteurs* (1971) et *Triptyque* (1973), il n'y
a pratiquement plus d'écart entre le niveau de l'énonciation et celui de
l'énoncé. Comme les bords d'une blessure qui se répare, les trous creusés
dans les romans par les perspectives infinies de la mémoire en tant que
domaine *métaphysique* disparaissent, le texte devenant comme la surface d'une
toile non-figurative: sans profondeur illusoire, apparemment intransitive.
C'est la réalisation, semble-t-il, du rêve ricardolien de
'l'autoreprésentation': un texte autonome, où chaque partie représente le
tout, où l'on ne peut plus faire de distinction entre 'forme' et 'contenu'.
Ainsi (théoriquement) chacun des trois 'panneaux' de *Triptyque* autres, le
texte s'autogénérant sans avoir besoin de l'appui, ou de l'autorité, de
'référents' non-fictionnels, et, à plus forte raison, de références à
l'histoire.

Et pourtant, comme je l'ai démontré à l'époque, ce texte ultra-moderne
contient d'étranges souvenirs, très fragmentaires, de romans antérieurs,
surtout *Le Tricheur* - publié en 1946, mais écrit avant 1940 (27) - souvenirs
enfantins surtout, se rapportant à l'époque où la mère cherchait toujours la
tombe du père. Et dans *Leçon de choses*, autre exercice de style
'matérialiste', la campagne de '40 est de nouveau très présente, cette
fois-ci sous forme de 'divertissements' brillants, comiques, sombres,
délirants, et très ironiques. Simon y utilise, dans un discours de soldat
truffé d'obscénités, un épisode de la retraite, lorsque son escadron
défendait un village belge contre les artilleurs allemands qui précédaient
l'infanterie (les panzers fonçaient, entretemps, sur les nationales). Même
dans ses textes les plus 'expérimentaux' ou 'formalistes', les souvenirs de
la défaite travaillent et fournissent de la matière à écrire.

L'écrivain 'moderne' des années '70, devenu un 'scripteur', interroge de plus en plus près son *médium*, le langage, mais son passé est toujours là. Lorsque les narrateurs des romans antérieurs se lamentaient de ne jamais savoir 'comment c'était, exactement,' ce qui les gênait, c'était le fait de ne voir et sentir qu'à travers des mots, c'est-à-dire des signes, mais à présent (par exemple dans *Orion aveugle* ou *Leçon de choses*) le 'scripteur' rappelle à ses lecteurs, en bon maître à écrire, que dans la littérature les signes s'inscrivent sur du papier. Peut-être oublie-t-il un peu que dans la vie les signes de la mémoire sont inscrits dans et sur le corps, et de façon indélébile. Toujours est-il qu'il déclare, à plusieurs reprises, que la sémiologie et la psychanalyse sont fatales pour la littérature.(28)

Cette période 'moyenne' se termine, inévitablement, par une brouille avec Jean Ricardou, principal théoricien du nouveau roman, qui avait encouragé Simon (à partir de 1967 environ), à écrire des textes plus 'modernes'. Dépréciant, implicitement, dans toute la production de Simon antérieure à 1960, ce qu'il appelle leur contenu 'référentiel', Ricardou cherche à gommer la distinction, cruciale, entre référent historique et référent de fiction.(29) A la suite de cette affaire, Simon se replongera, cinq années durant, dans un projet qu'il nourrissait depuis des années: tirer un roman des papiers de son ancêtre, le général Lacombe St Michel. Il publie *Les Géorgiques* en 1981, y reprenant, dans une série de fragments dispersés à travers ce très long roman, et entrecoupés de descriptions d'autres batailles datant de l'ère napoléonéenne, le récit de la réduction de son régiment, entre le 10 et le 17 mai 1940, à un escadron de quatre, et finalement deux cavaliers. Pour la première fois Simon fournit, très explicitement, des noms de lieu, et quelques dates.

C'est le début de ce qui pourrait s'appeler 'la phase récapitulative'. La question posée plus tôt, dans *La Route des Flandres*, ou *Histoire*, 'comment était-ce, exactement?', ne revient plus. La remémoration du passé et la description des souvenirs ne change rien à rien: à travers son narrateur, et utilisant la troisième personne, Simon réaffirme ce qu'il avait déjà dit en 1960 dans une interview, à savoir que si tout ce qu'il avait raconté dans *La Route des Flandres* n'était pas vrai, c'était tout de même un récit 'fidèle' à ses souvenirs, vingt ans après la bataille. Mais la réalité, c'est ce qui échappe (Lyotard); lorsque les narrateurs des romans de Simon essayent de reconstruire ou de réimaginer le passé, ils se retrouvent devant une double ou même une triple absence: celle de la représentation imaginaire qu'ils fabriquent, qui tend constamment vers l'autoréférence et qui, tel Narcisse, risque de se perdre sans son propre reflet, celle du référent historique, inexistant, et, finalement, celle du référent de fiction, inventé de toutes pièces. Le texte ne 'représente' rien: il fait rêver, il fait fantasmer et il stimule la mémoire: celle de l'individu, et à travers lui, toute la culture qui l'a formé. Pour Freud, le corps avait sa propre mémoire: l'inconscient. Cependant, à la différence de la mémoire des personnages de roman, la mémoire du corps ne connaît ni succession ni durée: tout y est contemporain. Le 'passé' que la mémoire semble ranimer est illusoire: c'est maintenant que *Ça* passe. Entre 1969 et 1981, Claude Simon semblait écrire à son corps défendant, pour ainsi dire, et c'est pour cela qu'il est nécessaire de voir sa déclaration, selon laquelle il aurait 'tout remis en question' dans *Les Géorgiques*, comme un défi aux puristes plutôt qu'une façon de dire qu'il 'revenait' à ses préoccupations d'antan: l'histoire, la mémoire, la guerre. En réalité, il n'avait jamais cessé de brasser ses souvenirs de la déroute, cherchant toujours d'autres façons de s'y prendre. Il avait toujours considéré le

point de vue idéal de l'historien, suspendu au-dessus des événements et hors
du temps, non comme absolument faux, mais inadapté à son 'désir de faire'.
De toute façon, la tâche de l'historien, au niveau de l'imaginaire, consiste
à recréer l'*ethos* d'une époque ou d'un événement, alors que le romancier qui
situe son récit 'dans' l'histoire se préoccupe surtout d'en communiquer le
pathos, privilégiant l'optique subjective et le détail, c'est-à-dire, chez
Simon, un chaos d'images, d'odeurs, de sons et de pensées.

Tour à tour jeune garçon, adolescent, conscrit, homme mûr et vieillard,
le narrateur qui se réincarne dans chaque texte, mais différemment, est donc
à la fois lui-même, un autre, et d'autres: un moi, un moi idéal, un surmoi,
leur famille - et leurs ancêtres aussi. C'est pourquoi toutes les ressources
du langage - figures, structures, rythmes, coupures, sonorités, aspects
visuels du texte imprimé - étaient bonnes lorsqu'il s'agissait de constituer
ce *corpus* textuel, ou corps verbal, qu'est l'oeuvre. Les structures
narratives complexes et même contradictoires des romans de Simon servent
également à parodier ce qui sous-tend l'angoisse temporelle et la crise
d'identité qui frappent les personnages du roman moderne: une vue
simplificatrice de l'histoire basée sur la fausse logique déterministe du
type de récit - fictionnel ou historique, biographique ou autobiographique -
qui passe sous silence le rôle de l'imagination et du fantasme dans toute
reconstruction, représentation ou description du passé. C'est peut-être
pourquoi, préoccupé par le côté 'moderne', novateur et expérimental de
l'oeuvre - qui peut, il est vrai, en rendre l'accès ardu - les commentateurs
ont en général évité d'analyser comment l'imagination romanesque de Simon
fonctionnait par rapport au domaine des faits historiques: il semblait aller
de soi que le romancier ne s'y intéressait pas. Ainsi, préférant se pencher
sur les transformations inter- et intra-textuelles d'images, de scènes, et
même de vocables isolés, la critique littéraire s'est souvent contenté de
noter que l'intense vie mémorielle et fantasmatique des narrateurs et des
personnages des romans était nourrie par les souvenirs de l'auteur, et que
l'on avait affaire, par conséquent, à des 'fictions autobiographiques'.

Mais qui parle, au juste, ou qui écrit, plutôt, dans un texte dit
'autobiographique'? Qui est-ce, ce 'sujet' qui se rappelle et qui se
raconte? - les questions que posait à la littérature la critique
structuraliste me paraissent toujours cruciales ici, quoi qu'en disent ceux
pour qui la théorie littéraire est une affaire classée. Le 'sujet' véritable
du texte, n'est-ce pas en réalité les images, les souvenirs, et les paroles
qui remontent du passé pendant que l'écrivain travaille? Une fois
transformées en mots, les 'impressions' originales de l'auteur qui cherche à
les communiquer cessent de se rapporter à lui, rejoignant l'archive
historique et culturelle commune de la mémoire collective où se fondent
conscience historique et souvenir individuel. Il se peut même que les
impressions 'originales' de l'auteur - nous le verrons tout à l'heure -
soient moins originales qu'on ne le pense: comme n'importe quel autre
citoyen, sa façon d'envisager le passé est influencé par les événements
contemporains, et par la continuelle remise en question, par hommes
politiques, historiens, journalistes et particuliers, de ce passé qu'il
(l'auteur) a vécu mais qu'il ne peut revivre que par le moyen, si peu
fiable, de la réminiscence. Les distinctions théoriques entre récit
autobiographique, récit historique et récit romanesque sont donc déjà
instables, floues, et historiquement variables. Il n'y pas de représentation
directe de la réalité dans un texte, à moins que ce soit une réalité
linguistique, une copie (un faux même). Comme Barthes l'a noté, dans *La
Chambre claire*, seules les photographies sont capables de faire s'abolir,

tel un souvenir, un rêve, ou un fanstasme intensément vécu, l'écart temporel entre alors et maintenant.(30)

Essayant toujours de comprendre ce qui autorisait la transformation, chez Simon, de souvenirs physiques en *mémoire textuelle*, j'ai donc cherché à trouver un dénominateur commun entre *corps* et *corpus*. Et c'est de nouveau Barthes (dans ses essais sur la chanson) et des études psychanalytiques de *rythmes musicaux*, qui m'ont aidé à comprendre qu'il s'agissait surtout, chez le romancier, de *souffle*. Je ne suis pas le seul, bien entendu, à avoir noté ce phénomène, mais personne, à ma connaissance, n'a considéré jusqu'ici le rythme des *retours, reprises, répétitions* et *tranformations* des scènes de guerre *par rapport à la biographie de l'auteur* car le *corpus* est nécessairement en rapport d'homologie partielle avec le *corps* de l'écrivain lui-même. C'est pourquoi il faut parler ici de *La Corde raide*.

Claude Simon fut pendant longtemps très peu enclin à parler ce cet essai d'autobiographie artistique, maintenant une extrême discrétion concernant la période de sa vie qui précéda son émergence, autour de 1957, dans le groupe de nouveaux romanciers réunis par Jérôme Lindon aux Editions de Minuit. Toujours est-il que *La Corde raide* est l'oeuvre, me dit Simon en 1969, d'un homme un peu confus, mais surtout en proie à des angoisses 'atroces'. C'est un texte-symptôme, ou un texte-cri, le produit, manifestement, d'un profond conflit psychique et même d'un état physique maladif (c'est à cette époque que, suite à un diagnostic qui révéla une tuberculose avancée, Simon fut opéré d'urgence, sans anésthésie, perdant l'usage de la moitié de l'appareil respiratoire au cours d'une tentative de regonflement d'un poumon affaissé).

Mélangeant récits personnels et commentaires plus généraux sur les moeurs et les valeurs de l'homme moderne, dit civilisé, le texte tourne néanmoins, de façon obsessive, autour de trois sujets: la mémoire, la mort et la valeur finale de l'activité artistique. Malgré le ton emphatique, désinvolte et sarcastique qu'il adopte, l'auteur de *La Corde raide* est très préoccupé par les problèmes de style que lui posent son essai autobiographique. Dès l'incipit, le texte témoigne du désir contradictoire d'écrire d'une manière à la fois libre et littéraire: 'Autrefois je restais tard au lit et j'étais bien' (p. 9). Le résultat ressemble à une parodie involontaire d'*Oblomov*, ou à une mauvaise pastiche de la première page des *Plaisirs et les jours*. La page finale n'est d'ailleurs pas plus réussie, car c'est dans une sorte de rêverie vaguement panthéiste et une tentative d'inversion de la perspective temporelle 'naturelle' de l'autobiographie que se clôt *La Corde raide*: 'Les branches passent à travers moi, sortent par les oreilles, par ma bouche, par mes yeux, les dispensant de regarder et la sève coule en moi, m'emplit de mémoire, du souvenir des jours qui viennent me submergeant de la paisible gratitude du ciel' (p. 187).

Si ce texte gênait Claude Simon en 1969, et le gêne encore, c'est parce que la voix qui parle sonne faux, révèlant, entre autres, un sentiment de culpabilité très vif concernant 'celle qui m'a trop aimé' (p. 187): c'est déjà l'un des *leitmotifs* d'*Histoire*. Ne sachant pas trop à qui s'adresse son texte, le narrateur ventile ses opinions au hasard de sa plume et se lance, tel un acrobate mal entraîné, sur une corde raide tendue au-dessus du précipice du sublime, du ridicule - et de l'intimité. L'image de la corde suspendue sur un vide illustre néanmoins le caractère du défi artistique de Simon, un écrivain qui ne réussit à se faire reconnaître, et à écrire comme il le voulait, que dix ans plus tard, après *L'Herbe*. Son programme était simple, pourtant: 'essayer de me rappeller ce qui s'est passé pendant le moment où j'écrivais' (p. 178). Et encore maintenant, par exemple en répondant à la question, 'quels conseils donneriez-vous à un jeune écrivain', Simon a tendance à donner une réponse semblable: 'allez dans la rue pendant dix minutes, retournez dans votre chambre, et décrivez tout ce que vous avez vu, ressenti et pensé.'(31) La simplicité même, dirait-on. Mais en 1947, toujours en colère contre ceux pour qui il avait failli mourir tant de fois pendant la déroute et après son évasion d'un *stalag* allemand, Claude Simon n'arrive pas encore à écrire comme il le voudrait. Aussi se contente-t-il de raconter des anecdotes, commençant à décrire des épisodes de guerre, mais attaquant surtout l'inauthentique sous toutes ses formes.

L'exemple de Paul Cézanne, modèle, depuis *L'Oeuvre* de Zola, du peintre incompris par les bourgeois de son temps, lui fournit une cible toute faite. S'en prenant aux préjugés esthétiques et moraux des défenseurs de valeurs artistiques traditionnels, le narrateur de *La Corde raide* affirme que pour comprendre le réel, il faut réapprendre à percevoir le monde, de préférence avec des yeux de peintre. Manifestement, pour Simon, rien ne compte, à trente-quatre ans et la guerre finie, en dehors de la vie du corps et de l'ouverture des sens à la beauté du monde. La reconnaissance par la partie la plus pauvre de la machine corporelle et mentale - la raison - de la tragique fuite du temps et de l'irréversible perte de sens qui en résulte est ressenti comme une blessure ouverte d'où coule, en permanence, la signification de nos actes. Un tableau de Cézanne dit tout cela, mais n'a pas à le mettre en mots, et les formules brutales employées dans cette première tentative d'autobiographie témoignent de la frustration d'un autodidacte (son propre terme) cherchant à exprimer une philosophie esthétique très personnelle, mais très simple aussi:

Si, lorsque vous vous trouvez devant un tableau, un sentiment de joie, de tumulte ou de calme ne naît pas en vous avant même que vous ayez pu distinguer ce qui est représenté, c'est, ou bien que le peintre est complètement nul, ou bien que vous êtes infirme et qu'il vous manque un sens. Alors vous pouvez faire votre deuil de la peinture et chercher des satisfactions ailleurs.(*La Corde raide*, p. 99)

Dire quelque chose, raconter ce qu'on pense, c'est obligatoirement énoncer des opinions et porter des jugements, mais à force de se raconter et de commenter les choses de la vie, on finit par ressembler à tout le monde. D'où la conclusion du narrateur de *La Corde raide* que l'autobiographie conventionnelle est une entreprise vouée à l'échec, une vaine tentative en vue d'arrêter le temps. Le livre s'arrête, comme par hasard, au moment précis où le narrateur aborde ce problème, celui de la paradoxale présence/absence du passé dans le présent qui marche. De toute façon, objections éthiques et esthétiques abondent: le fait de parler de soi est un acte indécent, et on n'écoute bien, de toute façon, que les bons raconteurs, qui trichent systématiquement. Comment faire alors, lorsqu'on est à la fois révolté, mais pas si jeune, rentier, mais pas si riche, et ancien combattant, quoique pas si vieux? Qui s'intéressera à vos petites histoires, à part un éditeur complaisant, quelques amis et une poignée de lecteurs? Pourquoi faire mine de rejeter les valeurs de monsieur-tout-le-monde alors qu'en réalité, on ne fait que chercher, dans la solitude de l'acte créateur, sa voix d'écrivain?

Est-ce pour ces raisons que dans *La Corde raide* Claude Simon invective si violemment contre les auteurs de récits truqués, qui trichent avec le temps, les créateurs de spectacles en trompe-l'oeil et autres faux-semblants? Face aux difficultés que j'ai énumérées, il semble que l'écrivain ait choisi, comme tant d'apprentis autobiographes, et probablement sans y réfléchir, de jouer un personnage dans *La Corde raide*:

celui, comme par hasard, du jeune homme en colère. Porteur, pendant un an, de la carte du PCF, le réserviste de '39 et le rescapé d'une débâcle qui, prétend-il toujours, fut le fait de la 'trahison' des hommes politiques et des généraux, risquait donc fort de se retrouver, dans le miroir de ses 'souvenirs' écrits, sous les traits d'un   classique anarchiste. De droite ou de gauche, peu importe: il devenait un personnage, et cessait - dans son texte - d'être une personne. D'où quantité de remarques, dans *La Corde raide*, niant, de façon très rimbaldienne, la notion d'*identité*. Les remarques sur la société ou sur la politique que l'on retrouve dans *La Corde raide* sont également négatives, grinçantes, et pessimistes   - et pas très convaincantes. Le narrateur est pris dans un tourniquet: il ne croit plus en l'espoir d'un avenir meilleur, ou d'une société plus juste, mais ça le gêne d'avoir à le dire si crûment. Il a conclu, semble-t-il, comme Flaubert, que l'oeuvre d'art est seule capable de témoigner de la valeur d'une vie humaine. L'intensité avec laquelle l'écrivain - ou le peintre - enregistre ses impressions et exprime la violence de son désir de sentir tout, jusqu'au bout, contre la mort, constitue la seule raison d'être de l'oeuvre. Peu importe si la maladie qui le cloua au lit cinq mois durant entraîna un état dépressif ou vice versa: Simon souffrait encore et des conséquences morales de la défaite et des suites de son emprisonnement en Allemagne.

Le narrateur qui se penche sur son passé dans *La Corde raide* est ainsi arrivé à un tournant dans sa vie, et le fait d'écrire ses 'souvenirs' constitue un essai, cette fois-ci dans le sens d'une tentative assez désespérée, pour sortir d'un état devenu intolérable. Tâchant de voir, à travers le récit indirect de ses déboires personnels et celui, plus franc, du désastre de 1940, une issue et une solution à 'son désir de faire', c'est-à-dire de créer, il se relança dans l'écriture. *Le Tricheur*, son premier roman, paru en 1946 mais écrit en 1939, n'avait pas eu de succès, éclipsé par *L'Etranger* de Camus, auquel certains critiques l'avaient comparé. Revenant à lui-même, pour ainsi dire, ce rescapé du désastre, dont l'apparence, à l'automne de 1940, après son évasion du camp de prisonniers effraya tant le garçon de café lorqu'il débarqua du train un beau matin à Perpignan, et terrifia ses vieilles tantes (qui croyaient, justment, voir un fantôme, (*L'Acacia*, p. 342)) décida d'écrire à peu près n'importe quoi: il suffisait de s'y remettre.

Si *La Corde raide* contient peu de détails contextuels, consistant surtout en impressions et en anecdotes, et s'il n'y a aucune tentative de synthèse des souvenirs de l'auteur concernant la défaite, c'est donc pour deux raisons principales. D'abord, le narrateur ne sait pas comment réconcilier son désir de faire avec les exigences du langage, qui oblige à dire. Il a tout de même toujours envie d'écrire, ayant abandonné ses études de peinture avant la guerre. Ce qui fait défaut, tout bêtement, c'est l'envie de se raconter et de soumettre ainsi sa vie, son passé, aux lois de la narration. Chronologie, ordre, voix, focalisation: rien de tout cela ne compte, son seul désir étant de décrire les impressions qu'il a enregistrées, si réelles qu'il croit être douée de ce que les psychologues appellent 'la vision éïdétique', les images persistant sur sa rétine plus longtemps que chez le commun des mortels. Ce n'est que vers la fin des années cinquante, après avoir 'travaillé vingt ans dans le noir', que cela lui sautera aux yeux, pendant qu'il s'efforce, avec *La Route des Flandres*, de trouver une forme adéquate, convenant à son désir de montrer 'comment c'était', qu'il se rendra compte que c'est avant tout une affaire de composition, de rythme, et de souffle.

Dans *La Corde raide*, le narrateur était engagé dans ce qu'il appelait
'une course de vitesse', arrivant plus ou moins bien au bout de ses phrases,
désespérant de tout noter, essayant tant bien que mal de capter le flux de
ses pensées et de ses humeurs. Dans sa tardive maturité, et avec un poumon
de moins, le 'scripteur' qu'il sera devenu produira des phrases, ou des
périodes, bien plus longues que celles de l'asthmatique du boulevard
Haussman. Paradoxal à première vue, ce rapport inversé entre le corps de
l'auteur et ce que Didier Anzieu appelle 'le corps de l'oeuvre', entre le
souffle créateur et le souffle vital, tend à justifier les hypothèses
psychanalytiques selon lesquelles des lois inflexiblement contradictoires
règlent le travail de l'inconscient, du rêve et de la création artistique.
La période de l'après-guerre correspondrait chez Simon, selon la théorie
d'Anzieu, au moment du 'saisissement créateur':
> 'Le saisissement créateur peut survenir à l'occasion d'une crise
> personnelle (un deuil à faire ... une maladie grave, une
> liberté reçue ou conquise qui élargit le champ des possibles,
> la crise d'entrée dans la jeunesse, la maturité ou la
> vieillesse). (...) Son contenu psychique s'étend de la
> représentation unique, dotée d'une grande vivacité, à un flot
> déferlant de sensations, d'émotions, d'images'.(32)

La Corde raide est en effet le récit d'une crise très semblable. Simon y
raconte, pour la première fois, des événements qui lui fourniront, pendant
près de cinquante ans, de la 'matière à écrire'. Il remplit aussi quelques
blancs: le réserviste de *L'Acacia* qui a fait des études de peinture, épouse
une jeune femme qui pose pour lui; brièvement, et de façon toujours anonyme,
la disparue de *La Corde raide* et *Histoire* retrouve sa place dans la galerie
des revenants.

De même que le détail des épisodes de guerre resta vague pendant au
moins quarante ans, c'est-à-dire jusqu'aux *Géorgiques* de 1981, de même le
réquisitoire personnel qu'il finit par dresser contre les hommes politiques
qui imaginèrent la stratégie de l'avance jusqu'à la Meuse grâce à laquelle
son régiment fut anéanti en mai 1940 demeure inédit, figurant dans une
correspondence avec l'auteur suscitée par ma demande de précisions
concernant des noms de lieu dans *La Route des Flandres*.(33) Depuis la
défaite, Simon est retourné dans les Flandres au moins une fois, et il a
interrogé d'autres témoins. Il a maintenant (en 1991) 78 ans et il ne faut
pas s'étonner si cette 'phase récapitulative' l'amène à remplir des blancs,
revoir et corriger le récit de son long apprentissage d'écrivain. Dans *La
Corde raide*, par contre, le futur Prix Nobel ne s'était pas encore rendu
compte qu'un texte quelconque, autobiographique ou non, s'adresse en fait à
son expéditeur et aux fantômes qui habitent son inconscient, et non au
destinataire, vaguement imaginé, qu'est le lecteur empirique éventuel. Le
narrateur de *La Corde raide* écrit trop fort, pour ainsi dire, et, mal visé,
son texte n'arrive pas à son but: lui-même et ses autres. L'autobiographe
aussi est un revenant - un autre soi-même qui revient sur ses propres
traces. *La Corde raide* correspond donc à un double défi: se défaire d'un
passé récent traumatisant, et se lancer dans le vide d'une carrière
d'écrivain. Pour la première fois, Simon essaie de décrire des scènes de la
débâcle: la retraite jusqu'à la Meuse, la course à pied dans la tranchée de
chemin de fer, la mort du colonel. Mais c'est décousu, informe - et il pose
des questions trop directes à l'histoire.

Et c'est là que nous voyons, de façon très claire, la racine du
problème, car malgré tout le travail d'écriture effectué entre 1947 et 1989,
les textes n'apportent jamais de réponses aux questions qu'ils posent, et

Claude Simon n'arrive toujours pas à comprendre comment il sortit vivant du guet-apens que tendirent à l'armée française les auteurs du Plan Jaune: Von Mannheim, et Hitler lui-même. En 1947, en tout cas, c'était toujours trop proche, trop absurde:

> Un après-midi de printemps (...) je me suis tout à coup trouvé tout seul, en train de courir lourdement sur un ballast, au fond d'une tranchée de chemin de fer du haut de laquelle, un peu en arrière de moi, des types me visaient. J'avais, pendant les quarante-huit heures précédentes, parcouru environ deux cents kilomètres à cheval, à peu près rien mangé, encore moins dormi et été soumis aux secousses nerveuses habituelles dans ce genre de circonstances. J'étais de plus, saucissonné de courroies, bretelles, harnachements, et trimballais sur moi un attirail brinqueballant, supposé nécessaire et suffisant pour le rôle auquel on me destinait. C'est-à-dire qu'en courant j'arrivais à me déplacer un peu plus vite qu'un couple de retraités en promenade, un peu moins vite qu'un marcheur pressé. (*La Corde raide*, p. 49)

NOTES

1. *1940 l'année terrible*, Jean-Pierre Azéma, (Paris, Seuil, 1990), pp. 9-10.
2. Paris, Minuit, 1960, 1967, 1981.
3. *Ibid*, 1989.
4. Par exemple, *Histoire*, p. 61.
5. 'Histoire d'une lecture - lecture d'*Histoire*', dans *Le Lecteur et la lecture dans l'oeuvre*, (Clermont-Ferrand, Association des Publications de la Faculté des Lettres et Sciences Humaines, 1982, pp. 185-6).
6. Voir notre article, 'Du *Tricheur* à *Triptyque* - et inversement', *Etudes littéraires*, 9, 1976, pp. 137-160, où sont étudiés un certain nombre de 'transitions' significatives pour l'étude du travail de la mémoire chez Simon.
7. Voir 'Claude Simon: fiction and the question of autobiography', *Romance Studies*, 8, 1976, pp. 81-96, où nous analysons le thème de la 'coupure' temporelle.
8. Voir notre article 'Facing the matter of history: *Les Géorgiques*', dans *Claude Simon New Directions*, ed. A.B. Duncan, (Edinburgh, Scottish Academic Press), 1986, pp. 113-130 pour une réflexion sur ce passage.
9. La base théorique de cette approche est posée dans les articles cités ci-dessus, notes 5 et 6.
10. *Ibid*.
11. *Les Géorgiques*, p. 47.
12. *Art. cit*, note 5.
13. *Art. cit*, note 8, pp. 126-129.
14. *Ibid*, pp. 121-126.
15. Voir le chapitre intitulé 'Fiction, history, text and context' que nous avons contribué au collectif *Cross-References*, (The Society for French Studies, 1987), pp. 111-122.
16. *Art. cit,*, note 8, pp. 126-129.
17. En juillet 1984.

18. Paris, Editions du Sagittaire, 1947.
19. Voir le travail cité ci-dessus, note 15.
20. La phrase est citée par S. Sykes dans *'Les Géorgiques*: une reconversion totale?', *Romance Studies*, 2, 1983, pp. 80-89.
21. Voir notre article, 'La tentation autobiographique chez les anciens nouveaux romanciers', *La Chouette* (Birkbeck College, University of London), 17, 1987, pp. 32-42.
22. Voir l'article très pertinent de P. O'Kane, *'La Route des Flandres*: the rout(e) of the reader?', dans *Claude Simon New Directions* (note 8).
23. *Art. cit.*, note 7, p. 92. Le terme *alterbiographie* a l'avantage de souligner le rôle de l'autre dans l'autobiographie, les changements que l'écriture effectue au niveau du 'moi écrivant', et la différance (la distance) entre autobiographie et biographie.
24. Voir, dans 'L'illusion romanesque', de Cleusa Rios Pinheiro Passos, *Texte* 10, 1990, pp. 121-134, la section intitulée *'un miroir inquiétant'* et *'l'identité: un risque angoissant'*, pour un commentaire utile sur la question du double et des reflets (pp. 123-127).
25. Epuisé depuis très longtemps, ce texte n'a jamais été republié, sans doute à cause des sentiments de l'auteur à son égard.
26. Paris, Calmann-Lévy, 1954; Livre de poche, 1975.
27. Paris, Sagittaire, 1946 (épuisé).
28. Par exemple devant une assemblée franco-anglaise à The Institute of Contemporary Arts, Londres, en 1985.
29. Voir notre travail 'Claude Simon et la route de la référence', *Revue des sciences humaines*, 220, 1990, pp. 23-45.
30. Paris, Seuil, 1980.
31. Réponse à une question de l'auditoire, Colloque de Genève, 1986.
32. Didier Anzieu, *Le Corps de l'oeuvre*, (Paris, Gallimard), 1981, p. 91.
33. Voir l'article cité ci-dessus, note 29.

IMAGE AND COUNTER-IMAGE: ANDRE GIDE AND THE OCCUPATION

Michael Tilby

After the Fall of France, the English literary world not surprisingly maintained a keen interest in the fate of French writers and in the various ways in which they succeeded in making their voices heard.(1) In certain circles, there was an especial interest in the war-time activities of André Gide, as he moved first to the unoccupied South, then to Tunis, where after a while he was encouraged to go into hiding, and finally to Algiers. This interest in Gide was above all true of the critics and men of letters who came into the orbit of Cyril Connolly's francophile literary review *Horizon*, the title of which, if Stephen Spender is to be believed, derived from the frequency with which the word *horizon* appeared in Gide's *Journal*. For Connolly and Spender, as for kindred spirits such as Raymond Mortimer, John Lehmann, and E.M. Forster, Gide occupied a privileged position among French writers, essentially for the values that in their view made him a humanist and, in many cases also, for his public stance on the question of homosexuality. Their admiration for Gide was based solidly on his pre-war utterances, but, as we shall see, they united in a view of him that stressed in addition what they saw as his distinguished contribution to the preservation of France from the insidious values of the Vichy government. (This was in spite of the fact that in 1940 Gide had declined Spender's invitation to become a contributor to *Horizon*, saying 'j'ai fait voeu de silence.')(2) Connolly in particular shared Gide's belief that it was essential in wartime to keep alive an interest in the civilising values of literature and the arts. But there was a general ambition in this circle to prise from the ageing French writer contributions for their literary ventures, whether as editors or translators, and once travel became possible, Gide was visited in Algiers by Constantine Fitzgibbon, Mortimer, Jiri Mucha (John Lehmann's collaborator on *New Writing*), and Harold Nicolson. Spender went straight to see Gide in Paris after the latter's return to France in the summer of 1945, and it was presumably at Mortimer's instigation that Gide in 1943 replied to a questionnaire for the *Sunday Times* about the state of France.

As is well known, E.M. Forster took Gide as the subject of one of his radio broadcasts in 1943 and spoke for many of the writers already mentioned when he highlighted the four qualities that made Gide a humanist: 'curiosity, a free mind, belief in good taste, a belief in the human race'.(3) Forster was also commissioned by the British Council to write a 'Homage to André Gide' for the Cairo edition of the Free French newspaper *Marseillaise*, though the paper appears to have been suppressed before Forster's piece could appear.(4) Although the 'Homage' bears much similarity to the radio broadcast, it also contains certain significant references of more contemporary interest. Gide is described as having condemned defeatism. An unspecified passage from his *Journal* is adduced as evidence for the view that he 'demolishes Vichy a quarter of a century before Vichy existed'. Forster goes on to say: 'How natural that, to-day, such a mind should be with the Free French. [...] We English writers have not yet been tested as French writers have been tested. If the hour of our trial comes, may we remember the example of Gide.'

He protests that it is not his intention to cast Gide in the mould of a hero, for Gide himself would have disclaimed such a rôle, but there is no mistaking Forster's desire to emphasize Gide's courage in adversity:

'Returning to unoccupied France, he continued to espouse truths which he alone, owing to his prestige, was able to get printed. Instead of playing for safety, he used his high position to uphold still higher the torch of freedom. Then Hitler advanced again and occupied the south. Gide got away to Tunis.'

This desire on the part of Forster and other English men of letters to see Gide as a pillar at least of opposition, if not of resistance, was not wholly lacking in supporting evidence. His credentials as patriot were emphasized by the attack on him that was published on 9 July 1940 by *Le Temps*,(5) a paper that until taking up residence in the Midi he had read on a regular basis. The leading article in this particular issue was devoted to the new educational reforms proposed by the Vichy Minister, M. Rivaud, but the author took the opportunity to proclaim: 'On ne peut nier l'influence exercée sur la littérature contemporaine et sur l'esprit de la jeunesse par les ouvrages d'André Gide. C'est contre cette influence considérable, mais néfaste, qu'il faut aujourd'hui réagir. L'auteur séduisant de *L'Immoraliste* et du *Traité de Narcisse* a fait une fâcheuse école. Il a formé une génération orgueilleuse et déliquescente; il l'a élevée sous prétexte de sincérité, dans la perversion du sens moral.' Arnold Naville, who brought Gide a copy of the newspaper from the town of Vichy itself, encouraged Gide to reply but the latter saw little point.(6) He realized that the article in *Le Temps* might well lead to the banning of his works, but it was up to his young readers to defend him. As for the ancient charge of 'corrumpere juventutem', it was, he noted, so often ill-founded and much more likely than fulsome praise to put the accused 'du bon côté de la gloire'. He further pointed out that the texts of his that had been singled out for castigation had appeared before the First World War and that the young men of that generation had in fact 'assez vaillamment combattu.'

In November 1941 *Horizon* published a letter from an anonymous French correspondent reporting on the now well-known fiasco surrounding the lecture that Gide had agreed to give in Nice that May on the poetry of Henri Michaux, a further example of these strident attempts to lay the blame for France's defeat on Gide's pernicious influence on French youth.(7) The lecture, which Gide later described to Valéry as 'la plus anodine des conférences',(8) had been organized by the young homosexual Jewish writer Roger Stéphane.(9) A lengthy letter - and one which Gide evidently came close to admiring - from the propaganda section of the Alpes Maritimes branch of the Légion Française des Combattants gave further credibility to Gide's opposition rôle by issuing veiled threats of what might happen if he went ahead with his lecture.(10) The author of the letter described the situation in which France found herself as the most pertinent criticism possible of Gide's work. Having heaped scorn on Gide's pale and indecisive 'personnalité politique', this *ancien combattant* went on to claim that politics anyway was a dirty word from the past and that his action was not motivated by political considerations. Defending himself in advance against the charge of philistinism, he asked the author of *Les Nourritures Terrestres* to ensure that Nathanaël and all his family were well and truly forgotten. The letter was opened by Roger Stéphane, who was then joined by Martin du Gard, and at the latter's suggestion, André Malraux. It was Malraux who declared that Gide would have to cancel the lecture and read a brief statement in its place attacking his opponents. A change of heart by the Légion was an unwelcome complication, but it was decided that Gide's statement should make it clear that, either way, no decision he took would be dictated by the Légion. If he was not now going to give his lecture it was in order to avoid civil disorder: 'j'ai trop grand souci des intérêts de la France pour engager une lutte sur un malentendu'. It took Gide five minutes to read his ten-line statement amid stupendous applause and cries of 'A bas la Légion'. A certain wry satisfaction was to be gained when it was learnt a few days later that there had been 165 resignations from the Légion. Gide none the less regretted that, as a result of censorship, reports had made it seem as if he had given way to pressure from the Légion thereby recognizing the errors of his ways. In reality it was only the local newspapers that had distorted the affair - the Vichy press itself described it rather more accurately.

In London the *Review of the Foreign Press*, then compiled by the Foreign Research and Press Service of the Royal Institute of International Affairs (and later by the Research Department of the Foreign Office), noted in August 1941 that just as defeatism had produced some strange bedfellows, so opposition had thrown together Gide and Thierry Maulnier, contributor to the *Action Française*, in that both had penned 'brilliant attacks' on the defeatism of Jacques Chardonne's *Chronique privée de l'an quarante*. They had thus both given evidence of 'moral courage and intellectual independence'. The point was derived from an article by Claude Roy who had noted that while *L'Action Française* insisted on placing their trust in Pétain, they were just as ready to attack the 'totalitarian mystagogy which is spreading from Paris to Vichy' as their traditional democratic targets.(11)

There was also the fact that after momentary hesitation Gide had broken with the *Nouvelle Revue Française* now that the editorship had passed into the hands of Drieu la Rochelle.(12) Instead, his name was to appear in Seghers's *Poésie 41*, thereby enhancing his image as a potential resistant. In 1944 excerpts from his *Journal* relating to the liberation of Tunis appeared in the second volume of the anonymous *Chroniques interdites* published by the clandestine *Editions de minuit*. There were those in London who were ready also to attribute to him the authorship of *Le Silence de la mer*, which, under the then unfamiliar pseudonym Vercors, had likewise been published by Minuit. This was something of a party game: Forster kept Vercors's work within the original NRF group by attributing it to Jean Schlumberger.(13) Others similarly thought it might be by Roger Martin du Gard. The Gidean attribution was doubtless encouraged by the introductory note that accompanied the serialization of *Le Silence de la mer* in the then London-published *Marseillaise*.(14) Not only was it attributed to 'un grand écrivain', tribute was paid to 'la claire pureté de cette langue, la noble et logique ordonnance du récit'. Still in London, Gide's obituary for Pierre Viénot, the son-in-law of his Luxemburger friends the Mayrisches, was published in *La France libre* and in the volume of Viénot's *Discours et messages* printed on behalf of the Gaullists. Thus at each stage of the war there was something to keep alive the image of Gide the resistant, provided the observer was so inclined.

In fact not all were so inclined. As we shall see, there were those who were determined to form a very different image of Gide in wartime, while an examination of both his behaviour and his writing reveals a much more complex position than Forster and some of Gide's other London admirers were in a position to appreciate.

Certain murmurs of dissent may be seen to surface behind the scenes in London as a result of a little known plan to bring Gide to England in the summer of 1943.(15) In a lecture he gave in Edinburgh that year, Cyril

Connolly spoke of the need for Britain to import one or two Frenchmen
rather than allow Europe's artistic talent always to cross the
Atlantic.(16)   With or without knowledge of this lecture, Raymond Mortimer
wrote to an old schoolfriend who was Anthony Eden's Principal Private
Secretary asking him whether he might use his influence to bring about
Gide's wish to come to Britain. The BBC French Service was keen to have him
and he added: 'My concern is to have him write for English papers about
French resistance and culture. We have no first-rate French writer in this
country and we need one.' Desmond McCarthy reported on the possibility of
Gide's visit in the *Sunday Times*(17) and added his voice to those who would
welcome it. The impending visit was also advertised, though with decreasing
certainty, by Forster in the successive published versions of the broadcast
already mentioned. It all points to a concerted effort.

   An early Foreign Office memo states as received opinion that Gide was
the author of *Le Silence de la mer* and described him as having shown
'considerable moral courage' in some of his wartime writings. Britain's
Resident Minister in Algiers, Harold Macmillan, was asked to find out
whether Gide was drawn to the idea of coming to Britain. He reported that
'owing to his age and health he obviously will not be able to do much
propaganda work and you of course realize that he has strong Gaullist
sympathies.' The British Council's newly appointed representative, Austin
Gill, himself sent word that Gide was in fact enthusiastic about the idea.
He announced that Gide's attitude since June 1940 had been one of 'courage
and dignity', but he too emphasized Gide's advanced age and stated a
preference for inviting Gide's fellow Algiers resident Max-Pol Fouchet, the
editor of *Fontaine*, though he recognized that Fouchet could not reasonably
be invited if Gide were not. The Foreign Office took the view that they
could hardly take exception to 'strong Gaullist sympathies', but it was
decided that it would be prudent to ascertain the views of Gide's old
friend Enid McLeod who, in all but name, was in charge of the French
section of the Ministry of Information. This was wise. McLeod was keen to
see Gide in London and she thought his presence alone would be of
propaganda value. Yet she feared that an official invitation would lead the
Foreign Office to expect concrete results in return for their money. She
warned: '[Gide] has never in all his life had to do anything he did not
want, and he is by nature the sort of person who immediately wants to do
the   opposite from anything that is suggested to him. I am sure that it
would be utterly impossible ever to get him to sit down and write a
pamphlet for PWE or give a lecture for the ministry.' As for the Gaullist
question, she went on to add: 'some telegrams have seemed to suggest that
he was very Gaullist, while others intimated that he did not want to come
under their auspices. However I know that he is a very old friend of Pierre
Viénot's and that he attaches great importance to Gide's visit.' Even
Forster had been prepared to recognize the essentially apolitical nature of
the figure he was proposing for his readers' admiration: 'But, oh my Free
French friends, you have with you a very unusual bird! His plumage is not
political and never will be. He was hatched in an aviary which produces
birds as different from him as Montaigne, Voltaire and Renan, three of the
eagles of France.'

   At the Foreign Office there was considerable toing and froing of
memos. By now there were officials who were decidedly opposed to Gide's
visit, clearly worried about Gide's reputation. There were financial
problems also. Meanwhile on 5 August Gide lunched with Duff Cooper and
Harold Macmillan (Noel Coward, whom, according to Anne Heurgon, Gide much

admired, was also present and sang his new song: "Don't let's be beastly to the Germans") and the Minister cabled to London that Gide was becoming very 'fretful and sulky at receiving no news about his proposed trip to England.'(18)   Eventually after much dragging of feet, it was decided that the British Council could invite him for a week and that he might be allowed to stay on for a month or so as a private visitor. This is the last trace of the matter. Gide did not come. Max-Pol Fouchet did.

It is understandable that McLeod should be uncertain about Gide's Gaullism. In Algiers Gide had the opportunity of dining with de Gaulle on more than one occasion. The General undoubtedly made a strong impression on him. Gide's diary entry for 26 June 1943 reveals that they discussed, albeit in vague terms, the need for 'une nouvelle revue qui groupât les forces intellectuelles et morales de la France libre ou combattant pour l'être' and he confided to himself: 'Je ne ferai pas de difficulté pour raccrocher à lui mes espoirs.' Yet at one luncheon party given by de Gaulle, it appears that his mood was rather different.(19)   Finding himself next to Harold Nicolson, he turned and said: 'Vous ne m'avez pas demandé à quoi je travaillais en ce moment.' To which Nicolson replied: 'Mais, maître, entre écrivains, cela ne se demande pas.' 'Demandez-le-moi tout de même, à voix haute, je vous prie', Gide insisted. Nicolson duly obliged and Gide trumpeted the reply 'A une biographie de Pucheu.' (Pucheu, the hated member of Doriot's PPF, had been executed by the Gaullist authorities, probably at the instigation of the communists whose comrades had largely formed Pucheu's victims.) Was it on this occasion that Gide broke a long silence by asking de Gaulle: 'Mon général, dites-moi, quand avez-vous eu envie de désobéir?' Max-Pol Fouchet, who claimed to have acquired this story from those who were present, related that 'l'insinuation était géniale [...] et machiavélique, voire satanique. Le regard de l'écrivain se posait, rieur, sur le général, comme s'il avait joué un bon tour. Et d'ailleurs, c'en était un'.(20)   Fouchet also claimed to have expressed to Gide his fears that de Gaulle was becoming too authoritarian. His memory was of Gide being a true Gaullist at this time and, as such, reluctant to take note of anyone who did not approve of the leader *dévotieusement*. (Anne Heurgon later claimed that under Jean Amrouche's influence in Algiers, which was considerably more extensive than that of Saint-Exupéry, 'Gide se croyait ou se voulait gaulliste ... les boutades souvent très spirituelles de Saint-Exupéry contre le général ne l'amusaient pas.')(21) On this occasion Gide is alleged to have replied: 'Ce qui m'inquiéterait, moi, c'est qu'il ne le fût pas assez, autoritaire.' Fouchet concluded that Gide, who had done so much to arouse in his generation an awareness of freedom, was at heart 'un homme singulièrement épris d'autorité'. The fact remains that Gide's involvement with the Gaullists, does not seem to have been all that great.

But the questioning of Gide's usefulness or the emphasis on his apolitical nature was nothing compared to the outright hostility he attracted from certain other quarters. And notably from the communists who had never forgiven him his 'U turn' with regard to the Soviet Union in the mid-1930s. On 6 July 1944 there appeared in *Liberté* an attack on Gide motivated by his diary entry for 9 July 1940, which had appeared in the latest number of Gide's Algiers review, *L'Arche*, and in which Gide had written that a high proportion of Frenchmen would accept the German invader if the latter could guarantee them food in abundance: 'Si la domination allemande devait nous assurer l'abondance, neuf Français sur dix l'accepteraient; dont trois ou quatre avec le sourire. Et il n'y a pas à s'en indigner, non plus que de ce que j'en dis.'

The outraged journalist contrasted Gide's success at eating his fill with the resistants in France who each day faced death on an empty stomach. There followed a threat issued in the form of a prediction: 'Gageons que M. Gide rira moins, demain, en France libérée.' The following day in the Consultative Assembly, the Communist Resistance Delegate for Corsica, Arthur Giovoni, drew the Assembly's attention to the entry in Gide's *Journal* for 13 July 1940, in which the writer had claimed that solidarity between citizens was too abstract a notion for people to be able to feel it easily. Gide was once again brutally frank: 'moins de sucre, dans le café, et moins de café dans les tasses; c'est à cela qu'ils seront sensibles.' The French farmer would willingly accept that Descartes and Watteau had been Germans if it were a way of getting a better price for his corn. No less offensive to Giovoni was the provocative way in which Gide had opened his entry for Bastille Day 1940: 'le sentiment patriotique n'est du reste pas plus constant que nos autres amours.' The Communist delegate asked Bonnet, the Commissaire à l'Information, whether the publication of such sentiments should be tolerated and then went on to proclaim that if Clemenceau had been alive, Gide would have been arrested and bought before the Military Tribunal under the article of the code prescribing the death penalty for treason in wartime, the review would have been suppressed, and its allocation of paper transferred to one of the few 'journaux et revues patriotiques d'Alger.' Bonnet adopted the obvious defence, that Gide's comments had been written in special circumstances when all communications, both internal and external, had been cut off and at a moment when 'une lourde oppression s'appesantissait sur la France'. Giovoni had taken these remarks out of context; other, slightly later diary extracts that Gide had published in *L'Arche*, expressed his delight that the French people had not rallied to Vichy. Bonnet took the opportunity to claim that only a handful of writers had rallied to Vichy and that 'l'immense majorité', 'la quasi-totalité d'entre eux', including Gide, had spurned Vichy's blandishments. Giovoni was not satisfied and turned his attention to Gide's 'narcissistic' consideration of himself to be 'au-dessus de la mêlée'. Gide was guilty of defeatism, he had located patriotism in Frenchmen's stomachs, advocated working for Hitler and Pétain, insulted the French peasant and all those Frenchmen who were in prison camps, and in general had judged the French people in the way he had judged the peoples of the Soviet Union. The communist deputy claimed to have been told also that the manuscript of the *Journal* contained the statement: 'Ce qu'on nomme aujourd'hui collaboration et trahison pourrait s'appeler bon sens.' He ended by calling for Gide's imprisonment. His answer to those elderly ladies and ephebes who would be scandalized by such a call was to offer them solace from the idea that in prison Gide would produce writings superior to those of Silvio Pellico, the author of *Le mie prigioni*. What is particularly striking about this attack is the way that it also talks of Gide's deplorable influence ('influence morbide') on a sector of French youth in terms that would have beeen perfectly at home in the mouth of a Pétainiste. Giovoni thus castigates 'la manie de cet homme "de naviguer contre le courant", pour "épater" le lecteur, sa manie de l'original et de l'excentrique, son immoralisme érigé en système, la perversité de ce protestant qui a mal tourné, cette perversité qui lui fait écrire une défense de la pédérastie'.

Others were prepared to come to Gide's defence, notably the columnist Claudine Jaques, who wrote a piece for the 'Left Catholic' weekly *Quatrième République* under the heading 'Faut-il fusiller Gide?'(22) Though the editor prefaced her article with a note to the effect that it was not to be seen as an apologia for Gide's work, Jaques was determined to judge Gide solely on the totality of the extracts he had published from his diary, observing that you don't have a man shot on the basis of a manuscript you haven't read. Elsewhere in the published extracts, Gide had made it abundantly clear that soon after the summer of 1940 he came to regret his previous remarks.(23) It was, she observed, a *mea culpa* all the more meritorious in that Gide could have had no idea of the *épuration* that was in store. Sadly, Giovoni's attacks recalled, she said, the Vichyite attack on Gide at the time of his lecture on Michaux and the Légion's subsequent use of violence in the name of 'Travail, Famille, Patrie' to sabotage a *Lettres Françaises* exhibition in Fès that had included the work of 'les écrivains de la corruption Marcel Proust and André Gide': 'Ils voulaient, déjà, ces totalitaires fascistes, tout comme M. Giovoni, "faire de la littérature une arme de guerre", alors qu'elle est une arme de culture.'

Giovoni was ill-advised to include in his attack invoking the spirit of Clemenceau a jibe at *les vieilles dames* among Gide's admirers, for it was none other than Clemenceau's octogenarian niece who was moved to write to Gide on the very day of the attack to claim that Clemenceau's tiger's claw would have been reserved not for him but for the false patriotism of Giovoni, whom she variously described as 'sinistre imbécile' and 'crétin présomptueux'.(24) Clemenceau, she told Gide, shared his view of the 'égoïsme étroit de la paysannerie'.

There is no doubt that the attacks on Gide in *Liberté* and by Arthur Giovoni were Moscow-inspired and that, more specifically, they were the result of the influence of Gide's former associate Ilya Ehrenburg, whose view of Gide as a traitor went back to the publication of the latter's *Retour de l'URSS*. Ehrenburg was a frequent contributor to the Algiers press and on more than one occasion used his articles to attack Gide in terms that are by now familiar. In June 1944, as the Soviet correspondent of *Marseillaise*, he attacked the first number of *L'Arche*.(25) Or rather its writers, whom he denounced as aesthetes moved by the slaughter and bloodshed of the war that was still being waged. In placing themselves 'au-dessus de la mêlée', they were lining up with 'les héros du marché noir, les fournisseurs d'aluminium du Comité des Forges, ces messieurs de Vichy'. The job of 'soldats de plume' was to 'attiser le feu de la haine'. The review's manifesto was guilty of equating the Russian Revolution with the fascist seizure of power in Germany and Italy, a commonplace, Ehrenburg adds, in the PPF and Vichy press. Less than a week later *Liberté* reported in great detail a lecture Ehrenburg had given in the Trades Union Palace in Moscow the previous month and in which he had begun by describing Algiers pointedly as 'l'arche de Noé', adding 'nous nous rappelons que, dans l'Arche il était entré de tout: du propre et du pas propre'.(26) In his *Marseillaise* article, Ehrenburg claimed that he had been motivated by an assertion he had heard during a radio broadcast that the creation of *L'Arche* was to be counted an event, a symptom of the rebirth of France, and the triumph of culture (Mme Théo observed that there was no shortage of things to be saved by the Ark!)(27), whereas it was in fact 'un symptôme de la maladie incurable qui a frappé certains éléments de la société française'. It was the similarly warm reception accorded to *Le Silence de la mer* that led Ehrenburg to mount an equally venomous and largely contestable campaign against Vercors's story.(28) When he claimed 'seul un André Germain pouvait ainsi décrire des officiers allemands', was this perhaps perhaps a way of signalling that he too wondered whether the story was in fact the work of another A.G.: André Gide?

There was, it seems, little for this orthodox Communist that was 'propre' in Algiers and plenty that was 'pas propre'. He certainly inveighed against *Fontaine* in the pages of which 'des esthètes sauvés du déluge et nourris d'un peu de saucisson américain y dogmatisent que l'art doit être au-dessus des passions et que l'on n'a pas le droit de se laisser séduire par la haine du Boche.'(29)   Before the foundation of *L'Arche*, Gide had contributed to *Fontaine* (though not when first approached in July 1940), but neither this nor the fact that the two reviews elicited almost identical invective from Ehrenburg, brought them into close alliance. One of *Fontaine*'s editors, Henri Hell, while protesting friendship for Gide, indeed expressed considerable misgivings about the manifesto of *L'Arche*, precisely on the grounds that it paraded a definition of France to which no-one could object, not even Maurras, above all, not Maurras, he said.(30) Hell went on to accuse *L'Arche* of ignoring certain 'réalités internationales'. It is easy to appreciate the irritation of the *Fontaine* team. Their review had braved the authorities in much more difficult times and the risk of being eclipsed by a new review as a result of the international prestige of its patron was all too apparent to them.(31) They were jealous of a pedigree that would allow historians subsequently to emphasize *Fontaine*'s heroic defence throughout German and Vichy rule of 'l'honneur de l'homme' and 'la liberté de l'esprit'. Good submissions were not plentiful and it was not clear that there was room for two literary reviews in Algiers. This was very much the line taken by Max-Pol Fouchet in his autobiography published in 1968, but he went much further, launching into an extraordinarily personal and vindictive attack on Gide twenty-five years after the event, partly as an attempt to counter what he considered to be the over-sympathetic (but in fact not entirely contradictory) portrayal of Gide that had recently been published by the latter's Algiers hostess, Anne Heurgon, daughter of Paul Desjardins, with whose Pontigny décades Gide had been closely involved in the years leading up to the First War.(32)   Fouchet chose to paint a picture of a disagreeable and self-absorbed figure, who cheated in order to avoid losing at chess, strutted around in the brightly coloured striped shirts given to him by English and American soldiers, was an incorrigible 'pique-assiette', and who while claiming that *L'Arche* had been created for Jean Amrouche who had been so good to him, in fact saw it as the answer to his obsession with having his own review.

With the liberation first of North Africa and then of Paris, there seemed little room for Gide to make a contribution. Those who now wielded power and influence included some who had been no less critical of him than Vichy had been. At the end of August 1944, Gide was quick to send a 'message amical' to the editor of the *Figaro* expressing not his own joy as an individual, but that of North Africa at the news of Paris's new-found freedom and the republication of the newspaper.(33)   During the years in which freedom of speech had been impossible both writer and paper had, he maintained, nonetheless been united 'de coeur et d'esprit' but 'au point que je ne trouve aujourd'hui rien de particulier à dire'. That autumn, while still in North Africa, he joined the Comité National des Ecrivains. *Les Lettres Françaises* marked the event by publishing extracts from his *Délivrance de Tunis*. But this provoked a long and furious response from Aragon, whose work Gide had in fact gone out of his way recently to support.(34)

Aragon recognized that Gide had not actually written for *Je suis partout* and that he had not gone on from his *Retour de l'URSS* to recruit for the L.V.F., but he was adamant that *Les Lettres Françaises* had not been created with such courage and amid such dangers in order to accommodate the triumphal home-coming of André Gide, who had done so much to try and separate France from her Soviet friends. Those returning from North Africa had had some unpleasant things to relate about Gide but he will restrict himself to what Gide had written since 1940. He finds much in Gide's wartime journal that disturbs him, starting with Gide's determination to study the German language and with what is seen by him as Gide's reading and re-reading of Goethe out of a sense of duty in the face of German military success. The admiration for Hitler is said to be unmistakable in some of the diary entries and he claims 'admirer le génie hitlérien est la marque de ce genre de conscience que nous avons déjà connu sur son retour de l'URSS'. These were precisely the entries in the *Journal* to which Ehrenburg had taken exception in yet another attack he had launched on Gide, this time in *Pravda* the month before Aragon's article.(35)   Aragon goes on to quote some of the entries that had earlier scandalised Ehrenburg and the communists in Algiers, including the entry of 5 September 1940 which Giovoni had known only second-hand and had therefore been able to reproduce only in approximate fashion. What Gide had actually written was : 'Composez avec l'ennemi d'hier, ce n'est pas lâcheté, c'est sagesse; et d'accepter l'inévitable.' Detecting an unconscious alexandrine in one of the statements that follow, Aragon is led to observe: 'Il y a une poésie de la bassesse, sachons-lui gré de nous y faire accéder.' In a postscript he addresses those who have died in Europe: 'O Saint-Pol Roux, Bergson, Basch, Pulitzer, Marc Bloch, Max Jacob, Benjamin Crémieux! Et vous, les autres, qui importez si peu à M. Gide, les sans-noms, de Tulle, d'Oradour-sur-Glane, d'Ascq, de Fresnes, de Montluc, de Compiègne, d'Auschwitz ou de Lublin, que dites-vous de la vertu de M. Gide, esprit libre?'

English expectations of Gide and above all E.M. Forster's admiration for Gide as a symbol of moral courage appear to have been without their counterpart in France. If we look at Gide's record, there is perhaps little that allows us to hold on to the view of him as a key figure in opposition to Vichy or the German invader. There is much to suggest that this septuagenarian's over-riding concern was with his personal comfort and safety. Planes were ready to take him to London in 1943 and to Rome in 1944 but he preferred to remain in North Africa. He was slow to return to Paris after the Liberation. His commitment to Gaullism has not left much of a trace. In conversation with Roger Stéphane as late as December 1941, he revealed that although he wished for the rebuilding of France, he had difficulty in believing in it for the time being. (36) It was France's lot to be protected either by Germany or by the Anglo-Saxons. He had always been a partisan of a Franco-German alliance and it was true that Hitler's grandiose plan impressed him. (It was nevertheless not impossible, he confided to Stéphane, that a victorious Hitler would turn into an Augustus, 'prisonnier de la grandeur de son personnage'.) But the concerted effort by the Communists to use entries from his *Journal* to turn him into all but a collaborator does them little credit. This illustrates how the fate of France allowed old divisions and antagonisms to be given still more violent expression. A more dispassionate reading of the *Journal* shows Gide, the devotee of Montaigne, determined to retain an individual and honest voice in contradistinction to the false languages being spoken around him. There is little doubt that for this reason he found Vichy more deeply antipathetic than the German invader.

And it is at this point and as a form of conclusion that we have to remark on a surprising omission in the French reaction to Gide's war-time pronouncements, namely the 'imaginary interviews' that he contributed to *Le Figaro* in 1941 and 1942. It was these texts that were almost certainly the basis of the official British view in 1943 that Gide had shown courage in his opposition to the regime. At first sight, these discussions of linguistic usage, literary genre, and metrics and prosody might seem to represent, as the character who is being interviewed indeed pretends, a total ignoring of political questions.(37)   (Arthur Koestler, though no longer a Communist, certainly alleged that they made for 'distressing reading'.)(38) Yet in fact these fictional interviews, a form which Gide had first tried in *L'Ermitage* in 1905, have not received the attention they deserve. They invite a reading as examples of double entendre that succeed in revealing Vichy values for the sham that they are. An un-responsive reading, such as that of the censor, will feel that Gide is working with categories that are acceptable to the ideology of the regime, but what these texts show is Gide recovering from Vichy concepts and terms that the regime had misappropriated. The attentive reader is led to realize that the interviewee is using language in fundamentally different ways from the interviewer, whose Pétainist qualities in the process become increasingly clear. It may be that Gide's opponents on the Resistance Left, in ignoring these satires on Vichy, were continuing the process of selectivity they practised with regard to the *Journal*. More likely, perhaps, is that they failed, as did Koestler, to realize what kinds of texts these were, since the language they spoke was in essence much closer to that of Vichy than to that spoken by Gide. For such readers the mere presence of a subject or a particular word is immediately indicative of the political acceptability or otherwise of the writer. Gide seems, in contrast, to imply that the rebirth of France was dependent on an activity that broke out of the very conceptual framework that was common to both ends of the spectrum in order to build the world afresh. As he makes clear in both the *Journal* and the *Interviews imaginaires*, to try to rebuild straightaway using existing concepts was to build on sand. It was not an approach that those actively involved in contemporary political action and polemic in France could perhaps be expected to accommodate. It is surely no concidence that it was to a much greater extent Gide's English readers, and notably Enid Starkie and George Painter,(39) who later showed themselves alive to the particular suggestiveness of these far from anodine texts.

Notes

1.   Gide's relations with the English literary world in this period form part of the more detailed study of Gide and England on which I am currently engaged.

2.   See the unpublished letter of Gide to Stephen Spender of 18 December [1939], now in the Humanities Research Center of the University of Texas at Austin.

3.   E.M. Forster, 'Gide and George' in *Two Cheers for Democracy* (Abinger edition), edited by Oliver Stallybrass (London: E. Arnold, 1972), pp. 220-23.   There exist various texts, published and unpublished, of this broadcast (see ibid., p. 370).   See also Michael Tilby, 'André Gide, E. M. Forster, and

G. Lowes Dickinson', *Modern Language Review*, 80 (1985), 817-32. (My conjecture in this article, based on an interpretation of a statement in Francis King's biography of Forster, that Gide and Forster met twice before the War was incorrect: they met but once, in 1935.)

4. The manuscript of this article is now in the Humanities Research Center, Austin, Texas.

5. This was not the first attack on Gide after the defeat of 1940. On New Year's Day 1941, Peyrade, writing in *La Croix*, inveighed against 'un romancier de l'immoralité qui, nous l'espérons bien, n'aura plus de lecteurs' (quoted by W.D. Halls, *The Youth of Vichy France* (Oxford: Clarendon Press, 1981), p.163; Halls mentions similar attacks by Guéhenno and others; see also on this subject H.R. Kedward, *Resistance in Vichy France* (London: Oxford University Press, 1978).)

6. See Gide's diary entry of 16 July 1940.

7. *Horizon*, IV, 23 (November 1941), p. 344.

8. André Gide-Paul Valéry, *Correspondance 1890-1942* (Paris: Gallimard, 1955), p. 523 (letter of 21 August 1941). See also Gide's diary entry for 14 June 1941.

9. See Roger Stéphane, *Chaque homme est lié au monde* (Paris: Editions du Sagittaire, 1946), and Maria van Rysselberghe, *Les Cahiers de la Petite Dame* (Paris: Gallimard - *Cahiers André Gide*, 1975), III, pp. 246-47.

10. The text of the letter is given by Stéphane, pp. 285-86.

11. A member of the occupying forces, Bernhard Payr, referring to Gide's attack on Chardonne, spoke of 'le fin et pénétrant, mais aussi malveillant André Gide, toujours aussi déconcertant' as having published 'une critique heureuse très violente' (see Gérard Loiseaux, *La Littérature de la défaite et de la collaboration d'après Asche oder Asche de Bernhard Payr* (Paris: Publications de la Sorbonne, 1984), p. 236). Chardonne was defended by Maurice Martin du Gard (in *La Dépêche de Toulouse*, the selfsame paper to which Anthime Armand-Dubois contributes his scientific articles in *Les Caves du Vatican*).

12. Gide's break with the NRF was directly related to the position adopted by Chardonne, (see Gide's postscript to his letter to Dorothy Bussy of 30 March 1941 - *Correspondance André Gide-Dorothy Bussy*, III (Paris: Gallimard - *Cahiers André Gide*, 1982), p. 196). The first number under the new editorship contained texts by Alain, Eluard, Gide, and Valéry, but several of these had of course been commissioned or submitted before Drieu took over.

13. E.M. Forster, *Commonplace Book*, edited by Philip Gardner (London: Scolar Press, 1985), p. 155. Forster had been given the book to read by Raymond Mortimer and recorded that he had 'read it without much admiration though with plenty of sympathy'.

14. *Le Silence de la mer* was serialized in *Marseillaise* in February and March 1943.

15. Much of the following information on the projected visit of Gide to London comes from a Foreign Office file now in the Public Records Office at Kew (series FO 371/36287-file Z5519 of 1943). I am greatly indebted to Dr Tony Kahane for bringing

this file to my attention. Dr Kahane has himself drawn on this file in his article 'André Gide in North Africa during the Second World War', *European Gay Review* (forthcoming). Included in the file is a typescript of Forster's 'Homage to Gide' that differs only slightly from the manuscript already mentioned.

16. Cyril Connolly, 'French and English Cultural Relations', *Horizon*, June 1943 (reprinted in *The Condemned Playground* (London: Cape, 1945)).

17. *Sunday Times*, 27 June 1943.

18. This was almost certainly the luncheon to which Anne Heurgon-Desjardins refers when she relates the remark made by another guest, André Maurois, about Gide's behaviour in Coward's company: 'Quel curieux homme que cet André Gide!... Comme il est peu aimable! Au déjeuner de l'ambassadeur où j'étais son voisin de table, il n'a fait devant moi que vanter les films des autres' ('Gide à Alger' in Marcel Arland & Jean Mouton (eds.), *Entretiens sur André Gide* (Paris & The Hague, Mouton, 1967), [1]- 12 (p. 5).)

19. What follows is based on the account given by Roger Stéphane, *Fin d'une jeunesse* (Paris: La Table ronde, 1954), pp. 111-12.

20. Max-Pol Fouchet, *Un Jour, je m'en souviens* (Paris: Mercure de France, 1968), p. 133.

21. Heurgon-Desjardins, art.cit., p. 6.

22. *Quatrième République*, 22 July 1944.

23. Gide's belief that resistance was hopeless was indeed shortlived. (Note also his opening comment in his letter to Dorothy Bussy of 5 January 1945.)

24. For the text of Mme Berthe Zuckerkandl's letter, see André Gide, *Journal 1939-1949. Souvenirs* (Paris: Gallimard - Bibliothèque de la Pléiade, 1954), p. 346.

25. *Marseillaise*, 3 June 1944.

26. *Liberté*, 8 June 1944.

27. Maria van Rysselberghe, *Les Cahiers de la Petite Dame* (Paris: Gallimard - Cahiers André Gide, 1975), III, p. 313.

28. *Marseillaise*, 27 May 1944.

29. *Liberté*, 8 June 1944.

30. *Fontaine*, 33, p. 351.

31. Loiseaux notes (p. 563) 'Dès la signature de l'armistice Max-Pol Fouchet entamait la lutte dans la revue *Fontaine*, créée quelques années auparavant à Alger.'

32. Fouchet, *Un Jour, je m'en souviens*, pp. 124ff.

33. 'Un message d'André Gide', *Le Figaro*, 10 September 1944.

34. *Les Lettres françaises*, 25 November 1944.

35. A translation of the *Pravda* article of 2 October 1944 may be found in the Foreign Office file already mentioned.

36. Stéphane, *Chaque homme est lié au monde*, p. 94.

37. Thus Jean-Jacques Thierry speaks of 'une suite de chroniques grâce auxquelles [Gide] se promène librement dans le jardin de la littérature' (*André Gide* (Paris: Hachette, 1986), p. 170). Gide's interest in the alexandrine at this time was motivated by the close attention he paid to his daughter, Catherine's training to be an actress (see, for example, his letter to Valéry of 15 August 1941 and his letter to Dorothy Bussy of 14 March 1941).

38. 'Gide's writings have always shown a touch of esoteric arrogance; there is a thin, rarefied atmosphere about him and his books. His influence on the younger French generation was deplorable (not because of his twisted eroticism, for which the Vichy Fascists reproached him: one does not become an invert by reading books), but because of the arrogant spiritualism it imparted, an attitude of being initiated, the illusion of belonging to some exclusive order, of sharing some exquisite values, which, however, if you tried to define them, ran like sand through your fingers, Gide's message to the young intelligentsia was like the Emperor's new clothes: nobody dared to confess that he could not see them [...] Judged by his *Imaginary Interviews*, Gide has changed little, if not for the worse. There is the same ethereal boredom, a pale fluorescence which throws no shadow and has no substance behind it. I read them some months ago and cannot remember a single phrase or thought: the sand has run away and all that remains is some vague fragrance, Yet if the word message applied to literature has any meaning, it is this that its gist should remain in your memory after the words have faded' ('The French 'Flu' in *The Yogi and the Commissar* (London: Cape, 1945), first published in *Tribune*, November 1943 under the title 'Literary Idolatry'). The antagonism was not mutual: Gide had approved of Koestler's *Spanish Testament* when he read it in French translation several years previously (see his *Journal* entry for 9 February 1941).

39. See Enid Starkie, *André Gide* (Cambridge: Bowes and Bowes, 1953), p. 52, and George D. Painter, *André Gide, A Critical Biography* (London: Weidenfeld & Nicolson, 1968), pp. 125-26.

JULIEN GRACQ AU BOIS DORMANT:

AUTOBIOGRAPHIE, POESIE ET LA DROLE DE GUERRE

Peter Whyte

Publié en 1958, *Un Balcon en forêt* est une contribution tardive à la littérature consacrée à cette période traumatisante pour la France qui s'étend de la *drôle de guerre* à la débâcle de mai et de juin 1940. Pourquoi Julien Gracq, qui fut mobilisé à la fin du mois d'août 1939 comme lieutenant dans le 137ième régiment d'infanterie, qui se battit en Hollande et en Belgique aussi bien que dans le nord de la France, qui fut prisonnier de guerre en Silésie et finalement rapatrié à la suite d'une affection pulmonaire,(1) avait-il attendu si longtemps avant d'entamer un sujet aussi important dans sa vie et dans celle de son pays? Il est vrai qu'il ne partageait pas le goût de ses contemporains pour le roman historique, encore moins pour le récit de guerre ou le roman dit 'existentialiste', mais la raison n'est pas là. Gracq explique dans *Lettrines* que, bien qu'il ait 'fait Dunkerque', l'expérience, désagréable en elle-même, fut peu fructueuse pour lui en tant qu'écrivain.(2) N'ayant rien pu tirer de l'expérience brute de la guerre, qu'il trouva être parfois 'fantasmagorique',(3) il dut la filtrer, la transposer, afin de lui donner rétrospectivement un sens. C'est que l'écrivain avait besoin de prendre ses distances vis-à-vis de la réalité historique:

> J'ai toujours pensé, déclarait-il en 1972, que j'écrirais sur la guerre et sur ce climat très particulier qui était la drôle de guerre, mais il fallait une maturation, il fallait une décantation, il fallait un recul, et cette période s'étant terminée en 1940 j'ai attendu dix-huit ans avant d'écrire sur elle. Probablement il fallait un certain tassement des souvenirs, une mise en place qui se fait seulement avec le temps. Ainsi j'ai écrit ce livre très tard et cette guerre dont j'ai eu l'expérience du côté de la Mer du Nord, je l'ai située dans l'Ardenne française.(4)

Une fois venu le moment de raconter sa guerre, il trouve alors impossible de situer son histoire dans le même cadre géographique où appartiennent les souvenirs personnels auxquels il fait appel.(5) Au mois d'octobre 1955, il entreprend donc un voyage éclair dans les Ardennes,(6) où il fait une marche de vingt-cinq kilomètres, depuis la gare de Revin aux Hauts-Buttés, puis à Monthermé, où il reprend le train. Cette visite d'une seule journée, dont il gardera toujours un souvenir indélébile, lui fournit un élément essentiel du récit qu'il commence à rédiger quelques mois plus tard, au printemps de 1956.

Bien que Gracq eût, de son propre aveu, parcouru la Vallée de la Meuse vers 1947,(7) il ne connaissait même pas à cette époque l'existence des maisons fortes en Ardenne, dont la présence ne lui fut révélée que par la lecture des *Communistes* où l'on retrouve une description qui annonce dans tous ses détails celle de la maison-forte de Grange.(8) Mais s'il est vrai que Gracq a puisé le prétexte de son récit dans le volumineux roman d'Aragon, où celui-ci décrit des spahis se délectant de longs mois d'existence paisible dans les environs de Monthermé, avec son paysage bien 'exotique' à leurs yeux,(9) et où le capitaine Balpêtré et ses officiers mènent à Malemort une 'vie féodale' et 'hors du temps',(10) il ne fait pas de doute qu'*Un Balcon en forêt* soit 'né de l'expérience directe de la guerre de 1939-40'.(11)

Bien entendu, il est difficile, même pour l'écrivain, de délimiter la part de l'autobiographie dans un ouvrage où il a utilisé ce qu'il appelle 'un souvenir émotionnel global plutôt que des souvenirs concrets'.(12) D'ailleurs, Julien Gracq a toujours reproché son outrecuidance au critique qui rechercherait les 'sources' d'une oeuvre littéraire, au sujet desquelles seul l'écrivain saurait nous renseigner de façon satisfaisante sinon exhaustive. L'image mentale qu'un auteur se fait de son ouvrage, et qui peut être bien différente de celle qu'il finira par transmettre à ses lecteurs, consiste pour Gracq en cette suite de possibilités, souvent non réalisées, et en tout cas inaccessibles au critique, que sont 'les fantômes de livres successifs que l'imagination de l'auteur projetait à chaque moment en avant de sa plume',(13) fantômes qui hantent toujours les pages du livre achevé. Ainsi, il avait écrit la première partie d'*Un Balcon en forêt* 'dans la perspective d'une *messe de minuit aux Falizes*, qui devait être un chapitre très important, et qui aurait donné au livre, avec l'introduction de cette tonalité religieuse, une assiette tout autre'.(14) Au critique alors de rêver à ce que ce chapitre-fantôme aurait apporté à l'aventure d'un jeune officier dans les Ardennes lors de la *drôle de guerre*. Non qu'il soit sans intérêt, en ce qui concerne la genèse de l'oeuvre d'en rapprocher l'écrivain, dans la mesure où celui-ci nous a livré quelques-uns de ces secrets de la composition littéraire normalement consignés au néant. *Un Balcon en forêt*, sans être au sens strict un ouvrage autobiographique, encore moins un reportage réaliste, représente une transposition subtile de données réelles. Historien de profession, Julien Gracq ne s'intéresse pas ici, cependant, aux événements de mai 1940 en eux-mêmes mais plutôt à un phénomène de psychologie collective. En fait d'activité militaire, ne sont décrites que les journées du 10-13 mai; l'auteur se livre, par contre, à une analyse détaillée de l'état d'esprit de son héros qui succombe à l'enchantement de la forêt au cours de ces longs mois d'attente à partir de l'automne de 1939. André Breton admirait tout particulièrement la manière dont Gracq rend ici 'l'atmosphère si spéciale des premiers mois de la guerre', lui reconnaissant une 'incomparable mémoire affective',(15) ce qui a dû faire plaisir à un auteur qui avait déclaré deux ans plus tôt que 'dans une oeuvre dite d'imagination la mémoire ne joue pas moins de rôle que dans une oeuvre réaliste'.(16) En transposant une expérience personnelle en aventure imaginaire, Gracq part alors d'un fait 'concret' mais 'inventé'.(17) Le récit est tiré de 'l'image des Ardennes', donc d'un souvenir récent, et 'du souvenir d'un certain climat', c'est-à-dire de 1939-40.(18)

Pour avoir fait la guerre dans des conditions bien différentes de son héros, Gracq n'en insère pas moins des réminiscences personnelles dans son *récit*. (Le terme *récit*, soit dit en passant, ne comporte pour l'auteur aucune connotation historique mais évoque 'une histoire d'une ligne simple, sans les ramifications et l'intrigue plus compliquée que suggère l'idée de roman'.)(19) Trop de détails concordent pour qu'on ne trouve dans l'aspirant Grange, avec ses trois camarades de fortin - un chasseur de canards de la Brière (Hervouët); un journalier de Questembert presque illettré (Gourcuff); un chef d'équipe aux chantiers navals de Penhoët (Olivon) - le reflet du lieutenant d'infanterie Louis Poirier qui commandait en 1939 une section de Bretons leur ressemblant.(20) On pourrait multiplier les points de comparaison entre l'auteur et son héros en se reportant aux souvenirs de la guerre recueillis dans les deux volumes de *Lettrines*. Gracq partage avec Grange l'impression d'être coupé non seulement des liens familiaux mais encore de la vie réelle, au point même d'envisager la guerre comme 'des vacances de luxe au bord de la mer'.(21) Il est amusant de constater que l'auteur fait lire à son héros pendant l'hiver de 1939-40 le premier volume du *Journal* de Gide, qui venait alors de paraître, et les *Mémorables* de Swedenborg, ouvrages qu'il lisait lui-même en octobre 1939.(22) Ce sont de telles interférences entre 'une histoire imaginaire'(23) et la vie de son auteur qui lui ont fait admettre qu'*Un Balcon en forêt* ne ressemble pas tout à fait à ses livres précédents et se demander en même temps si un sujet qu'il croyait si 'clair et si réel' ne s'est pas 'complètement transformé (...) sous ma pensée et sous ma plume'.(24)

Les opinions des journalistes qui rendirent compte du livre lors de sa publication en septembre 1958 étaient partagées sur le problème du caractère autobiographique d'une oeuvre qui est, à bien des égards, poétique autant qu'historique. André Rousseau mettait bien en évidence ce côté poétique du récit,(25) André Billy n'y voyait cependant qu'un exercice de style(26) et Pierre de Boisdeffre croyait avoir affaire à une version remaniée du *Rivage des Syrtes*;(27) André Wurmser, au contraire, considérait que le roman faisait un pas vers le réalisme,(28) Emile Henriot attribuait au texte un vif intérêt documentaire,(29) Claude Roy retrouvait le 'mauvais rêve' que la France avait fait en 1940 (30) et Maurice Nadeau y voyait presque des mémoires de guerre.(31) Dans des critiques plus nuancées, Dominique Aury cherchait à confronter l'élément onirique du récit et 'le document de guerre de premier ordre',(32) Henri Hell évoquait l'exactitude d'une documentation qui lui semblait cadrer mal avec les descriptions poétiques du décor,(33) et Gaëtan Picon constatait un flottement constant entre réel et imaginaire, histoire et mythe, dans un livre qui prenait pour sujet la *drôle de guerre* mais en la déréalisant.(34) Dans les trente dernières années, la critique universitaire a insisté sur cette tendance à désamorcer l'historicité du récit. Marie Francis, par exemple, prétend que '(...) la guerre est là non pour exprimer la réalité d'une époque mais pour nourrir le rêve de son personnage, pour alimenter son attente'(35) et N. Dodillé va jusqu'à dire que le discours historique ne sert pas à vraisemblabiliser une fiction mais, au contraire, à 'viabiliser en vue d'un destin romanesque des données historiques'.(36) Il est sans doute vrai que le héros, qui focalise la presque totalité du récit, vit un temps mort et bascule hors du réel, mais il y a, au delà du *monologue intérieur* et du *style indirect libre*, une autre forme de discours qui appartient au narrateur et qui fournit en sourdine un commentaire historique, presque, croirait-on, à l'insu de l'auteur, qui insiste toujours que son récit à lui n'est 'ni un document, ni un témoignage'.(37)

Comme beaucoup de ses contemporains, Julien Gracq reconnaît que l'effondrement de la France en 1940 'est la conséquence d'un désastre qui a déjà eu lieu'.(38) Il a parlé à ce propos du 'coup de masse que la société française avait reçu (...) de la Marne et de Verdun', phénomène qui n'atteint l'Angleterre qu'avec un retard d'un quart de siècle, au moment de Dunkerque et du *blitz* de 1940.(39) Mais de tout cela il n'en souffle mot dans *Un Balcon en forêt*, où l'évocation de la première guerre mondiale ne sert qu'à établir quelques contrastes de détail. On n'y trouvera aucune référence à la décadence morale ou politique (chère à Vichy), ni à la dénatalité, à la cinquième colonne ou à la carence des alliés. Parmi les nombreux phénomènes qui passent généralement (et peut-être à tort) pour être les causes de la débâcle, Gracq n'en retient que deux: l'armement désuet de l'armée française et les défaillances, en matière de stratégie et d'organisation, de l'état-major.

On sait que la supériorité des Allemands en blindés et en aviation leur permit de percer rapidement les défenses françaises dans les Ardennes. Le narrateur d'*Un Balcon en forêt* suggère par petites touches l'infériorité du matériel de guerre français. On apprend dès le début du récit que les embrasures de la maison forte ne sont pas encore munies de leurs trémies réglementaires mais de simples sacs à terre (p. 29-30).(40) Ce détail reviendra comme un *leitmotif*. Un album de photographies reproduisant les différents types de casemates de la ligne Siegfried révèle, par contre, des embrasures 'avec la collerette plus claire de leur curieux encadrement à soufflet' (p. 46). Le capitaine Varin, qui tempête en vain après les trémies introuvables, 'souffrait de ces blocs sans paupières comme d'une mutilation' (p. 133). Les sacs de terre s'ébouleront au premier obus allemand, tuant deux occupants du *blockhaus* - 'Varin avait raison pour les trémies' (p. 252) conclut notre héros, lui-même au seuil de la mort. De même, les réseaux de barbelés, toujours en voie d'achèvement à l'automne de 1939 (p. 27), ne seront terminés que le 11 mai 1940 (le lendemain de l'invasion de la Hollande, de la Belgique et du Luxembourg) et, dérisoirement, avec du fil *Brun*, c'est-à-dire sans barbelés mais avec 'de gros boudins nickelés en accordéon' (p. 189). La D.C.A., lit-on, 'ne faisait jamais mouche: c'étaient des tubes de 75 vétustes qui avaient canardé les taubes de la dernière guerre' (p. 130). Les mines anti-char ne fonctionnent pas mieux; la *destruction* installée près du *blockhaus* ne sautera pas, au grand scandale de Grange, qui se met en colère pour la première fois (p. 205). Dans 'cette armée qui muait avec trente ans de retard' (p. 77), une arme sur deux n'est pas en état de tirer à la fin de l'hiver, selon Varin (p. 134).

L'infériorité matérielle va de pair avec la sclérose des commandants. Si le portrait du capitaine Magnard frise la caricature (p. 42-43), même les bons officiers de carrière, comme les capitaines Vignaud et Varin, ne pourront rien faire contre le manque de résolution de leurs chefs, imbus de la stratégie défensive de la ligne Maginot, là où les Allemands affichent la doctrine offensive de la guerre-éclair. La maison forte, pourvue d'une mitrailleuse et d'un canon anti-char, est censée interdire aux blindés allemands 'l'accès des pénétrantes descendant de l'Ardenne belge vers la ligne de la Meuse' (p. 20), de 'détruire les chars' et de 'renseigner sur les mouvements de l'ennemi' qu'on doit arrêter 'sans esprit de recul' (p. 24). Il est évident cependant que ce *blockhaus* isolé, au nord-est de la ligne Maginot et sur la rive droite de la Meuse, ne pourra rien faire contre les Panzer, comme l'explique un jour un lieutenant de Cavaliers en des termes qui rappellent encore *Les Communistes* (Voir note 8); Grange cherche à se rassurer en ripostant que les chars ennemis pénétreront difficilement la forêt (p. 80-81). Au cours l'hiver, il commencera cependant à s'inquiéter de la manière dont l'état-major précise les itinéraires de repli (p. 124-25). Lors de l'attaque du 10 mai, la cavalerie française passe en Belgique mais l'infanterie ne la suit pas (p. 188). Cette impression de n'être pas 'soutenus' (p. 156), l'absence d'ordres au moment de la crise du 13 mai (p. 194), constituent aussi un commentaire amer sur la conduite de 'cette guerre sans âme et sans chansons, qui n'avait créé d'état de foule' (p. 145).

Il faut comprendre que les éléments proprement historiques de la diégèse servent le plus souvent à souligner l'abîme qui sépare nos protagonistes de la fausse guerre de la vraie qui va se faire. L'écoute des émissions radiophoniques du *traître de Stuttgart* renforce 'toute l'irréalité de la guerre qui fusait à travers le brouillage avec cette voix mince et acide qui prenait le temps de ses répliques comme un *troisième couteau*' (p. 37). Les journaux ne fournissent que des bribes d'information légèrement parodiques ('Pourquoi ne jouons-nous pas quelques mesures de *la Marseillaise* à la suite de *God save the King*, demande aux Communes le brigadier général Spears' (p. 91)), voire incompréhensibles ('Que pouvait bien signifier une guerre en Finlande?' (p. 92)).

A la différence des romans antérieurs de Gracq, *Un Balcon en forêt* est situé dans un temps précis et il n'est pas difficile de rétablir la chronologie interne du texte, parfaitement consistante. Il n'en est pas de même de l'espace géographique.

L'on savait que l'auteur d'*Au château d'Argol*, d'*Un beau ténébreux* et du *Rivage des Syrtes*, 'foncièrement allergique au réalisme',(41) préférait aux décors réels, légèrement transposés de sites authentiques, que lui suggéraient ses souvenirs et son imagination. Il convient alors de signaler à ceux qui ont voulu voir en *Un Balcon en forêt* un ouvrage de pure documentation, que le décor du récit est imaginaire, point sur lequel Gracq tient à insister depuis 1958.(42) Le *blockhaus* commandé par Grange est situé près de la frontière belge aux environs de Moriarmé, nom inventé (comme le sont quelques autres noms de lieu) mais qui rappelle pour Gracq la ville ardennaise de Monthermé(43) qui était 'un des points chauds de la bataille de la Meuse' en mai 1940.(44) Rien d'ailleurs n'est situé avec précision, bien que la petite région où se déroule l'histoire puisse être identifiée sans trop de difficulté.(45) Un lecteur ardennais a même cru pouvoir reconnaître, en cette Ardenne de fantaisie, la maison forte des Hautes Falizes,(46) mais on comprend dès le début du récit que, quelque réaliste que paraisse le décor par ses effets de réel, quelque reconnaissable que puisse sembler le cadre géographique, il s'agit d'un paysage fabuleux. Le train qui passe par Charleville à la première page du livre entre dans un domaine mythique que signale une référence au *Domaine d'Arnhem* d'Edgar Poe. (L'orthographe laisse rêver: s'agit-il d'une simple coquille, Poe et son traducteur Baudelaire écrivant *Arnheim*, ou Gracq cherche-t-il à évoquer la désastreuse opération aéroportée des alliés en 1944?)

Agrégé d'histoire et de géographie, l'auteur se complaît à établir des descriptions topographiques sans pour autant s'adonner à un réalisme descriptif. Son goût de la nature, en dépit de sa passion pour la géologie et la botanique, est assez limité: 'Ce qui m'intéresse ce sont les ensembles, les grands paysages'.(47) Il entraîne son lecteur dans un monde qui ne fait que franger l'authentique. 'Dans un paysage, dit-il, je ne vois guère que les lointains'.(48) Il s'agit alors d'évoquer une certaine atmosphère, cette même atmosphère mystérieuse et inquiétante qui baigne tous ses livres et qui est destinée ici à reproduire, symboliquement, le climat bizarre de la *drôle de guerre*. Les Ardennes sont pour Gracq un pays 'légendaire, fabuleux et féerique',(49) à la fois 'la forêt galante de Shakespeare' (p. 227) et une forêt de conte (p. 19, 50), où les manoeuvres des blindés et des dragons portés se transforment en grandes chasses sauvages et en hautes chevauchées (p. 70) des temps héroïques. C'est encore la forêt 'languissante' du *Roi Pêcheur*, celle, plus funèbre, d'*Au château d'Argol*, le royaume interdit de l'ancien château perdu parmi les forêts tristes de la Baltique dont rêve Henri dans *Un beau ténébreux*, lieux solitaires et symboliques, à l'instar de la forêt de Brocéliande et des forêts enchantées du romantisme allemand, de Wagner ou de Jünger,(50) domaines à la fois fascinants et redoutables, prometteurs d'une réintégration à la vie profonde ɑe la nature. 'La traversée d'une forêt, nous confie Gérard dans *Un beau ténébreux*, je n'ai jamais pu m'imaginer autrement l'approche d'un pays de légende'.(51) Cette forêt de l'Ardenne, à l'écart de la vie réelle, et qui enferme Grange dans un cercle magique dont il ne sortira plus, constitue aussi une de ces régions frontalières qui fournissent un thème majeur de l'oeuvre gracquienne. Particulièrement dans *La Rivage des Syrtes* et dans *La Route*, retrouve-t-on cette même obsession du 'petit clan en marge' et du 'goût du large'. La forêt, surnommée 'le Toit' par Grange (p. 39), toit dont on eût 'retiré l'échelle' (p. 29), est aussi un de ces hauts lieux tentateurs mis en évidence dans *Les Yeux bien ouverts* et *Un beau ténébreux*. *Un Balcon en forêt* trouve, en partie, son origine dans cette puissante image du 'haut plateau' où l'on subit 'l'appel irrésistible du vide'.(52) La forêt deviendra pour Grange l'image même de sa vie (p. 52, 154), telle une 'île heureuse' (p. 84), espace privilégié du bonheur et de l'angoisse. Comme déjà dans *Au château d'Argol*, il s'établit une complémentarité poétique entre la forêt et la mer,(53) ces deux 'résidences secondaires' des personnages des romans de Gracq,(54) de sorte que la rêverie du héros en forêt appelle des images récurrentes d'un flottement sur les eaux.

Le titre même du récit est une métaphore révélatrice, qui fait penser non seulement à la situation géographique du *blockhaus* haut perché, mais encore à l'idée du spectateur passif qui ne fait qu'attendre l'événement(55) et pour qui c'est 'la guerre au sous-sol et la paix au premier étage'.(56) Par association d'idées, des images théâtrales ('le rideau baissé' (p. 111), 'les feux de la rampe' (*ibid.* et p. 188)), viennent renforcer cette impression. 'Le théâtre de la guerre ... songea Grange. Le mot n'est pas si mal trouvé' (p. 188). Le fait même d'avoir fait imprimer *en forêt* en caractères italiques sur la page de titre de l'édition originale semble valoriser une expression banale et lui conférer, parodiquement, le sens d'une villégiature.(57) Le *blockhaus* lui-même, décrit comme 'Le bizarre accouplement [d'un] *mastaba* de la préhistoire avec une guinguette décatie de la pire banlieue au milieu du bric-à-brac des bohémiens en forêt' (p. 21-22) est pour Gracq 'un symbole expressif de la drôle de guerre' et d'une 'paix blanche',(58) de ce qu'il qualifie de '*farniente* de neuf mois au-dessus d'une soute à munitions'.(59) En plus, ce haut lieu est aussi un lieu clos, celui de la tombe et, par extension, de l'utérus.

Le sentiment puissant du peu de réalité de la fausse guerre qui envahit Grange trouve bien son parallèle dans la vie de Gracq, qui avait trouvé cette époque 'somnambulique',(60) 'une espèce de rêve éveillé',(61) termes qui conviennent parfaitement à l'état d'âme de son héros. Gracq raconte:

> J'ai été extrêmement frappé par le climat qui régnait en France pendant les années 1939-40, cette impression d'être au bout du rouleau, de laisser courir cette désintégration consentie. On attendait l'événement avec une espèce de stupeur magique, comme une fin du monde indéfiniment suspendue. Tant et si bien qu'on avait fini par s'y faire: à l'intérieur on ne parlait presque pas de la guerre.(62)

De tels recoupements de la vie et de l'oeuvre concernent d'ailleurs toute la production romanesque de l'auteur. *Un Balcon en forêt* reprend aux romans antérieurs d'autres thèmes qui attestent la continuité de l'inspiration gracquienne. Grange partage avec Aldo ce même sentiment de l'irréalité en face des choses et subit le même envoûtement de 'l'attente pure' (p. 162,

225). En insistant sur le parallélisme d'*Un Balcon en forêt* et du *Rivage des Syrtes*, Gracq constate: 'J'ai cherché, en effet, dans ces deux livres, à creuser cette impression bizarre suscitée par la drôle de guerre'.(63) Ainsi le thème majeur du *Rivage des Syrtes* se trouve ramené dans *Un Balcon en forêt* à l'une de ses origines véritables. Le thème de l'attente est, selon Gracq, comme un rythme fondamental qui régirait l'ensemble de son oeuvre romanesque,(64) la *drôle de guerre* n'étant même qu'un phénomène qui incarnait en quelque sorte un sentiment pré-existant, car l'Histoire, disait-il en 1972, 'pendant quelques mois a ressemblé à la situation dans laquelle j'aime à me retrouver'.(65) Dix ans plus tard, il renchérit: 'L'histoire pendant la drôle de guerre, s'est faite un moment attente pure, je me sentais en communication avec elle. Dans le genre noir, bien entendu.'(66) Le choix de l'Ardenne est donc encore une façon de véhiculer un thème 'moteur', auquel s'attachent certains éléments stéréotypés - le lieu clos (château d'Argol, Hôtel des Vagues, forteresse de l'Amirauté, *blockhaus*, maison de campagne à Braye la Forêt ...), le groupe isolé, la quête mystérieuse. Il s'agit, selon toute évidence, de se délivrer de certaines obsessions en les objectivant en images: '(...) l'idée qui a suscité *Un Balcon en forêt* est celle de la solitude. De la solitude dans la guerre. Et de l'attente'.(67)

Cette fausse guerre, dont le caractère insolite dépayse complètement notre jeune héros, délivre aussi des servitudes de la vie de tous les jours et apporte un prolongement du monde enchanté de l'enfance. Grange rêve la guerre plus qu'il ne la vit. Ce qui compte, c'est la camaraderie de la maison forte et l'exaltation de la liaison avec la jeune veuve Mona, qualifiée de 'fadette' et de 'sorcière' (p. 53), d'être 'surnaturel' (p. 96), d'espèce 'fabuleuse' (p. 119) et de 'Sibylle enfant' (p. 121), et qui est comme l'initiatrice aux mystères de la forêt.

La guerre elle-même garde jusqu'à la fin un caractère parodique, comme si on était en plein *comique troupier* (p. 205), n'arrêtant pas, comme dans *Le Rivage des Syrtes*, de 'se cacher derrière ses fantômes' (p. 250). La participation de Grange à la guerre active ne durera que quelques brefs instants. La destruction d'un camion allemand (où deux soldats ennemis sont tués) se révèle être dérisoire (le camion ne transportait que des livrets matricules) et n'apporte aux occupants du *blockhaus* que le sentiment d'une faute, la conviction qu'il seront punis pour avoir touché 'aux arcanes' (p. 234). Sur le plan historique, Grange vit, sans doute, cette 'période de schisme entre l'homme et le monde'(68) dont Gracq a parlé; il est victime de 'l'écart désormais insondable, sidéral, entre l'action individuelle et le résultat collectif'.(69) Et pourtant l'expérience du héros n'est pas que négative. Sans qu'on puisse définir avec exactitude ce que la vie *en forêt* apporte de précairement consolateur au jeune aspirant, il est évident que le fait de rester sur place fait de lui une sorte de héros bien qu'il soit, sur le plan spirituel, 'un déserteur' (p. 139), comme le comprend bien son officier supérieur. Sans rechigner à la besogne, il ne participe pas d'instinct (p. 14). Il refuse d'être muté au régiment non par patriotisme mais parce qu'il se plaît là où il est (p. 138). Il fait la guerre sans raison, de mauvaise foi, sachant qu'il est 'complice' en se laissant aller au charme du *fil de l'eau* (p. 157), en refusant de suivre les conseils d'un cavalier en retraite qui lui annonce le 12 mai que les Allemands sont à dix minutes (p. 204), en restant à son poste quand il ne peut recevoir l'ordre du repli, le téléphone étant coupé,(70) donc en choisissant sa propre fatalité. Pris dans des sentiments contradictoires (à propos desquels Gracq n'a pas voulu éclairer ses lecteurs),(71) où une angoisse apocalyptique s'accompagne d'un sentiment de sécurité irréelle (p. 209), le tout médiatisé par des images du Déluge et de l'Arche de Noé, notre héros paradoxal effectue un retour à l'enfance; '(...) la peur des enfants perdus dans la forêt crépusculaire' (p. 209) alterne avec la joie enfantine d'être seul à 'faire ce que je veux' (p. 210). Un puissant sentiment de *lâchez tout*, qui lui fait tenir des propos d'un optimisme délirant à un réfugié belge (p. 211), l'impression qu'il ne 'relève plus de rien' (p. 218), se résolvent en ce désir de rester là, quoi qu'il advienne (p. 223).

Héros existentialiste face à un monde absurde ou héros romantique redécouvrant l'unité secrète de l'homme et de la nature? Nul doute que Gracq, pénétré du mythe du Graal, qu'il désigne comme une quête 'terrestre',(72) ne soit attiré par cette ambition de fusion avec les choses qui est celle d'un Novalis, aussi bien que par le sentiment de 'paradis perdu' qu'il considère comme caractéristique du surréalisme.(73) Les mots de *Parsifal* cités en exergue à *Un Balcon en forêt* sont cependant ironiques. Pour Grange, qui trouvera un bonheur interdit, la quête se réduit autant à une chimère délicieuse et éphémère qu'à une véritable révélation. De là le paradoxe du thème de la mort chez Gracq. Que Grange meure ou non à la fin du récit, peu importe - il ressent un plaisir délicieux à être 'sorti de toutes les ornières' (p. 249). Il s'endort 'comme pour un sommeil éternel'.(74) 'Sa courte aventure de guerre' (p. 249) a pris fin; il a trouvé, par la voie de la rêverie, la paix intérieure, il est 'revenu' (p. 251). C'est ainsi qu'à certains moments privilégiés le monde 'racheté, lavé de l'homme' (p. 97) se remagnétise et baigne dans 'une lumière meilleure' (p. 212). Sans partager l'opinion de Gérard Mourgue(75) qui voudrait voir dans le dénouement du récit 'un acte de foi' au sens religieux, là où il faudrait voir plutôt une mutation ontologique du sujet, nous croyons que le critique a raison de voir en l'amour de Grange pour Mona et 'la camaraderie chaleureuse unissant le chef et ses hommes' une résurgence du *sacré*, du moins au sens où le récit entend ce terme: venant mourir dans la chambre de son amante partie, Grange effectue un transfert maternel, sa fin prenant la forme du phantasme rassurant d'une enfance retrouvée au ventre de la mère.

En sacrifiant toute préoccupation anecdotique à l'analyse d'un état d'âme et à la peinture d'un dépaysement qui devient, obscurément, moyen de connaissance, Julien Gracq a réussi un beau roman poétique, fortememt marqué par des tendances régressives et chargé d'une atmosphère qui invite à atteindre le monde à l'un de ces 'noeuds cachés'(76) qui permettent 'une entrée en résonance universelle'.(77) Le récit reproduit un état de rêverie où peut s'effectuer le jeu des *correspondances*. C'est en ce monde 'entièrement soluble dans la poésie'(78) d'*Henri d'Ofterdingen* que notre héros, pénètre dès son arrivée dans les Ardennes de 'béatitude songeuse' (p. 31), trouve, à l'approche de la mort, dans le désir même du néant (p. 182) et de la solitude (p. 186), 'dans l'attente angoissée d'une catastrophe inévitable et peut-être desirée'(79), sa voie.

La débâcle de 1940 revue par le surréalisme ou le réalisme magique? Il est certain que si Gracq prend appui sur des données historiques, c'est pour en tirer une légende.(80) En évoquant cette 'armée au bois dormant' (p. 157), 'armée rêveuse' (p. 161), cette 'allée du château de la Belle au bois dormant' (p. 198), il fait revivre les fantômes de son propre passé. Une fois son récit terminé, ayant dit ce qu'il avait à dire sur 1940, Gracq trouve que 'des souvenirs très vivants, très intenses de la guerre' sont déjà 'plus flous, et surtout inertes, sans écho, sans prolongement' car 'en écrivant on s'appauvrit'.(81) *Un Balcon en forêt* serait alors un ouvrage thérapeutique, sorte d'exorcisme du réel par la poésie, où l'écrivain chercherait à dire sa guerre, tout en ne la disant pas? Pour Gracq, réalité et légende s'interpénètrent. L'Ardenne reste à la fois paysage mythique et *paysage-histoire*, comme il le constate dans un passage remarquable où il évoque le passage de la Semois par les Allemands en mai 1940, deux jours avant le nouveau désastre de Sedan:

> *Le Sombre Mai!* Encore 1940! Il est vrai, jamais je ne traverse ces terres méhaignées, ce *pays gât*, ces forêts si splendidement vertes, qui en l'an quarante ont couvert et camouflé jusqu'à la dernière minute comme autrefois la forêt de Dunsinane, l'armée d'invasion, elle-même toute enguirlandée de branches, sans que le souvenir de la guerre ne vienne las repeupler d'une vie fantôme. J'ai parlé autrefois de l'existence de *paysages-histoire*, qui ne s'achèvent réellement pour l'oeil, ne s'individualisent, et parfois même ne deviennent distincts, qu'en fonction d'un épisode historique, marquant ou tragique, qui les a singularisés, les faisant sortir une fois pour toutes de l'indistinction, en même temps qu'il les a consacrés. L'Ardenne est pour moi un de ces *paysages-histoire*: elle ne parlerait pas, quand je la vois et que je la traverse, aussi fort qu'elle le fait à mon imagination, si, à la seule image de la forêt d'Hercynie sans chemins et sans limites que nous ayons conservée chez nous, elle ne superposait celle de la forêt de Teutoburg, inquiétante à force de silence, par trois fois grosse des légions d'Arminius.(82)

Notes

1. Pour la biographie de Julien Gracq, on se reportera à la *Chronologie* établie par Bernhild Boie pour les *Oeuvres Complètes*, 'Bibliothèque de la Pléiade' (Paris, Gallimard, 1989), t. I.
2. *Lettrines* (Paris, Corti, 1967), pp. 104-105.
3. *Ibid.*, p. 120.
4. *Cahiers de l'Herne*, pp. 20, 1972, 215. (Entretien avec Gilbert Ernst sur *Un Balcon en forêt*).
5. *Ibid.*, p. 214.
6. *Ibid.*, p. 216. Voir aussi *Chronologie, Oeuvres Complètes*, t I, LXXVI-LXXVII.
7. *L'Herne*, p. 215.
8. Voir à ce propos les remarques de Gracq dans des entretiens avec J.-L. de Rambures (*Le Monde*, 16 mai 1970, V) et Gilbert Ernst (*L'Herne*, p. 215). Le passage en question est le suivant: 'C'est un châlet comme un jouet d'enfant, où peut vivre un petit ménage bien gentil qui a trouvé ça tout plein mignon de venir faire sa lessive, et mettre ses enfants à s'ébattre en plein no man's land de la frontière, à un croisement de routes stratégiques dans la forêt. Sauf que le rez-de-chaussée fait resserré, avec le premier étage qui le déborde, tout autour, si on ne remarque pas tout de suite qu'il est en béton armé gris sous la maisonnette pimpante pour conte de fée, et qu'il a de drôles de fenêtres du genre embrasure, créneau, pourquoi voulez-vous que le conducteur de

panzer qui arrive dessus s'en méfie? On appelle ça une maison forte, et ça en a fait couler, de l'encre! Trois hommes et un aspirant sont là-dedans avec leurs armes automatiques, seuls, après le repli des postes. Il n'y avait qu'une chose à quoi on n'avait pas pensé: que des éléments avaient pu s'infiltrer en arrière par une sente, et tandis que les quatre hommes surveillaient en avant par les fenêtres du blockhaus, un Allemand a jeté par une des embrasures arrière une grenade à l'intérieur de la maison forte. Tout a sauté, les hommes sont morts, ils n'auront pas à utiliser l'ingénieux boyau creusé sur quelques mètres pour assurer leur retraite sous le couvert des bois ...' (*Les Communistes* (Paris, Editeurs français réunis, 1951), t. III, 'mai 1940', ch. v, pp. 78-79.

9. Ce dernier rapprochement a déjà été signalé par Carlo Bronne, qui n'a pas cependant fait état des autres, plus significatifs selon nous. Voir 'L'Attente de la forêt. A propos d'un texte de Julien Gracq, *Académie royale de la langue et de la littérature française de Belgique*, pp. 3-4, 1971, 263-64. Il convient de donner la référence précise, qui manque chez Bronne: *Les Communistes*, t. III, 'Mai 1940', ch. viii, p. 151.

10. *Les Communistes*, t. II, 'Novembre 1939-mars 1940', ch. III, p. 50.

11. Jean Carrière, *Julien Gracq: qui êtes-vous?* (Lyon, La Manufacture, 1986), p. 146. (Entretien avec Gracq).

12. *L'Herne*, p. 218.

13. *Lettrines*, p. 27.

14. *Ibid.*, p. 28.

15. *Le surréalisme et la peinture*, édition définitive, (Paris, Gallimard, 1965), p. 257. Cité par Serge Gaubert, 'Julien Gracq et le temps perdu', *L'Herne*, p. 324.

16. 'Les Yeux bien ouverts' in *Farouche à quatre feuilles* (Paris, Grasset, 1954), p. 110. Texte repris dans *Préférences, nouvelle edition augmentée* (Paris, Corti, 1969), p. 67.

17. R. Poulet, *Aveux spontanés* (Paris, Plon, 1963), p. 119. (Entretien avec Gracq, publié dans *Carrefour*, pp. 9-15 juillet 1958).

18. J.-R. Huguenin, *Une autre jeunesse* (Paris, Editions du Seuil, 1965), p. 74. (Entretien avec Gracq, publié dans *Arts*, 17 septembre 1958).

19. Lettre de Gracq du 15 mars 1968 à l'auteur du présent article.

20. *L'Herne*, p. 214.

21. *Ibid.*, p. 218.

22. *Lettrines 2* (Paris, Corti, 1974), p. 142.

23. *Nouvelles littéraires*, 11 septembre 1958, p. 1. (Entretien avec A. Bourin).

24. R. Poulet, *Aveux spontanés*, p. 119.

25. *Le Figaro littéraire*, 6 septembre 1958.

26. *Le Figaro*, 3 septembre 1958.

27. *Revue de Paris*, décembre 1958, pp. 165-66.

28. *Lettres françaises*, 18-24 septembre 1958.

29. *Le Monde*, 8 octobre 1958.

30. *Libération*, 26 novembre 1958.

31. *France Observateur*, 18 septembre 1958.
32. *Nouvelle Revue Française*, novembre 1958, pp. 881-84.
33. *La Table Ronde*, février 1959, pp. 173-74.
34. *Mercure de France*, décembre 1958, pp. 659-63. Texte repris dans *L'Usage de la lecture* (Paris, Mercure de France, 1961), t. II pp. 247-51.
35. *Forme et signification de l'attente dans l'oeuvre romanesque de Julien Gracq* (Paris, Nizet, 1979), p. 152.
36. 'Figures et fonctions de la guerre dans *Un Balcon en forêt*' in *Julien Gracq. Actes du Colloque International, nouvelle édition* (Angers, Presses Universitaires d'Angers, 1982), p. 85.
37. *Magazine littéraire* 179, décembre 1981, p. 19. (Entretien avec Jean Roudaut).
38. Jean Carrière, *Julien Gracq: qui êtes-vous?*, p. 65.
39. 'Souvenirs d'une ville inconnue', *Le Nouveau Commerce*, automne 1976, p. 35.
40. *Un Balcon en forêt* (Paris, Corti, 1958). Toutes nos références renvoient à cette édition.
41. *L'Herne*, p. 219.
42. *Nouvelles littéraires*, 11 septembre 1958, 1. (Entretien avec A. Bourin).
43. Gracq m'a expliqué dans sa lettre du 15 mars 1968: 'Les noms de lieux sont faits ici pour rappeler, mais un peu changés, les noms réels de la région de Monthermé où visiblement se déroule l'histoire. Aucun lieu, je crois, n'est identifiable avec précision, mais il ne fait aucun doute pour le lecteur qu'il s'agit de cette petite région dans son ensemble.' A coté de vrais noms de lieu de l'Ardenne française, on retrouve des toponymes fictifs dérivés de noms réels. Il a dit dans une interview que Moriarmé est une contraction de Monthermé et de Morialmé (en Belgique) et que les Hautes Falizes dérivent de la Falizette (*Givre*, I, mai 1976, p. 25). Il introduit aussi des noms étrangers à la région; voir, à ce propos, Michèle Monballin, *Gracq: création et recréation de l'espace* (Bruxelles, De Boeck, 1987), pp. 59-60.
44. *Givre*, I, mai 1976, pp. 25-26. (Entretien avec Julien Gracq).
45. '(...) si on se promène de Revin aux Hauts-Buttés et de là à Monthermé, on a sous les yeux tout le cadre du récit. C'est la seule promenade que j'avais faite en Ardenne quand j'ai écrit ce livre' (*Ibid.*, p. 26).
46. *La Grive*, janvier-mars, 1959, p. 14. Voir, sept pages plus loin, la photographie du blockhaus.
47. *Nouvelles littéraires*, 11 septembre 1958, p. 1. (Entretien avec A. Bourin).
48. *Nouvelles littéraires*, No. 1265, novembre 1951, p. 1.
49. *L'Herne*, p. 215.
50. On sait l'importance, pour *Le Rivage des Syrtes* aussi bien que pour *Un Balcon en forêt*, des *Falaises de Marbre* d'Ernst Jünger, livre que Gracq avait lu en 1943. Jünger prétend que Gracq ne voulait pas se laisser influencer, sous l'occupation, par un écrivain allemand. Voir *La Quinzaine littéraire*, pp. 15-31 janvier 1969, p. 11. (Entretien avec Ernst Jünger).

51. *Un beau ténébreux* (Paris, Corti, 1945), p. 73.
52. *Ibid.*, p. 119.
53. Voir à ce propos les remarques de Gracq lui-même (*L'Herne*, p. 220).
54. *Lettrines*, p. 32.
55. Voir la réponse de Gracq à la question posée par G. Matoré, *L'espace humain* (Paris, La Colombe, 1962), p. 115 note. Cette image est à rapprocher de la *loge de mer* dans *La Presqu'île* (Paris, Corti, 1970), p. 116.
56. *Le Monde*, 16 mai 1970, V. (Entretien avec J.-L. de Rambures).
57. Il ne semble pas que les critiques qui ont mis en évidence l'emploi de l'italique chez Gracq aient relevé cet exemple capital du procédé. On trouvera néanmoins des remarques intéressantes à ce sujet dans les articles d'Hubert Juin, 'Julien Gracq et le fil des images', *L'Herne*, pp. 328-36, et de Jacqueline Michel, 'La puissance imageante de l'italique dans les récits gracquiens' in *Julien Gracq. Actes du Colloque International*, pp. 420-30.
58. *L'Herne*, pp. 217, 218.
59. *Givre*, I, 1976, p. 26.
60. J.-R. Huguenin, *Une autre jeunesse*, p. 74.
61. *L'Herne*, p. 219.
62. J.-R. Huguenin, *Une autre jeunesse*, p. 74.
63. *Nouvelles littéraires*, 11 septembre 1958, p. 1.
64. Comme il constatait, lors de la publication du *Rivage des Syrtes:* 'Il me semble qu'il y a toujours, en effet, dans chacun de mes livres, une progression lente, une attente indéfiniment prolongée, des pressentiments - ce qui m'intéresse c'est l'au-delà, le lointain, ce qui se cache derrière un personnage ou un paysage'. (*Nouvelles littéraires*, No. 1265, novembre 1951, p. 1).
65. *L'Herne*, p. 214.
66. *Magazine littéraire* 179, décembre 1981, p. 19. (Entretien avec Jean Roudaut).
67. *Nouvelles littéraires*, 11 septembre 1958, p. 1. (Entretien avec A. Bourin).
68. *Le Nouvel Observateur*, 29 mars 1967, p. 33. (Entretien avec Guy Dumur).
69. *Nouvelles littéraires*, 11 septembre 1958, p. 1. (Entretien avec A. Bourin).
70. Comme dans le rêve prémonitoire (p. 131).
71. En réponse à la question de J.-R. Huguenin, *Une autre jeunesse*, 75, Gracq se contenta d'évoquer le mancenellier qui figure dans son récit (p. 227).
72. *Un beau ténébreux*, p. 66.
73. Voir 'Le surréalisme et la littérature contemporaine', *Nieuw Vlaams Tijdschrift* (Anvers), mai 1950, p. 1113. Texte repris en 1972 dans *L'Herne*, pp. 189-204, et en 1989 dans *Oeuvres Complètes* t. I, pp. 1009-1033.
74. Comme l'a très bien dit J.-P. Vaillant 'De George Sand à Julien Gracq: *Un Balcon en forêt*, *La Grive*, 1969, p. 15. Léon Roudiez avait parlé de 'sommeil mythique' dans son article de 1959 (Julien Gracq: *Un Balcon en forêt*', *The French Review*, février, 1959, pp. 384-86).

75. *Dieu dans la littérature d'aujourd'hui* (Paris, France-Empire, 1961), p. 103.
76. *Honneur à Saint-John Perse* (Paris, Gallimard, 1965), p. 159.
77. *Lettrines*, p. 75.
78. *Préférences, nouvelle édition augmentée*, p. 269.
79. René Lalou, *Le roman français depuis 1900* (Paris, P.U.F., 1966), p. 121.
80. Comme le font, dans *La Nuit de San Lorenzo*, les frères Taviani: 'Ce n'est pas un film sur la seconde guerre mondiale. Ce n'est pas non plus un film historique. Il traduit au contraire un désir actuel: celui de raconter une histoire, non pas l'histoire mais simplement une belle histoire: une fable ou peut-être une légende ou une chanson de geste. (...) Et puis, vous savez, nous sommes de très mauvais historiens: nous partons d'un fait réel pour inventer une métaphore.' (*Le Nouvel Observateur*, 30 octobre 1982). Passage cité par J.-M. Adam, *Le Récit* (Paris, P.U.F., 1984), p. 119.
81. *Le Monde*, 16 mai 1970, v.
82. Texte publié pour la première fois par Jean Carrière, *Julien Gracq: qui êtes-vous?*, p. 179. Les légions en question furent en réalité celles de Varus détruites par Arminius. La transposition est peut-être significative? Par contre, la référence à la forêt de Dunsinane, là où il faudrait strictement parler de Birnham Wood est sans doute le fruit d'une simple inadvertance?